The Virginia Hostess

Junior Woman's Club of Manassas, Inc.

Manassas, Virginia

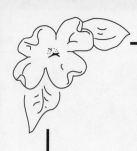

We gratefully acknowledge the generous efforts and contributions of everyone involved in the creation of this cookbook.

First Printing	5,000 copies	December, 1991
Second Printing	5,000 copies	July, 1993
Third Printing	5,000 copies	August, 1996

Printed in the USA by

WIMMER

The Wimmer Companies, Inc.

Memphis

TABLE OF CONTENTS

CLUB HISTORY

The Junior Woman's Club of Manassas was founded in 1931 by thirteen prominent young women under the auspices of the Woman's Club of Manassas. At the time the Club was formed, Manassas was a small farming community.

The aim of the Club was and continues to be "social and cultural advancement." Through the years, the Juniors have strived to recognize the needs of the community and to meet those needs through community action.

The Club has passed its golden anniversary as Manassas and Prince William County have transformed into a larger metropolitan area. This growth brings with it new challenges to the thriving suburb of Washington, D.C. The Club's members continue to strive to meet the needs of the community and to live by its pledge "...by living each day trying to accomplish something, not merely to exist." Through the sales of this cookbook the club endeavors to meet these growing needs.

ABOUT THE ARTISTS

Lu Wyer Harris - Cover Watercolor

Lu, a native of California, resides in Manassas and exhibits her work at the Center Street Gallery in Old Town. While she is best known for her pastels, Lu works extensively in water colors, oils, acrylics and mixed media. Her work can also be seen at the Torpedo Factory in Alexandria.

After studying at the Northern Virginia Community College and George Mason University, Lu attended a variety of extended workshops, including several with the well-known pastel painter, Albert Handell. She also studied at the Instituto Allende, San Miguel Allende in Mexico.

The Junior Woman's Club of Manassas extends its gratitude to her for the original pastel donated for our cover.

Richard Guy - Historical Sketches

Richard Guy grew up in Chevy Chase, Maryland and began working with a portrait artist at the age of 12. He was graduated from Syracuse University with a degree in Fine Arts. After settling in Manassas, Virginia, Mr. Guy became interested in the history of the area and has created a number of black and white drawings of popular sites throughout picturesque Virginia.

ACKNOWLEDGEMENTS

Chris Althoff
Maribel Alvarez
Rose Armstrong
Catherine Arrington
Janet Bailey
Lindsey Bailey
Connie Barnett
Kris Barrett
Joy Basham
Sheryl Bass
Betty Bell
Susan Bixby
Debbie Blum
Terre Boepple
Lois Bolton
Tracy Boone
Paige Bradford
Barbara Breeden
Nancy Breeden
Katherine Brooks
Patty Browne
Sheri Bush
Carol Butler
Lisa Campbell
Marie Canton
Jody Carpenter
Deborah Carter
Wanda Castellaw
Frieda B. Cathey
Barbara Caudle
Susan Clark
Jackie Corbin
Anne Marie Courchaine
Donna Crnkovich
Jennifer Darrah
Elizabeth S. Davies

Linda Davis
Lynn DeFazio
Mary Dellinger
Jane Dennin
Debbie Dever
Joyce D'Eugenio
Ann DiMaria-Haines
Alison Dixon
Becky Dowell
Susan Dowell
Patti Dunegan
Sheron Dunn
Susan Ecker
Louise Edsall
Susan English
Ann Faust
Cathy Ferramosca
Dale Fisher
Diane Fontana
Ann Forest
Marianne Fox
Nancy Fox
Martha Ann France
Pam Gay
Anna Marie Green
Charlene Greene
Sue Groundwater
Shelia Hainline
Susan Hanifin
Kelly Harman
Anne Harrington
Ann Walser Harrover
Margaret Hart
Judith Hill
Rebecca Hill
Debbie Hodges

Julie Hohns
Lisa Holman
Amy Howard
Alissa Hudson
Sandra Jackson
Debbie Jamba
Lynne Jennings
Joyce Johnston
Jennifer Kane
Katy Kimbrell
Ramona Kite
Krista Klemens
Suzanne Knieriem
Leslie Kohn
Debbie Krawczyk
Deborah Kuhn
Leslie Lahue
Vicki Latimer
Freda Lawrence
Nancy Lawson
Joan Leggett
Maryann Lesnick
Laura Lundquist
Frances Lynch
Mary Beth Lynch
Pam Magee
Karen Maltman
Georgean Martin
Naomi Martin
Anita Martindell
Jo Matthews
Julie McCauley
Nancy McClellan
Debbie Milligan
Annette Mohl
Pam Monder

Patti Monroe
Loretta Moran
Kathy Mumma
Robyn Murphy
Karen Nolan
Lynn O'Neill
Susanne O'Neill
Diane Oristian
Marianne Overs
Susie Parker
Debra Parrish
Lorene Parrish
Ann Patterson
Terrie Patullo
Toni Payne
Sue Pelkey
Fanelle P. Polen
Molly Powell
Mitchell Price
Jane Rabatin
Sharon Race
Kathy Rea
Shelley Rector
Jeanne Rhoads
Leigh Anne Rhoads
Colleen Richards
Elise Riedel
Linda Riggles
Gerri Rigney
Lelia Ringler
Jody Ritner
Laura Robinson
Charlene Rogers
Margaret Rogosienski
Cheryl Rosko

Phyllis Sakole
Lana Schinnerer
Holly Shaughnessy
Suzanne Shepard
Sue Shlanta
Anne Sievers
Jane Oliver Smith
Kris Spitler
Susan Spitler
Mary Delia Stokely
Anne Stultz
Jane Sumner
Claire Sutherland
Bonnie Tazewell
Jackie Thamm
Lisa Thoma
Megan Tokash
Patti Townsend
Marie Turner
Barbara Van Doren
Dolly Webb
Sharon Weber
Terrie Wells
Beverly White
Diane White
Rita White
Betsy Willett
Helen Williams
Rachel Wist
Donna Wittenauer
Linda Womack
Leslie Wood
Nancy Wood
Kay Worley
Agnes Yeaman

The Pleasure
of Your Company

R. Guy

Manassas Railroad Station - City of Manassas

Requesting the "pleasure of your company" might be considered the "first stop" in a hostess' entertaining plans. The "first stop" in a traveler's itinerary may be a historic railroad station.

Manassas had its birth at the completion of the Orange and Alexandria Railroad (now the Southern) about 1853. The first train station was located near the Presbyterian Church on Fairview Avenue. The little town was then known as Tudor Hall. The present train station, located between West and Battle Streets in downtown Manassas, was the town's third depot. Built in 1915, it is on the same site as a train station that burned earlier. The present one-story brick station with ceramic-tiled hip roof partly incorporates the walls of the burned 1904 depot. Its architectural design typifies the charm of a bygone era.

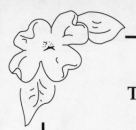

The Pleasure of Your Company

Whatever the occasion for entertaining, an experienced hostess organizes her event before extending the invitations. Consider the formality and style of the event, the facilities available to you, the time of day and season, and your budget. The following generally accepted definitions are helpful to suggest the variety of style and expense:

COCKTAIL PARTY: Finger hors d'oeuvres and open bar. Cocktail plates or napkins suffice. Guests stand. Invitation specifies starting and ending time.

COCKTAIL BUFFET: Guests expect more than hors d'oeuvres. Serve platter of meats, slices of breads and accompanying dishes. Plates are optional depending on the type of food offered. Guests stand. Invitation gives the arrival time only, since guests are expected to linger longer. The arrival time may be later since this takes the place of dinner.

BRUNCH BUFFET: Combination of breakfast and lunch relies heavily on breakfast menu, but is served closer to lunchtime. Informality is the rule.

SEMI-BUFFET (breakfast, lunch or dinner): Guests serve themselves from a sideboard at a chosen mealtime, and then sit together at the dining table or additional tables set up for the meal.

BUFFET (breakfast, lunch or dinner): Guests serve themselves from a sideboard at their convenience and sit and eat wherever they choose. Places for everyone to sit must be available, but do not need to be at tables.

SIT-DOWN (breakfast, lunch or dinner): Guests are seated at tables and are served at the chosen mealtime. Generally, if help is unavailable, the number of guests is limited to eight. If you select a sit-down dinner, the serving style may range from the most formal to the least formal, family style. The hostess chooses the serving style to complement the nature of the occasion, keeping in mind the resources available to her. You may consider four basic alternatives in your decision:

> **FORMAL:** By definition, formal dining requires efficient and well-trained servants, minimally a cook, a butler and a footman. If your household does not have a staff available, you can hire temporary help. A truly formal meal is only served by men. Everything on a formal table is geometrically spaced. Plates are

spaced two feet from center to center. Silver is placed so that one uses the utensils farthest from the plate first; no more than three forks and knives are at a setting at any time. Napkins are placed flat on each plate. Courses consist of soup or fresh fruit or melon or shellfish, fish, the entree, salad, dessert, and coffee.

INFORMAL: Servants or help are not required. Allow 20 to 30 inches width for each place setting. Again, silver to be used last is placed nearest the plate. Forks are to the left in the order of their use and dinner knives are to the right. A bread and butter knife is straight across the top. The napkin is placed either to the left of the forks or in the center of the setting. If used, the bread and butter plate is placed above the forks. Salad bowls are optional; dinner salad may be placed on the bread and butter plate. Water goblets are lined up above the tip of the knife. When wine is served, place the glass to the right of the water glass, slightly forward, forming a diagonal line. For an informal sit-down meal, you may serve your guests in English style or family style.

ENGLISH STYLE: The main dishes are served at the table by the host or hostess. Stack the plates at the end of the table in front of the host. Place the serving utensils next to the host's silver. Place the food within easy reach. The host carves the meat. Before the plates are passed the host or hostess may serve the vegetables. The table is cleared before the dessert course: first the serving dishes and then the plates. Serve the dessert, providing any additional silverware if needed.

FAMILY STYLE: The food is placed on the table in serving dishes at the beginning of the meal and each person at the table helps himself to the desired portions.

If you select a buffet service, plan for easy access to the serving table by placing it in the middle of the room. Set the table in a logical sequence so that guests may serve themselves effortlessly (i.e. dinner plates, main dish, salad, vegetables, rolls, silverware, napkins). Place the serving pieces near the edge of the table within easy reach. Leave space near the serving dishes for setting down plates, if needed. For a large group, prepare twin arrangements on both sides of the buffet table and form two serving lines. For a semi-buffet, arrange small tables in another room with the flatware, napkins, and water glasses.

The seating of the guests at a sit-down meal is also part of the planning. The host and hostess are seated at opposite ends of the table. The female guest of honor sits to the right of the host and the male guest of honor sits to the right of the hostess. Men and women usually sit in alternating fashion around the table and married couples are separated.

Once these basic decisions are made, the guests need to be invited. With today's busy lifestyles, two to four weeks in advance are required for social invitations. While you await your guests' response, organize your party using three essential lists:

• Menu Planning

• Inventory of supplies

• Countdown of activities

The use of these lists helps any hostess increase her skill and efficiency in entertaining with ease.

Menu Planning

Just choose one complete menu from the variety available in this cookbook, or mix and match recipes to create your own.

Keep in mind the following guidelines when selecting any menu.

Keep it simple with no more courses than you can manage. The simplest meal is two courses: the main course with salad and dessert with coffee. A more elaborate presentation is the three course menu: soup or salad, main entree with vegetable and dessert with coffee.

Buy within your budget. Once the menu is determined, make a shopping list and purchase items that may be easily stored a few weeks or days ahead such as the necessary staples, wines, liquors, mixers and paper products. This spreads the cost over a period of weeks if time allows. Serve items in season if possible; fresh is best.

Be generous in estimating portions. It is always better to have too much than to commit the ultimate sin of sending the guests home hungry. An abundant table is a true sign of Virginia hospitality.

Avoid monochromatic color schemes. Vary not only the food selections on the plates but the table setting itself. Remember the basic design rules in combining texture, color and patterns of all the elements working together on the table. Not all your plates need to match but they should tie together with similar colors and patterns.

Present your food with a little flair and flourish. Use familiar items in unfamiliar ways. Bake a cake in a clay flowerpot, serve ice cream or cold soups in wine goblets, arrange flowers, candles or dips in gourds or vegetables, use an old quilt or a new rag rug as a tablecloth, or tie large damask napkins to the handles of a galvanized tub to be used as a wine cooler. The list is only limited by your imagination and is shaped by the mood you intend to create.

Remember the garnishes. Kale makes a nice "bed" for salads, meats, sandwiches or cheeses and it is much more substantial than the usual lettuce. You do not have to take a catering course to curl carrot slivers, twist a lemon or squash slice, flower the ends of green onions or simply place a few edible flowers around the top of a special cake or platter of fruits and cheeses. Some safe flowers are nasturtiums, roses and violets; grape leaves and numerous types of herbs may be tied together with a pretty ribbon.

Inventory of Supplies

With the menu planned, now turn your attention to the equipment needed to prepare, serve and present your meal. Inventory all of the serving pieces, linens, glassware, china, silver, tables, chairs and warming plates you have on hand. It is a good idea to have a permanent equipment list for reference. If necessary, additional items may be purchased, borrowed from family members and friends, or rented. Determine if you need flowers (what style of arrangements and how many), extra decorations, candles, lighting or entertainment. Most importantly, decide what you will wear and try it on in advance. Let the nature of the event guide you in all of these decisions, remembering to allow the theme, the holiday, or the cause for celebration to prevail.

Countdown of activities

The major list to compile next is a timetable of "things to do". Use the following suggestions to complete your schedule. Note that reference tables are provided in the back of the book to assist you in calculating food quantities for twenty-five or fifty people, food equivalents and substitutions just in case something is omitted.

Above all else, try to remain flexible as you march towards your goals and to keep your sense of humor. Remember to enjoy your own party.

One week ahead:
- Start to make ice and/or ice rings and store in the freezer
- Order fresh flowers
- Polish silver and put in plastic bags
- Make sure linens are cleaned and pressed
- Clean and clear a shelf or two in your refrigerator and save this space for items made in advance
- Develop the timetable for food preparation
- Post the menu by serving order in a highly visible spot
- Arrange for a neighborhood teen to help in the kitchen or to babysit
- Decide what to wear; look special

Three days ahead:
- Clean the house
- Rearrange any furniture
- Stock the guest bathroom with hand towels, soaps and necessaries
- Prepare any recipe that may be made in advance and store in the freezer or refrigerator to help eliminate as much last minute food preparation as possible (refer to freezing timetable in the reference tables)
- Set the table and pull out all serving pieces, glassware, etcetera
- Put notes where the food will go on the table

One day ahead:
- Shop for perishables and fresh items such as fruits and vegetables; wash and refrigerate them in plastic bags
- Set up bar
- Review family's responsibilities and assignments; older children can be very helpful with small duties and last minute errands

That day:
- Pick up flowers and allow time to assemble arrangements or have them delivered
- Use checklists and timetables to prepare the rest of the meal
- Plan time for yourself so you will be a relaxed, confident Virginia Hostess

When the Party Is Over

As you put away the crystal, take the time to reflect on your preparations and on the gathering itself. Did you prepare enough food? Was there time to arrange it attractively? Were you relaxed? Were the various dishes a pleasing combination of flavors and textures? What did the guests compliment?

Answers to these questions and many others are valuable to a hostess in planning her next party. A notebook or journal for recording this information is a terrific aid. Listing the date, theme, menu, guest list and special decorations or entertainment avoids future duplications, too. Essential to the record keeping is the evaluation of each occasion, indicating what worked or what you would do differently next time. Try to fill in the journal while your memory is clear.

Finally, as you read this cookbook, remember that each hostess must be herself and entertain in a way that suits her best, that works well in her house and that fits into her lifestyle. Whether it is an informal backyard barbecue or a festive holiday open house, the purpose of a party is to please others as well as yourself. Today there are no rules, only guidelines for giving parties. We hope you will enjoy and find useful the suggestions, menus and recipes in The Virginia Hostess, prepared by the Junior Woman's Club of Manassas, Virginia.

Beautiful Beginnings

Monticello - Charlottesville

Lavish hospitality was commonplace at Monticello, designed and built by Thomas Jefferson, author of the Declaration of Independence, third President of the United States and father of the University of Virginia.

Begun in 1769, Monticello was not completed until 1809. Jefferson directed every detail in the construction of his home. During the Revolution, Monticello was occupied by Union forces. The enemy "preserved everything with sacred care" thus showing enormous respect for Jefferson.

Restoration of the gardens began in 1925 and followed the directions found in Jefferson's Garden Book, a daily diary he kept for fifty-three years. Today Monticello is a shrine to a man whose individuality made an indelible impression on this nation.

Beautiful Beginnings

A late morning breakfast or early lunch, commonly referred to as the Brunch, is a popular entertaining option. Whether you serve a breakfast or lunch menu, a wonderful assortment of breads, preferably homemade, will tempt your guests. Complement them with marmalades, jams, jellies and preserves. An attractive fresh fruit bowl heaped with chilled melon balls, berries, red and green grapes and chunks of fruit makes a colorful centerpiece. Add to this an assortment of fine cheeses and vegetable relishes for a complete presentation.

Beverages
Apricot Shake
Banana Smoothee
Coffee Shake
Fresh Vegetable Cocktail
Grapefruit Pecos
Merry Brew
Mexican Hot Chocolate
Orange Breakfast Drink
Orange-Champagne Cocktail
Orange-Tomato Cocktail
Russian Tea
Sangrita
Southern Sangria
Sparkling Strawberry Mimosa
Spiced Tomato Juice
Strawberry Cooler
Tomato Cocktail

Breads
Angel Bread
Basic Waffles
Blueberry Muffin Batter and
    Variations
Breakfast Cake
Cranberry Muffins
Danish Puff
English Muffins
Golden Pumpkin Muffins
Old German Muffins
Orange Blossom Muffins
Orange Bread
Pancake Batter
Pop-overs

Refrigerator Muffin Mix
Rolled French Pancakes
Sausage Biscuits
Sopaipillas with Honey
Sour Cream Dill Biscuits with
    Boursin Cheese
Swedish Coffee Cake

Egg and Cheese Dishes
Breakfast Burritos
Broccoli-Ham Quiche
Cheese-Grits Casserole
Cheese Onion Pie
Cheese Soufflé
Poached Eggs Florentine with
    Mornay Sauce
Sausage-Cheese Strata
Sausage Fondue Casserole
Sausage Quiche
Scotch Eggs

Fruits
Baked Pineapple
Fried Shenandoah Valley Apple
    Slices
Hot Fruit Compote
Strawberry Jam

Vegetables
Broiled Parmesan Tomatoes
Fried Tomatoes
Hashed Brown Potatoes
Marinated Asparagus
Swiss Onion Tart

HUNT BREAKFAST

*After a rousing early morning hunt, riders and "hill toppers"
alike enjoy a hearty breakfast. Our hunt breakfast can be the
start or finish to any active occasion.*

Orange Champagne Cocktail

Sangrita

Tomato Cocktail

Sausage Fondue Casserole

Swiss Onion Tart

Hot Fruit Compote

Hashed Brown Potatoes

Orange Bread

Breakfast Cake

Orange-Champagne Cocktail

3½ cups champagne, chilled   2   cups orange juice, chilled
1   (28-ounce) bottle ginger
     ale, chilled

Combine above ingredients in a pitcher or punch bowl. Stir gently.
Garnish each serving with fresh fruits, if desired. Yield: 9 cups.

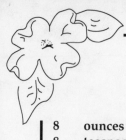

Sangrita

8	ounces tomato juice	4	teaspoons grated onion
8	teaspoons freshly squeezed orange juice		Pinch cayenne pepper or few drops hot pepper sauce
8	teaspoons freshly squeezed lime juice		

Combine all ingredients. Chill to blend flavors. Serve in old-fashioned glasses over ice, garnished with celery sticks. Serves 4.

Tomato Cocktail

1	cup tomato juice	⅛	teaspoon celery salt
1	teaspoon lemon juice		Dash hot pepper sauce
½	teaspoon Worcestershire sauce		

Combine all ingredients. Chill one hour or longer. Serves 1.

Sausage Fondue Casserole

2	pounds mild bulk sausage, browned and well-drained	4	eggs
1	(6-ounce) box Cheddar cheese croutons	2	cups milk
2	cups shredded Cheddar cheese	1	(10 ¾-ounce) can cream of mushroom soup, diluted with ½ cup milk

Place croutons in 13x9-inch (or larger) greased oven proof baking dish. Sprinkle cheese over croutons. Sprinkle sausage over cheese. Beat eggs and milk with a mixer until foamy. Pour over sausage, cover and refrigerate overnight. Before serving, mix soup with milk. Pour over casserole. Bake uncovered in 300 degree oven for 1 hour. Serves 10 to 12.

Swiss Onion Tart

2	slices bacon, chopped	1	teaspoon sugar
2	large onions, thinly sliced		Freshly grated nutmeg
3	tablespoons butter or		to taste
	margarine	⅓	cup shredded Swiss cheese
2	eggs, lightly beaten		Salt and pepper to taste
½	cup heavy cream	1	(9-inch) pastry shell, baked

Preheat oven to 375 degrees. Fry bacon until crisp, drain on paper toweling, and set aside. Sauté onions in heated butter or margarine in skillet until tender, being careful not to brown. Set aside. Combine remaining six ingredients in a bowl. Add onions, mix well, and turn into pastry shell. Top with bacon. Bake 35 minutes or until set and knife inserted into center comes out clean. Serve warm. Serves 6.

Hot Fruit Compote

2	(16-ounce) cans pears, drained and sliced	1	teaspoon cinnamon
		½	teaspoon nutmeg
2	(16-ounce) cans sliced peaches, drained	¼	teaspoon allspice
		½	cup firmly packed brown
1	(15 ½-ounce) can pineapple chunks, drained		sugar
		¼	cup orange-flavored
24	cooked prunes, pitted		liqueur (optional)
3	cups applesauce		

Purée cooked prunes in a food processor or blender. Combine pears, peaches, pineapple, prunes and applesauce in a saucepan. Add spices, brown sugar and orange-flavored liqueur. Mix well. Heat until warm. Serves 12.

Hashed Brown Potatoes

8 cups potatoes, diced
1 tablespoon chopped onion
3 tablespoons chopped fresh
   parsley

½ cup butter or vegetable oil
   Salt and freshly ground
   pepper

Combine potatoes, onion and parsley. Mix well. Heat butter or oil in a large heavy skillet. Spread potato mixture in skillet, pressing down with a spatula. Cook over medium heat until bottom is browned. Carefully turn potatoes over. Add salt and pepper to taste. Brown on other side. Serves 12.

Orange Bread

   Rind from 3 oranges
2 cups sugar, divided
1 cup water
1 tablespoon butter
2 eggs

3 cups flour
3½ teaspoons baking powder
1 teaspoon salt
1 cup milk

Peel oranges and cut rind into small pieces. Place in covered pan with water, cook until mixture boils; drain. Repeat this procedure three times. Drain and add 1 cup sugar and 1 cup water, boiling until approximately 1 tablespoon syrup is remaining. Cool. Cream remaining cup of sugar and butter. Add eggs. Sift dry ingredients together and add to mixture alternately with milk. Fold orange rind into bread batter and pour into a well-greased loaf pan. Bake in 350 degree oven for approximately 1 hour. Bread can be frozen. Serves 6 to 8.

Breakfast Cake

2	cups sugar	2	teaspoons baking powder
¾	cup margarine or	1	cup milk
	shortening		Jam
3	eggs		Confectioners' sugar
3 ½	cups flour		

Cream together sugar and margarine or shortening. Add eggs. Mix together flour and baking powder. Add flour mixture alternately with milk to sugar mixture. Batter will be thick. Pour batter into 2 greased 9-inch round cake pans. Bake at 350 degrees for 35 minutes. Cool 10 minutes in pans. Remove from pans and continue cooling on racks. When cool, slice through cake layers horizontally and spread bottom half with your favorite jam. Replace top and sprinkle with confectioners' sugar. Serves 8 to 10.

"DOWNHOME" VIRGINIA BREAKFAST

Offer this classic country breakfast when friends come to visit.

Spiced Tomato Juice

Fried Shenandoah Valley Apple Slices

Fried Tomatoes

Sausage Biscuits

Cheese Soufflé

Spiced Tomato Juice

⅔	cup sugar	1	quart tomato juice
½	teaspoon nutmeg	½	cup lemon juice
½	teaspoon cinnamon	2	cups hot water
	Several whole cloves		

Mix first four ingredients in a saucepan. Add tomato juice. Simmer until sugar dissolves. Add lemon juice and water. Simmer until flavors blend. Serve cold in wine glasses or goblets. Serves 8.

Fried Shenandoah Valley Apple Slices

12	tart apples (Granny Smith or Stayman)	1 ¼	teaspoons cinnamon
		1	teaspoon nutmeg
1	cup sugar	¾	cup butter

Peel and core apples and cut into eighths. Combine next three ingredients. Mix well. Melt butter in a large deep skillet. Add apple slices and spice mixture. Cook over low heat, stirring occasionally, until soft. Serve hot. Serves 12.

Fried Tomatoes

2	medium firm tomatoes	¼	teaspoon black pepper
¼	cup cracker meal	1	egg, beaten
½	teaspoon salt	3	tablespoons shortening

Slice tomatoes. Add salt and pepper to cracker meal. Dip tomatoes in beaten egg and then in cracker meal. Cook in hot shortening until golden brown on both sides, turning once. Drain on paper toweling. Serve hot. Serves 4.

Sausage Biscuits

1	pound hot bulk sausage	½	teaspoon salt
2 ⅔	cups flour	½	cup shortening
2	tablespoons sugar	1	package dry yeast
1	teaspoon baking powder	¼	cup very warm water
½	teaspoon soda	1	cup buttermilk

Cook hot sausage slowly. Do not overcook. Drain and set aside. Sift dry ingredients together and cut in shortening. Dissolve yeast in warm water for about five minutes. Add to buttermilk. Stir into dry ingredients and mix well. Roll to about ¼-inch thickness. Sprinkle sausage over half the dough. Fold over other half dough and pat or roll lightly with rolling pin. Cut with biscuit cutter. Place on greased cookie sheet and bake at 450 degrees for 12 minutes. These may be frozen before baking. Thaw in refrigerator overnight. Yield: 24 biscuits.

Cheese Soufflé

4	slices bread	4	eggs
1	teaspoon salt	2	cups milk
¼	teaspoon dry mustard		
2	cups shredded Cheddar cheese		

Crumble bread in buttered casserole. Add salt and dry mustard. Spread grated cheese over crumbs. Beat eggs, add milk and pour over cheese. Let stand overnight, covered, in refrigerator. Place casserole dish in pan of water about ½-inch deep. Bake at 350 degrees for 1 hour. Serves 6 to 8.

SUNDAY'S BEST BRUNCH

Dress up your table to suit this elegant Sunday brunch menu.

Sparkling Strawberry Mimosas

Orange-Tomato Cocktail

Danish Puff

Poached Eggs Florentine with Mornay Sauce

Sausage-Cheese Strata

Broiled Parmesan Tomatoes

Marinated Asparagus

Pop-Overs with Strawberry Jam

Sparkling Strawberry Mimosas

2 ½ cups orange juice, chilled
1   (10-ounce) package frozen
     strawberries, partially
     thawed

1   (26.4-ounce) bottle dry
     champagne, chilled
     Whole fresh strawberries
     (optional)

Combine orange juice and frozen strawberries in blender. Process until puréed. Pour into a pitcher. Add champagne and stir gently. Garnish each serving with a fresh strawberry, if desired. Serve immediately. Yield: 8 cups.

Orange-Tomato Cocktail

1 ½ cups tomato juice, chilled
1 cup orange juice, chilled
1 teaspoon sugar
1 tablespoon lemon or lime juice

½ teaspoon salt
¼ cup crushed ice
Crushed mint (optional)

Mix above ingredients. Garnish with mint, if desired. Serves 3.

Danish Puff

2 cups flour, divided
1 cup butter plus 2 tablespoons, divided
1 cup plus 2 tablespoons water

1 teaspoon almond flavoring
3 eggs
1 ½ cups confectioners' sugar
1-2 tablespoons orange juice
Blanched almonds

Mix 1 cup flour, ½ cup butter and 2 tablespoons water together. Divide dough in half. Place on baking sheet and roll out to ½-inch. Heat remaining butter and 1 cup water to boiling. Remove from heat, add almond flavoring and remaining flour all at once, stirring quickly so it does not lump. Add three eggs, one at a time. Spread mixture over the two dough halves. Mix remaining ingredients and spread on top. Bake at 350 degrees for 1 hour. Slice into strips to serve. Serves 10.

Poached Eggs Florentine with Mornay Sauce

2 (10-ounce) packages frozen chopped spinach, cooked and drained
¼ cup butter or margarine
⅛ teaspoon grated nutmeg
Salt and pepper to taste

16 warm poached eggs (soft or medium), drained
2 cups warm Mornay sauce (recipe follows)
¼ cup grated Parmesan cheese

Combine first four ingredients, mix well. Divide into 8 individual oven-proof baking dishes. Top with 2 eggs in each dish. Cover with Mornay sauce. Sprinkle with Parmesan cheese. Slide under heated broiler until bubbly hot and golden on top. Serves 8.

Mornay Sauce

¼ cup butter or margarine   ¾ cup shredded Swiss cheese
¼ cup all-purpose flour   Salt and pepper to taste
2 cups light cream or milk

Melt butter or margarine in a small saucepan, add flour, and cook 1 minute. Gradually add cream or milk and cook slowly, stirring until smooth and thickened. Stir in cheese and seasonings. Continue cooking until cheese melts. Yield: 2 cups.

Sausage-Cheese Strata

1 pound bulk sausage,   5 eggs
    cooked and crumbled   2 cups Half and Half
6 slices bread   1 teaspoon salt
    Softened butter (optional)   ½ teaspoon dry mustard
1 ½ cups shredded Cheddar
     cheese

Drain cooked sausage on paper toweling and set aside. Spread each slice of bread with butter (optional). Cut bread slices into cubes. Place bread cubes into a 13x9x2-inch baking pan. Sprinkle sausage over bread in pan and top with cheese. Combine remaining ingredients, beat well and pour over mixture in baking pan. Cover and chill at least 8 hours. Remove from refrigerator and bake at 350 degrees for 40 to 50 minutes or microwave at 70 percent power for 20 to 25 minutes until center is set. Let stand for 5 minutes. Serves 8.

Broiled Parmesan Tomatoes

¼ cup butter, melted and   1 teaspoon salt
    divided   ⅛ teaspoon pepper
½ cup fine dry bread crumbs   3 large peeled tomatoes, cut
½ cup grated Parmesan cheese   into 1-inch slices

Mix crumbs and half of butter. Stir in next three ingredients. Brush tomato slices with remaining butter and dip in crumb mixture. Arrange tomato slices on cookie sheet covered with aluminum foil. Broil 5 to 6 inches below heat source until lightly browned and warmed through. Turn carefully with pancake turner and brown on other side. Serves 6.

Marinated Asparagus

3	tablespoons vinegar	½	teaspoon salt
¼	cup oil	1	teaspoon dried parsley
¼	teaspoon white pepper	1	pound cooked asparagus

Mix all ingredients except asparagus. Marinate asparagus in mixture overnight. Serves 4.

Pop-Overs

1 ½	cups flour	2	eggs
½	teaspoon salt	2	teaspoons butter, melted
1 ½	cups milk		

Combine flour and salt in bowl. Add milk and eggs. Beat with a rotary beater for 3 minutes. Add melted butter and stir. Put in well-greased, hot muffin tins. Bake at 350 degrees for 40 minutes. Yield: 12 pop-overs.

Strawberry Jam

1	cup strawberries (frozen or fresh)	1	cup sugar
			Juice from ½ lemon

Mix all ingredients together. Cook to boiling, uncovered in a heavy pan for 12 minutes. Yield: 2 cups.

MEXICAN BREAKFAST

Start your day off with a sizzle. A Mexican breakfast buffet is a lively and colorful feast on a cool fall morning.

Breakfast Burritos

Sopaipillas with Honey

Mexican Hot Chocolate

Baked Pineapple

Breakfast Burritos

½	pound pork bulk sausage, cooked and crumbled	1	cup shredded Cheddar cheese (optional)
1	green onion, chopped		Tomato salsa
5	or 6 eggs		
4	flour tortillas (may substitute corn tortillas)		

Scramble onion and eggs into sausage. Heat tortillas per package directions. Place egg mixture in each tortilla. Sprinkle with cheese if desired. Roll up and pour salsa on top. Serves 4

Sopaipillas

4	cups flour	1	egg, beaten
4	teaspoons baking powder	1	cup water
1	teaspoon salt		Oil
1	tablespoon shortening		Honey

Sift dry ingredients together. Mix in shortening and knead. Add egg and water to form a stiff dough. Divide dough into 4 parts and roll out very thinly. Cut into 3-inch squares. Fry in deep hot oil at 350 degrees. The sopaipillas will puff up like little pillows. Serve immediately with honey. Serves 4 to 6.

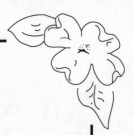

Mexican Hot Chocolate

1	(2-ounce) cake Mexican chocolate (or 2 (1-ounce) squares unsweetened chocolate, 2 tablespoons sugar, 1 teaspoon ground cinnamon and a pinch salt)	4	cups milk

Combine ingredients in a heavy saucepan and cook until chocolate melts. Remove from heat and beat until smooth and frothy. Pour into cups or serve from a pitcher. Serves 4.

Baked Pineapple

1	(20-ounce) can crushed pineapple	1	tablespoon butter
¾	cup sugar	3	tablespoons regular tapioca
2	eggs, slightly beaten		

Mix all ingredients. Bake uncovered in 350 degree oven for 1 hour. Serves 4.

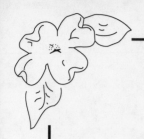

BRUNCH ENTREES

Create your own brunch menu from a delicious assortment of entrees. Change scrambled eggs and sausage or broccoli and ham into tasty casseroles in minutes.

Cheese-Grits Casserole

Broccoli-Ham Quiche

Cheese Onion Pie

Sausage Quiche

Scotch Eggs

Cheese-Grits Casserole

4	cups water	¼	cup margarine
1	teaspoon salt	2	eggs, slightly beaten
1	cup quick cooking grits		
1	cup shredded Cheddar cheese		

Preheat oven to 350 degrees. Heat water and salt to boiling in 3-quart saucepan. Gradually stir in grits. Heat to boiling and reduce heat. Simmer uncovered, stirring occasionally for 5 minutes and remove from heat. Stir in remaining ingredients. Pour into ungreased 1 ½-quart casserole. Bake approximately 50 minutes. May refrigerate up to 24 hours before baking. Serves 8.

Broccoli-Ham Quiche

1 (9-inch) pastry shell, unbaked
1 tablespoon butter, melted
½ (10-ounce) package frozen chopped broccoli
4 to 6 ounces Swiss cheese, shredded
¾ cup finely chopped ham
1 cup Half and Half
3 eggs
1 teaspoon salt

Brush pastry shell with butter. Chill pastry shell. Precook broccoli for 5 minutes. Drain well on paper towels. Layer broccoli, ham and cheese into pastry shell. In a small bowl, whisk together remaining ingredients. Pour over other ingredients. Bake at 375 degrees for 40 minutes or until knife inserted in center comes out clean. Serves 6.

Cheese Onion Pie

2 large onions, sliced
2 tablespoons butter
1 (9-inch) pastry shell, unbaked
½ pound Swiss cheese, shredded
1 tablespoon flour
3 eggs
1 cup milk
½ teaspoon salt
Dash pepper

Sauté onions in butter until tender but not brown and pour into pastry shell. Mix cheese and flour and sprinkle mixture over onions. Beat together remaining ingredients. Pour over cheese. Bake at 400 degrees for 20 minutes. Reduce heat to 300 degrees and continue baking for 25 minutes. Serves 8.

Sausage Quiche

½	pound bulk pork sausage, cooked and drained	2	tablespoons flour
½	cup chopped onion	2	teaspoons parsley flakes
1 ½	cups shredded sharp Cheddar cheese	1	(9-inch) pie crust, unbaked
		2	eggs, beaten
		⅔	cup evaporated milk

Preheat oven to 375 degrees. Combine sausage with next four ingredients. Mix well. Spread in unbaked pie crust. Beat together eggs and evaporated milk. Slowly pour over sausage mixture. Bake in oven on preheated cookie sheet 35 to 40 minutes or until filling is set. Serves 8.

Scotch Eggs

2	pounds bulk pork sausage	12	hard-cooked eggs, shelled
¼	cup chopped fresh parsley		Flour
¼	cup minced onion	2	eggs, beaten
¼	teaspoon cayenne pepper		Fine dry bread crumbs
	Salt and pepper to taste		Oil for frying

Combine first five ingredients and mix well. Roll out evenly on a piece of waxed paper. Dust each egg lightly with flour. Coat each hard-cooked egg with sausage mixture to cover completely. Roll each egg in beaten egg and then in bread crumbs. Fry in hot deep fat (375 degrees on frying thermometer) for about 5 minutes or until done. To serve, cut into halves. You can make beforehand and cook just before serving hot or cook beforehand and serve cold. Serves 12.

BREAKFAST BEVERAGES

Try an "out-of-the-ordinary" breakfast beverage for a start to a great day - a blended fruit juice, a spiced tea or spirited coffee.

Russian Tea

Merry Brew

Fresh Vegetable Cocktail

Southern Sangria

Orange Breakfast Drink

Strawberry Cooler

Apricot Shake

Banana Smoothee

Coffee Shake

Grapefruit Pecos

Russian Tea

6	cups water	1	teaspoon grated lemon rind
12	whole cloves		Juice of 2 oranges
2	tablespoons tea leaves		Sugar to taste
2 ½	cups pineapple juice		
	Juice of 2 lemons		

Boil water and cloves for 15 minutes. Add tea and steep for 2 to 4 minutes. Strain. Add remaining ingredients. Serve hot. Yield: 8 cups.

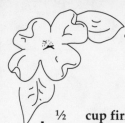

Merry Brew

½	cup firmly packed brown sugar	½	teaspoon whole allspice
¼	teaspoon salt	1	cup water
2	sticks cinnamon	2	quarts apple juice
1	tablespoon whole cloves	1	lemon, thinly sliced
		1	orange, thinly sliced

Combine sugar, salt, spices and water in a small saucepan and bring to a boil. Reduce heat and simmer 10 minutes. Combine remaining ingredients in a large saucepan and heat gently. Strain hot spiced liquid into apple juice and serve warm. Yield: 8 cups.

Fresh Vegetable Cocktail

3	cups unsweetened pineapple juice, chilled	⅓	cucumber, peeled and sliced
1	medium carrot, sliced	2	slices lemon
1 ½	stalks celery, sliced		Fresh mint (optional)

Combine all ingredients except mint in blender. Process until smooth. Chill. Garnish with fresh mint, if desired. Yield: 4 cups.

Southern Sangria

⅓	cup sugar	1	(25.4-ounce) bottle sparkling red grape juice, chilled
⅓	cup lemon juice		
⅓	cup orange juice		

Combine first three ingredients in a large pitcher and stir until sugar dissolves. Add grape juice and gently stir to mix well. Serve over crushed ice. Yield: 5 cups.

Orange Breakfast Drink

⅓   cup frozen orange juice   ½   cup water
concentrate, thawed and   ¼   cup sugar
undiluted   ½   teaspoon vanilla extract
½   cup milk   5   to 6 ice cubes

Combine all ingredients in electric blender and process until frothy. Serve immediately. Serves 2.

Strawberry Cooler

1   cup skim milk   2   tablespoons vanilla extract
1   cup plain lowfat yogurt   2   cups whole strawberries
2   tablespoons sugar   (fresh or frozen)

Combine first four ingredients in blender and process until smooth. Gradually add strawberries. Process until smooth and slightly thickened. Yield: 3 ¾ cups.

Apricot Shake

1   cup cold milk   ½   cup vanilla ice cream
1   cup apricot nectar

Combine ingredients in blender and blend until smooth. Serves 2.

Banana Smoothee

¾   cup milk   ½   cup vanilla ice cream
½   ripe banana, peeled and
cut-up

Combine ingredients in blender and blend until smooth. Serves 1.

Coffee Shake

1	cup strong coffee	Dash cinnamon
½	cup coffee ice cream	

Combine ingredients in blender and blend until smooth. Serves 1.

Grapefruit Pecos

1	egg, separated	1	tablespoon honey
1	cup grapefruit juice, chilled		Dash salt
			Grated nutmeg

Beat egg yolk in small bowl until creamy. Gradually add grapefruit juice, beating constantly. Add honey and salt. Beat egg white until stiff but not dry in a medium-sized bowl. Add grapefruit mixture. Pour into a chilled glass. Top with nutmeg. Serves 1.

BREAKFAST BREADS

Breakfast breads complement any occasion. A lace-lined basket filled with warm muffins is a pleasing treat to take when visiting friends or welcoming new neighbors.

Basic Waffles

Rolled French Pancakes

Pancake Batter

Blueberry Muffin Batter and Variations

Refrigerator Muffin Mix

English Muffins

Cranberry Muffins

Old German Muffins

Golden Pumpkin Muffins

Orange Blossom Muffins

Sour Cream Dill Biscuits with Boursin Cheese

Swedish Coffee Cake

Angel Bread

Basic Waffles

1 ½ cups sifted flour
2 ½ teaspoons baking powder
½ teaspoon salt
1 tablespoon sugar
2 eggs

1 cup plus 2 tablespoons milk
1 teaspoon vanilla (optional)
⅓ cup butter or margarine, melted and slightly cooled

Sift together dry ingredients into a large bowl. Place eggs in small bowl and beat on high speed about 30 seconds until fluffy. Add milk and vanilla, if desired. Beat to blend. Pour over dry ingredients and beat on medium speed about 1 minute until blended, scraping bowl as necessary. Beat in butter or margarine on low speed only until mixed. Preheat waffle iron, set at medium. Pour approximately 1 cup batter evenly over grids. Bake until golden brown. Remove waffle and repeat. Yield: 8 waffles.

Rolled French Pancakes

½ cup all-purpose flour
⅛ teaspoon salt
1 egg, beaten
1 egg yolk, beaten

½ cup milk
Vegetable oil
3 tablespoons jelly
Confectioners' sugar

Combine first five ingredients. Beat until smooth. Cover and chill 30 minutes. Brush a 5-inch skillet lightly with vegetable oil and place over medium heat until just hot, not smoking. Pour 2 tablespoons batter in skillet and quickly tilt in all directions so batter covers the bottom in a thin film. Cook about 1 minute. Lift edge of pancake to test for doneness. Turn pancake and cook about 30 seconds on other side. Spread each pancake with jelly and roll up jellyroll fashion. Place on baking sheet and sprinkle with confectioners' sugar. Place under broiler just until glazed. Yield: 8 pancakes.

Pancake Batter

1 ¼	cups flour		1	egg, beaten
3	teaspoons baking powder		1	cup milk
1	tablespoon sugar		2	tablespoons oil
½	teaspoon salt			

Sift together first four ingredients in a small bowl and set aside. Combine remaining ingredients. Add dry ingredients, stirring just until flour is moistened. Batter will be lumpy. Bake on hot griddle. Yield: 12 pancakes.

Blueberry Muffin Batter and Variations

½	cup unsalted butter		Pinch baking soda
2	eggs	1	cup milk
1 ⅛	cups sugar	1	teaspoon vanilla extract
3	cups flour, divided	2	cups blueberries,
3	teaspoons baking powder		sweetened as needed
½	teaspoon salt		

Grease 2 (12-muffin) muffin pans and set aside. Preheat oven to 400 degrees. In large bowl, cream together butter, eggs and sugar. Reserve 3 tablespoons flour. In medium bowl, combine remaining flour, baking powder, salt and baking soda. Add vanilla to milk. Alternately add milk and flour mixture to creamed butter and egg mixture. Place berries in large bowl, sprinkle with reserved flour and turn gently with large spoon until berries are lightly coated. Fold berries into batter. Fill each muffin pan ¾-full and sprinkle top with sugar. Fill any remaining empty tins ½-full with water. Bake 15 to 20 minutes or until muffins pull away from sides of pan and turn golden brown. To make Apple Muffins, substitute apple juice for milk and peeled, diced apples for berries. Sprinkle top of unbaked muffins with cinnamon and sugar. To make Raisin Spice Muffins, omit blueberries and add ¾ cup raisins, 2 teaspoons cinnamon and 1 teaspoon nutmeg to dough. To make Banana Muffins, substitute 3 mashed bananas for blueberries. Sprinkle top of unbaked muffins with cinnamon and sugar. Yield: 18 muffins.

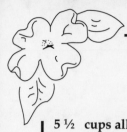

Refrigerator Muffin Mix

5 ½	cups all-purpose flour	1	quart buttermilk
2 ½	cups sugar	1 ½	cups cooking oil
3	cups natural wheat bran	4	eggs
2	cups bran cereal	½	cup molasses
3	tablespoons baking soda	2	cups raisins

In large bowl, combine all dry ingredients except baking soda. In another bowl, stir soda and buttermilk together. Add oil, eggs and molasses. Beat well with mixer. Make a well in center of dry ingredients, pour in liquid and stir well. Mix in raisins. Fill muffin cups ¾-full and bake at 375 degrees for 20 minutes. Store remaining mix in container with tight-fitting lid. Keeps in refrigerator 8 weeks. Yield: 4 dozen.

English Muffins

1	cup milk	1	egg, beaten
3	tablespoons shortening	4 ¼	cups all-purpose flour,
1 ½	teaspoons salt		divided
3	tablespoons sugar		Melted shortening
1	package dry yeast		
¼	cup warm water		
	(105 to 115 degrees)		

Scald milk and stir in next three ingredients. Cool to lukewarm. Sprinkle yeast over warm water, stir well and add to milk mixture. Add egg and 2 cups flour, mixing well. Turn dough out on a lightly floured board and knead in remaining flour until smooth and elastic. Place in a large greased bowl and brush with melted shortening. Cover and let rise in a warm place about 1 ½ hours. Turn dough out on a lightly floured board and roll to ¼-inch thickness. Cut with a 3 ½-inch round cutter and place on an ungreased baking sheet. Let rise in a warm place about 45 minutes or until doubled in bulk. Bake at 325 degrees about 8 minutes on one side, turn muffins and bake about 8 minutes on other side. Yield: 12 muffins.

Cranberry Muffins

1	cup sifted all-purpose flour	3	ounces orange juice
½	cup sugar	½	teaspoon grated orange peel
¾	teaspoon baking powder	1	egg, beaten
¼	teaspoon baking soda	½	cup coarsely chopped fresh cranberries
½	teaspoon salt		
2	tablespoons butter	¼	cup chopped walnuts

Preheat oven to 350 degrees. Grease a 12-cup muffin tin. In large mixing bowl, sift together dry ingredients. Cut in butter. In separate bowl, combine juice, orange peel and egg. Add to dry ingredients, mixing only enough to moisten. Fold in cranberries and nuts. Fill prepared muffin cups about ⅔-full with batter. Bake 15 minutes. Cool and wrap overnight. Warm and serve next day. Yield: 12 muffins.

Old German Muffins

¾	cup butter or margarine	2	teaspoons baking powder
½	cup sugar	2 ¼	cups flour
2	eggs	¼	cup ground almonds
1	tablespoon rum	1	tablespoon grated orange rind
1	teaspoon vanilla		
3	tablespoons milk	¼	cup raisins (optional)
½	teaspoon cinnamon		

Cream butter and sugar. Beat in eggs, rum, vanilla and milk. Mix dry ingredients. Add flour mixture to butter mixture. Gently mix in almonds, orange rind and raisins. Pour batter into greased muffin tins, filling ½-full. Bake at 375 degrees for 25 to 30 minutes, until browned. Yield: 18 muffins.

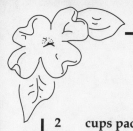

Golden Pumpkin Muffins

2	cups packaged biscuit mix	¾	cup milk
½	cup sugar	½	cup canned pumpkin
¼	teaspoon cloves	1	egg, beaten
½	teaspoon ginger	2	tablespoons oil
¾	teaspoon cinnamon		

In bowl, combine dry ingredients thoroughly. In another bowl, combine remaining ingredients. Stir into dry ingredients until blended. Fill greased muffin cups ⅔-full. Bake at 400 degrees for 20 minutes. Yield: 12 muffins.

Orange Blossom Muffins

1	(6-ounce) can frozen orange juice concentrate, thawed	2	cups packaged biscuit mix
		½	cup orange marmalade
¼	cup sugar	½	cup chopped toasted pecans
2	tablespoons salad oil or melted shortening		Cinnamon Topping (recipe follows)
1	egg, slightly beaten		

Preheat oven to 400 degrees. In medium-sized mixing bowl, combine first four ingredients. Add biscuit mix and beat vigorously for 30 seconds. Stir in marmalade and pecans. Grease muffin pan or line with paper bake cups. Fill each cup ⅔-full with batter. Sprinkle topping over unbaked muffins. Bake for 20 to 25 minutes or until toothpick inserted in muffin comes out clean. Yield: 12 muffins.

Cinnamon Topping

¼	cup sugar	¼	teaspoon nutmeg
1 ½	tablespoons all-purpose flour	1	tablespoon butter or margarine, room temperature
½	teaspoon cinnamon		

Combine first four ingredients. Cut in butter until crumbly.

Sour Cream Dill Biscuits

1 cup self-rising flour
¼ teaspoon baking soda
¾ cup sour cream
1 to 2 teaspoons dill weed

Sliced country ham
Boursin Cheese
(recipe follows)

Combine all ingredients in mixing bowl. Stir until smooth. Dough will be sticky, so flour hands and turn onto a floured surface. Pat dough until ½-inch thick. Cut with a 2-inch biscuit cutter. Place on greased baking sheet. Bake in 450 degree oven for 8 to 10 minutes or until golden. Serve with thinly sliced country ham and boursin cheese. Yield: 10 biscuits.

Boursin Cheese

1 (8-ounce) cream cheese
2 tablespoons butter
2 garlic cloves, crushed
½ teaspoon fresh lemon juice
  or to taste

1 teaspoon oregano
½ teaspoon basil
⅛ teaspoon salt
⅛ teaspoon cayenne pepper
2 tablespoons fresh parsley

Combine all ingredients (may be prepared in a food processor with steel blade) and blend thoroughly. Taste for flavor and seasonings. May be shaped into a ball and rolled in crushed pepper or put in serving dish and refrigerated overnight before serving. Boursin cheese may be frozen.

Swedish Coffee Cake

2	cups flour	1	(8-ounce) carton sour
1	cup sugar		cream
2	eggs		Chopped walnuts to taste
1	teaspoon baking powder		Cinnamon Mixture:
1	teaspoon baking soda	1	cup chopped nuts
1	teaspoon vanilla	1	teaspoon sugar
½	cup margarine	1	teaspoon cinnamon

Mix first nine ingredients. Divide batter in half. Put half of batter in bundt pan. Combine remaining three ingredients. Divide cinnamon mixture in half. Sprinkle half of cinnamon mixture over batter. Cover with remaining sour cream mixture. Top with remaining cinnamon mixture to form 2 layers. Bake at 325 degrees for 1 hour. Serves 8 to 10.

Angel Bread

5	cups flour	¾	cup solid vegetable
1	tablespoon baking powder		shortening
1	tablespoon baking soda	2	cups buttermilk
1	tablespoon salt	1	package yeast mixed with
3	tablespoons sugar		½ cup warm water

Sift dry ingredients together. Cut in shortening, add buttermilk and yeast. Mix and beat well. Do not let rise. Cover and put in refrigerator to use as needed. When ready to use, take out as much as needed. Roll on floured board to about ¾-inch thickness and cut. Allow to rise for length of time it takes to heat oven to 425 degrees. Bake about 10 minutes until golden brown. Dough will keep several weeks in refrigerator. This dough can also be used for dinner rolls, biscuits and small pizzas. Yield: 3 to 4 dozen biscuits.

Flowers and Flourishes

Christ Church - Alexandria

Seasonal colors abound on the grounds of historic Christ Church located on Cameron and Columbus Streets in Alexandria. Erected in 1767 on land donated by John Alexander of Stafford County, Christ Church is Georgian style, built of native brick laid in Flemish and English bond. The church claims some notable parishioners including George Washington and Robert E. Lee.

Following the Civil War, tax support of churches was removed. George Washington, together with other laymen, agreed to support the parish by purchasing pews and paying an annual fee to the rector. Christ Church is beautifully appointed with wooden panels, box pews and a wineglass pulpit.

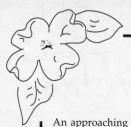

Flowers and Flourishes

An approaching wedding or birth, an anniversary, a reunion of friends or a first communion give us reasons to celebrate with a shower, a tea or a luncheon.

Beverages
Champagne Punch
Citrus-Tea Punch
Lime Sherbet Punch
Pink Punch for Ladies

Breads
Crescent Rolls
Crunch Rolls
Scones or Welsh Cookies

Desserts
Benne Seed Cookies
Neopolitan Sheet Cake
Old Fashioned Cheesecake
Raspberry Swirls
Southern Strawberry Pie
Sticky Butter

Entrees
Crab and Artichoke Casserole
Never Fail Cheese Soufflé
Open-Faced Crab Sandwiches
Uppercrust Chicken

Miscellaneous
Assorted Tea Sandwiches
Carrot Soup
Summer Squash Soup
Vegetable Sandwich Spread

Salads
Apricot Molded Salad
Blueberry Salad
Chicken Salad in Pineapple Shells
Colorful Coleslaw
Curried Chicken Salad
English Pea Salad
Orange Salad
Queen's Chicken Salad
Spinach Salad with Chutney
   Dressing
Taco Salad

Vegetables
Marinated Carrots
Spinach Souffle

Teas

Much credit is given to the British for raising teatime to an elegant affair. Freshly baked breads, fruit and cheese are good accompaniments to a steeping pot of your favorite tea blend.

Tips For The Perfect Pot of Tea

Selecting a good quality tea is the first step to creating the perfect pot of tea for your afternoon gathering. Choose one that complements your menu.

Darjeeling: Flavor of black currants.

English Breakfast: Blend of strong teas from India and Ceylon; goes well with sweets.

Formosa Oolong: Slightly peachy flavor; goes with foods that are not too sweet.

Lapsang Souchong: Hearty, smoky, and rich in flavor; goes with simple fare.

Orange Pekoe: "Pekoe" means little, referring to leaf size; originally flavored with orange blossom, but now a black tea varying widely in flavor.

Follow these steps for perfect brewing.

- Use "cold" tap water so tea is fresh and full of oxygen.

- If using an infuser or a tea ball, do not fill to the brim. Tea leaves need space to expand.

- Heat the teapot first by swirling in it a bit of hot water, then empty pot. This provides for the maintenance of the water's boiling point which is crucial for correct brewing.

- If using loose tea, use one teaspoon per serving, plus one for the pot.

- Do not overboil the water. This results in the loss of oxygen and tends to give tea a muddy taste.

- Normal steeping time is 5 minutes. Give the brew a stir, remove the infuser or tea bags and enjoy.

- Serve tea with sugar cubes, honey, milk or cream, mint or very thinly sliced lemon.

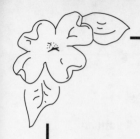

GARDEN TEA

Invite your club members for an afternoon of light conversation and tasty tea sandwiches. Take advantage of a gorgeous day by entertaining your guests on the terrace.

Assorted Tea Sandwiches

Scones or Welsh Cookies

Vegetable Sandwich Spread

Assorted Tea Sandwiches

Cottage cheese mixed with chopped tomato or raspberries

Cream cheese and chutney or jelly

Sardines, watercress and onion

Mashed avocado, crumbled bacon and chili sauce

Ladyfingers, split and spread with jam

Small canned shrimp, mashed with mayonnaise and onion

Snappy cheese mixture with chopped nuts and pimento

Date nut bread filled with cream cheese spread

Salami and slices of cooked potato on rye

Sliced chicken, asparagus spear, olive rings and tomato slice

Spread mixture on choice of bread to create an assortment of tea sandwiches.

Scones or Welsh Cookies

4	cups flour	½	cup shortening
1	teaspoon salt	¼	cup sugar
4	teaspoons baking powder	1	cup currants
1	teaspoon nutmeg	3	eggs
½	cup butter		Milk

Sift together flour, salt, baking powder and nutmeg. Cut in butter and shortening. Add sugar and currants and mix. Place eggs in 1 cup liquid measure; add milk to equal 1 cup. Beat and add eggs to dry ingredients. Turn onto a floured surface and knead 15 times. Dough can be prepared to this point and frozen. Roll out to ½ to ¾-inch thickness. Cut into biscuit-size wedges. Bake on ungreased cookie sheet at 425 degrees for 15 minutes. Yield: 2 dozen.

Vegetable Sandwich Spread

1	medium onion, finely chopped	1	cup finely chopped celery
1	medium cucumber, finely chopped	2	teaspoons salt
1	medium tomato, finely chopped	1	envelope unflavored gelatin
			Mayonnaise

Combine first four ingredients. Sprinkle with salt, stir and place in colander over a bowl to drain juice for 2 to 4 hours. Warm ½ cup of the juice and dissolve gelatin in it. Discard extra juice. Mix vegetables, gelatin and mayonnaise and let sit in refrigerator overnight. Spread on 60 to 90 finger sandwiches.

LUNCHEONS

One-dish entrees such as quiches or cold meat salads with fruits and vegetables are simple but elegant.

SPRING BRIDE'S LUNCHEON

Azaleas in full bloom provide a perfect background for this lively salad trio. The colors of spring reflected in fresh fruits and vegetables brighten the table. This is an ideal "do-ahead" menu.

Curried Chicken Salad

Blueberry Salad

Colorful Coleslaw

Never Fail Cheese Soufflé

Lime Sherbet Punch

Crescent Rolls

Curried Chicken Salad

12	cups Butter or Boston lettuce	6	cups diagonally cut asparagus
6	cups spinach	3	cups slivered carrots
2	cups alfalfa sprouts		Curried Salad Dressing
1	cup arugula lettuce		(recipe follows)
6	cups cooked chicken breasts, cut up		

In a large bowl, combine cleaned and dried greens. Cook asparagus and carrots in boiling water 2 to 3 minutes. Drain and rinse with cold water. Add chicken, asparagus and carrots to lettuce. Toss lightly with dressing. Serves 10.

Curried Salad Dressing

1	cup olive oil	1 ½	tablespoons curry powder
½	cup fresh lemon juice	1 ½	tablespoons basil
1	cup mayonnaise	8	scallions, minced
3	tablespoons honey	2	teaspoons salt

Mix well and toss with salad. Yield: 2 ½ cups.

Blueberry Salad

1	(8 ¼-ounce) can crushed pineapple, drained, juice reserved	1	cup sour cream
		1	(8-ounce) package cream cheese, softened
1	(6-ounce) package black raspberry gelatin	½	cup sugar
			Chopped pecans
1	cup boiling water		
1	(15-ounce) can blueberries, drained, juice reserved		

Add cold water to reserved blueberry and pineapple juices to equal 2 cups. Dissolve gelatin in boiling water. Stir in cold liquid. Chill until partially set. Fold in fruit. Pour into 12x8-inch pan. Chill until firm. Serves 10.

Colorful Coleslaw

1	large head cabbage, shredded	½	cup minced fresh parsley
		1 ½	cups cider vinegar
1	large onion, chopped	1 ½	cups vegetable oil
3	carrots, shredded	½	cup sugar
1 ½	cups chopped green pepper	1	teaspoon salt
		¾	teaspoon white pepper
1 ½	cups chopped red pepper		

Early in the day, combine first six ingredients in a bowl. Set aside. Combine vinegar and next four ingredients. Stir well. Add to cabbage mixture. Toss gently. Cover and chill. Serves 10.

Never Fail Cheese Soufflé

½	cup margarine	1	teaspoon salt
⅓	cup flour	2	cups shredded sharp
1 ½	cups milk		Cheddar cheese
	Dash cayenne pepper	6	eggs, separated

Make a white sauce with first three ingredients. Add seasonings and cheese, stirring until melted. Remove from heat and stir in egg yolks. Beat egg whites until stiff. Fold them gently into cheese mixture. Pour mixture into a 2 quart baking dish or 10 individual ramekins. Bake in preheated 300 degree oven for 1 hour 15 minutes for large dish or 30 to 40 minutes for ramekins until browned and puffed high. Serve as soon as possible. If soufflé must be held over, open oven door, turn oven off, and leave in oven with door open. Can hold in oven 10 to 15 minutes. Can be frozen. Cover with foil, place (uncooked) in the freezer. When you are ready to use, remove from freezer, remove foil and place in a pan of cold water about 1 inch deep. Bake in 350 degree oven 30 to 40 minutes. Will keep in the freezer for 10 to 12 weeks. Serves 10.

Lime Sherbet Punch

1	or 2 limes, sliced	1	(2-liter) bottle ginger ale,
¼	to ½ cup lemon juice		chilled
	concentrate	½	gallon lime sherbet
1	(48-ounce) can pineapple		
	juice, chilled		

Mix first three ingredients in punch bowl. Add ginger ale and sherbet just before serving. Serves 10.

Crescent Rolls

1	cup milk	4	cups unbleached flour,
¾	cup butter or margarine		lightly measured into cup
	(see Note)	2	eggs, room temperature
¼	cup sugar		Oil
½	teaspoon salt		Melted butter
1	envelope active dry yeast		Baking sheets
¼	cup warm water		
	(110 degrees)		

Heat first four ingredients until butter melts. Remove from heat and cool to lukewarm (85 degrees). Dissolve yeast in warm water in large bowl of mixer. Add milk mixture to yeast. Add 2 cups flour and beat at slow, then medium speed 2 minutes. (This is the secret in fine textured rolls. There should be no lumps.) Beat in eggs. When well blended, stop mixer and scrape down beaters and bowl. Slowly add 1 cup flour, beating at low speed 2 minutes (mixer may labor at this point). Remove beaters, stir in ¾ cup flour and beat with wooden spoon until dough is smooth and elastic. (Dough will not be as stiff as for bread or rolls kneaded on board.) Oil large bowl and turn dough into it. Brush top with oil and cover with plastic wrap, then cover with a towel wrung out in warm water. Set in warm draft-free place. Let dough rise until double in bulk (about 2 hours). Punch down dough and beat out all air bubbles by kneading. Divide dough into 4 equal pieces. Sprinkle remaining ¼ cup flour on board and roll each piece in circle ⅛-inch thick. Brush with melted butter, then cut each circle in 8 wedges. Roll each up from wide end to point and form a crescent. Arrange crescents on lightly oiled baking sheets point side down, allowing room for rolls to triple in size. Brush with more melted butter, cover with plastic wrap and set in warm place to rise (about 1 hour). Bake in preheated 400 degree oven 10 to 12 minutes or until pale gold. Remove to racks. When cool, bag airtight and refrigerate or freeze. Just before dinner remove as many rolls as you need. Arrange on baking sheets or foil and heat in 350 degree oven 10 to 15 minutes or until hot. Yield: 32 rolls.

Refrigerator Roll Dough: After dough has been beaten smooth, oil large bowl or plastic bag and place dough in it leaving room for expansion. Wrap airtight. Refrigerate up to 2 days, punching down whenever double in bulk (about every 9 to 10 hours). Remove from refrigerator 2 ½ to 3 hours before shaping, then shape as directed. Let rise until double, then bake as directed. (NOTE: Butter makes richer rolls; shortening makes fluffier rolls.)

COOL SUMMER LUNCHEON FOR HOT DAYS

Take a break from the heat of the day and serve a variety of refreshing beverages including old-fashioned lemonade, iced mint tea and chilled wines.

Summer Squash Soup

Spinach Salad with Chutney Dressing

Marinated Carrots

Crunch Rolls

Southern Strawberry Pie

Summer Squash Soup

1	medium onion, chopped	½	teaspoon poultry
¼	cup butter or margarine, melted		seasoning
		¼	teaspoon salt
6	medium yellow squash, sliced	¼	teaspoon pepper
		2	cups Half and Half
2	cups chicken broth		Chopped chives (optional)

Sauté onion in butter in large skillet until tender. Add squash, cover and simmer 5 minutes. Add chicken broth and seasonings, cover and simmer an additional 15 minutes. Process squash mixture in blender until smooth. Return mixture to a soup pot. Stir in Half and Half; cook just until thoroughly heated but do not boil. Garnish with chives. Serve hot or cold. Yield: 6 cups.

Spinach Salad with Chutney Dressing

1	(10-ounce) package fresh spinach	¼	cup dry roasted peanuts
2	cups sliced, unpeeled Red Delicious apples	¼	cup golden raisins
¼	cup very thinly sliced red onion		Chutney Dressing (recipe follows)

Wash spinach and remove stems. Toss with remaining ingredients in a large bowl. Just before serving, pour dressing over salad and toss gently. Serves 6.

Chutney Dressing

¼	cup white wine vinegar	⅛	teaspoon freshly ground pepper
½	cup olive oil		
½	cup salad oil	1	tablespoon chopped chutney
1	teaspoon salt		
1	teaspoon dry mustard	1	teaspoon curry powder

Combine first six ingredients in a covered jar. Shake well. Combine ⅓ to ½ cup dressing with remaining ingredients and shake. Add to reserved dressing. Let sit at room temperature a few minutes before serving. Yield: 1¼ cups.

Marinated Carrots

5	cups (2 pounds) carrots, sliced or julienned	½	cup salad oil
		¾	cup white vinegar
1	medium green pepper, cut in long slices (may substitute string beans, artichokes, or thin celery sticks)	1	teaspoon salt
		1	teaspoon pepper
		1	teaspoon dry mustard
		1	teaspoon Worcestershire sauce
1	medium onion, chopped	1	(8-ounce) can tomato sauce
¾	cup sugar		

Parboil carrots approximately 3 minutes. Combine first three ingredients in non-metal bowl. Combine remaining ingredients for marinade. Cover vegetables with marinade. Let stand at least 12 hours (24 hours is better). Serve chilled or at room temperature. Serves 8.

Crunch Rolls

1	package active dry yeast	1	egg
¼	cup warm water	1	egg yolk
1	cup milk, scalded	2 ½	cups sifted all-purpose
½	cup shortening		flour
¼	cup sugar	1	egg white, slightly beaten
1	teaspoon salt		Oatmeal Topping
1	cup quick or old-fashioned		(recipe follows)
	rolled oats, uncooked		

Soften yeast in warm water. Pour scalded milk over shortening, sugar and salt. Cool to lukewarm. Stir in oats. Add egg, egg yolk and softened yeast. Stir in flour and beat well. Cover; let rise in warm place until double in size, about 1 hour. Stir down. Fill greased muffin cups about ½ full. Cover; let rise in warm place until double in size, about 30 minutes. Brush tops lightly with egg white; sprinkle with topping. Bake at 375 degrees for 15 to 20 minutes or until golden brown. Yield: 18 rolls.

Oatmeal Topping

¼	cup quick or old-fashioned rolled oats, uncooked	¼	teaspoon salt

Combine oats and salt in small bowl. Crush slightly with mallet or bottom of small glass. Yield: ¼ cup.

Southern Strawberry Pie

¾	cup sugar	3	tablespoons strawberry
2	tablespoons cornstarch		flavored gelatin
2	tablespoons light corn syrup	1	quart fresh strawberries
1	cup water	1	(9-inch) pie shell, baked and cooled

Combine first four ingredients in saucepan. Bring to a boil. Cook, stirring constantly, until clear and thickened. Add gelatin, stirring until dissolved. Cool. Place strawberries in pie shell, pour in gelatin mixture. Chill until firm. Serves 6.

EASY LUNCHEON FOR FOUR

Keeping your party small allows time for good conversation or business planning.

Carrot Soup

Chicken Salad in Pineapple Shells

Old Fashioned Cheesecake

Carrot Soup

4	fresh carrots	¾	cup cream or milk
1	medium onion	1	teaspoon salt
1	stalk celery, sliced		Pinch cayenne pepper
1 ½	cups chicken broth	½	cup cooked potatoes

Combine carrots, onions, celery and ½ cup chicken broth. Bring to boil and simmer 15 minutes. Pour half of mixture into blender. Add salt, cayenne and potatoes and purée. Crush remaining vegetables in saucepan and add blender contents along with remaining chicken broth and cream. Serve warm or cold. Rice or pasta may be substituted for potatoes. Serves 6.

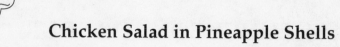

Chicken Salad in Pineapple Shells

1	chicken, whole	½	cup macadamia nuts,
2	celery stalks, diced		coarsely chopped
⅓	cup mayonnaise	1	green onion, diced
1	tablespoon milk		Chicory for garnish
2	medium pineapples		

Rinse chicken, giblets and neck. Place in 3-quart saucepan, add 3 inches of water. Heat to boiling. Reduce heat to low and simmer 35 minutes or until chicken is fork tender. Remove to plate and refrigerate for 30 minutes. (Refrigerate chicken broth for later use in soup.) Discard skin, bones, giblets and neck from chicken. Cut meat into bite-sized pieces. Place in large bowl, add celery, mayonnaise and milk. Toss gently. Add salt to taste. Cover and refrigerate salad. To serve: slice pineapple lengthwise in half from bottom to crown leaving on leafy crown. With small sharp knife, loosen fruit by cutting close to rind. Remove fruit, cut out core, cut fruit crosswise into ½-inch slices. Spoon chicken salad into shells. Arrange shells and pineapple on serving dish. Sprinkle salad with macadamia nuts and green onion. If desired, pecans can be substituted for macadamia nuts. Garnish with chicory. Serves 4.

Old Fashioned Cheesecake

3	eggs	4	eggs, separated
3	cups flour	1	teaspoon vanilla
3	teaspoons baking powder	1	cup sugar, divided
1	cup margarine	2	tablespoons flour
1	cup sugar		
2	(1-pound) containers cottage cheese		

Blend first five ingredients and spread in an ungreased jellyroll pan, starting in corners and filling in the rest of the pan. Beat cottage cheese with electric mixer; add egg yolks, vanilla, ½ cup sugar and flour. Beat egg whites separately with remaining sugar. Blend egg whites into cheese mixture. Pour cheese mixture evenly over cake crust. Bake at 350 degrees for 30 minutes or until golden brown. Serves 8.

OFFICE LUNCHEON BUFFET

*Invite your office staff for a lingering Saturday lunch -
be sure to keep shop talk to a minimum.*

English Pea Salad

Apricot Molded Salad

Spinach Soufflé

Queen's Chicken Salad

Sticky Butter

Raspberry Swirls

Citrus Tea Punch

English Pea Salad

2	(8 ¾-ounce) cans early June peas	¼	teaspoon pepper
			Dash garlic salt
2	ribs celery, finely chopped	½	teaspoon salt
¾	cup sharp Cheddar cheese, cubed	½	teaspoon mustard
		¾	cup tartar sauce
5	green onions, finely chopped		

Mix all ingredients together. May be served immediately, but is
better if marinated overnight. Serves 8.

Apricot Molded Salad

1	(29-ounce) can apricots, drained, juice reserved	4	ounces orange juice
½	cup crushed pineapple in heavy syrup, undrained	1	(3-ounce) package lemon flavored gelatin
½	cup pineapple chunks, well-drained	2	tablespoons lemon juice Dash salt
8	ounces apricot juice (from reserved juice)		

Smash apricots with fingers and drain. Combine apricots with crushed pineapple, and well-drained pineapple. Heat apricot juice and orange juice. Dissolve gelatin in juice mixture. Blend in lemon juice, salt, apricots and pineapple (in that order). Put in 5x8-inch greased mold. Refrigerate. Serves 8.

Spinach Soufflé

2	(10-ounce) packages frozen spinach	1	package onion soup mix
4	to 5 slices bacon	8	ounces sour cream

Heat oven to 350 degrees. Cook spinach as directed and drain. Fry bacon until crisp. Combine spinach, dry onion soup mix and sour cream together. Place in 8x8-inch baking dish. Crumble bacon pieces on top. Bake for 25 to 30 minutes until brown. Serves 5.

Queen's Chicken Salad

¾	cup mayonnaise	½	pound seedless green grapes
1	tablespoon curry powder		
2	tablespoons soy sauce	½	cup toasted slivered almonds
2	tablespoons lemon juice		
2	cups cooked chicken, cut into large chunks	1	(8-ounce) can pineapple chunks, drained
¼	cup sliced water chestnuts		

Mix first four ingredients. Combine remaining ingredients. Combine and chill several hours. Serves 5.

Sticky Butter

1	box yellow cake mix	2	cups confectioners' sugar
½	cup butter or margarine	1	teaspoon vanilla
1	egg	2	eggs
1	(8-ounce) package cream cheese, softened		

Cut butter into cake mix. Add egg. Pat down crust mixture in a greased 9x13-inch casserole dish. If mixture is too sticky, add a little flour. Pat on bottom and sides. Mix together remaining ingredients. Pour over crust. Bake at 325 degrees for 40 to 45 minutes. Serves 12.

Raspberry Swirls

3 ¾	cups flour	1	teaspoon vanilla
2	teaspoons baking powder	½	teaspoon lemon extract
1	teaspoon salt	1	cup raspberry jam
1	cup margarine	1	cup coconut
2	cups sugar	½	cup chopped nuts
2	eggs		

Sift dry ingredients together and set aside. Beat margarine and sugar until light and fluffy. Add eggs, vanilla and lemon extract. Beat well. Gradually add dry ingredients. Chill several hours. Divide dough in half and roll one portion into a 9x12-inch rectangle. Combine the remaining three ingredients. Spread with half the raspberry mixture and roll up like a jelly roll. Repeat with remainder of dough. Wrap rolls in waxed paper and chill overnight. Slice ¼-inch thick and place on greased cookie sheets. Bake at 375 degrees for 8 to 10 minutes or until slightly brown. Yield: 8 dozen.

Citrus-Tea Punch

1 ½	cups water	3	cups ginger ale, chilled
1	tea bag		Chilled orange and lemon
1 ½	cups orange juice		slices (optional)
1 ½	cups pineapple juice		Lemon rind strips
½	cup lemon juice		(optional)
1	cup sugar		

Bring water to a boil in a large saucepan; add teabag. Remove from heat; cover and let stand 5 minutes. Remove tea bag. Add fruit juices and sugar, stirring until sugar dissolves. Chill. Stir in ginger ale just before serving. Add orange and lemon slices and lemon strips, if desired. Yield: 2 quarts.

Showers

Planned in advance, a shower may be one of the most satisfying ways to entertain. Start with a theme, be creative and have fun!

Office Shower:
With many women working outside the home, there is less time available to prepare a shower. Consider hosting your shower at the office, over an extended coffee break or lunch hour. Box lunches may be ordered or co-workers may bring in easy make-ahead dishes. Bunches of balloons and streamers add a festive touch to a conference room or lunch room corner. Prepare invitations on inter-office memos.

Tie-A-Quilt Shower:
Memorable and sentimental, this shower works best among a close-knit group, such as a service club or religious circle. Each member makes a quilt square at home and then meets at the shower to sew and tie the quilt. This may be an informal affair with coffee, tea and desserts.

Rock Around the Clock Shower:
Each guest is asked to bring a gift pertaining to a particular hour of the day. Guests' invitations specify their assigned hours. For example, the guest with 7:00 - 8:00 A.M. on the invitation might bring juice glasses, a newspaper subscription or shower/bath accessories. Guests are asked to mark the time slot on the package so gifts are opened in sequence. Use various time pieces such as egg timers, antique watches, hourglasses and alarm clocks as the centerpiece.

All Year Round Shower:
Each guest is assigned a different month of the year. Suggest gifts suitable for entertaining or decorating. For April, bring an umbrella, garden tools and seeds. For July, give a picnic basket, beach towels or anything red, white and blue. Invitations may be written on different pages of a calendar.

Book Shower:
Books are unusual and useful gifts and might be the focus of a thoughtful shower. Books purchased could be new releases or old favorites. Select a Bible, a Dictionary or a First Aid Manual for a new household. Cookbooks, gardening books, an address book, a How-to Book or an old Classic are ideas for the Bride. Give the Mother-to-be a Mother Goose Nursery Rhyme Collection, a Baby Book or a Parenting Manual. Bookmarks, bookends, subscriptions and Book Club memberships are also good gifts. Decorate for the shower with book jackets and place your floral centerpiece among stacks of books.

Lend-A-Hand Shower:
Guests give coupons for services instead of the usual present. Services may include painting, house-sitting, tax assistance, silver polishing, yard work or teaching a decorative or handy skill. Mothers-to-be need baby-sitting, laundry service, errand running or a delivered meal. Purchase a file box or decorate a sturdy cardboard box. Send each guest, along with the invitation, two or three decorated filecards to be completed and returned.

Pantry Shower:
Provide a bride or a new homeowner with pantry and kitchen items. Guests bring food items as well as kitchen gadgets and essentials.

Garden Shower:
For the Bride who has a green thumb, plan your shower with a garden theme. A garden hat filled with fresh flowers and garden handtools can serve as your centerpiece. The hostess's gift of a wheelbarrow can serve to hold the other gifts. If you plan to play games, one idea is to have your guests list as many flowers or plants with names pertaining to love and marriage (bleeding hearts, bridal wreath, everlasting, and tulips).

A SHOWER OF BEST WISHES

Open-Faced Crab Sandwiches
Uppercrust Chicken
Crab and Artichoke Casserole
Taco Salad
Orange Salad
Benne Seed Cookies
Neopolitan Sheet Cake
Champagne Punch
Pink Punch for Ladies

Open-Faced Crab Sandwiches

Pumpernickel bread	Crisp bacon
Thousand Island dressing	Crabmeat
Tomato slices	Sliced swiss cheese

Spread pumpernickel bread with Thousand Island dressing. Add crabmeat, tomato slice and 2 strips of crisp bacon. Top with swiss cheese and broil until cheese melts.

Uppercrust Chicken

8	slices white bread	1	cup mayonnaise
2	cups chopped, cooked	2	eggs, slightly beaten
	chicken	½	teaspoon salt
1	cup sliced celery	½	teaspoon poultry
2	cups shredded, sharp		seasoning
	Cheddar cheese	1 ½	cups milk

Trim crusts from bread and reserve. Cut bread slices diagonally into quarters. Cut crusts into cubes. Combine bread cubes, chicken, celery, and 1 ¾ cups cheese; mix well. Spoon into 11 ¾ x7 ½-inch baking dish. Arrange bread quarters over chicken mixture. Combine mayonnaise, eggs, and seasonings; mix well. Gradually add milk, mixing until blended. Pour over bread. Sprinkle with remaining cheese. Cover. Refrigerate several hours or overnight. Bake, uncovered, at 375 degrees for 30 minutes. Garnish with celery leaves, if desired. Serves 8.

Crab and Artichoke Casserole

3	tablespoons butter	4	to 6 drops hot pepper
3	tablespoons flour		sauce, or to taste
1 ½	cups milk	4	hard boiled eggs, chopped
1	teaspoon salt	1	(16-ounce) can artichoke
⅛	teaspoon pepper		hearts, chopped
½	teaspoon Worcestershire	2	cups backfin crab meat
	sauce	⅓	cup Parmesan cheese
	Dash dry mustard		

Make a white sauce by melting butter in saucepan. Whisk in flour and add milk. Stir over medium heat. Add next five ingredients to white sauce. Add eggs, artichokes and crabmeat to sauce. Pour into 1 ½-quart casserole dish and top with parmesan cheese. Bake at 350 degrees for 30 minutes or until top is golden brown. This dish can be assembled a day ahead and baked before serving. Serves 4.

Taco Salad

4   ounces taco sauce
8   ounces Italian dressing
1   pound ground beef,
     browned, drained and
     cooled
½   (8-ounce) package
     shredded Cheddar cheese
1   head lettuce, shredded

2   tomatoes, cut into wedges
1   (16-ounce) can kidney
     beans, drained and rinsed
1   red onion, diced
1   (16-ounce) can medium
     olives, chopped (optional)
1   (16-ounce) bag corn chips,
     crushed

Mix taco sauce with Italian dressing, set aside. Mix all other ingredients together, except corn chips. Just before serving, mix in crushed corn chips and dressing. Serves 4 to 6.

Orange Salad

1   (3-ounce) package
     orange-flavored gelatin
1   (3-ounce) package
     lemon-flavored gelatin
1   cup boiling water
1   pint orange sherbet
1   cup crushed pineapple,
     undrained

1   (11-ounce) can mandarin
     oranges, drained
1   cup small marshmallows
½   pint whipping cream,
     whipped

Combine all ingredients except whipping cream. Fold in whipping cream. Pour into mold. Let set in refrigerator. Serves 12.

Benne Seed Cookies

¾	cup sesame seeds	1	cup sifted, all-purpose
½	cup butter, softened		flour
1	cup firmly packed light	¼	teaspoon salt
	brown sugar	1	teaspoon vanilla
1	egg		

Spread seeds out in a very shallow pan and toast in a 275 degree oven, stirring occasionally, until golden brown, about 10 minutes. Cool. Beat butter, sugar and egg in medium-sized bowl until light and fluffy. Stir in remaining ingredients until well mixed. Drop dough onto greased sheets, using rounded ½ teaspoonfuls spaced 2 ½ to 3 inches apart. (They spread considerably.) Bake at 350 degrees about 10 minutes or until cookies are a rich caramel color. Remove from oven; cool on cookie sheet or wire rack for about 1 minute only. Spread out on rack or brown paper, one layer deep, to cool completely. Store in airtight container. Yield: 3 to 4 dozen.

Neopolitan Sheet Cake

1	(3-ounce) package strawberry-flavored gelatin	1	(3-ounce) package instant vanilla pudding
1	marble cake mix	1 ½	cups cold milk
1	envelope whipped topping mix	1	teaspoon vanilla

Dissolve gelatin in ¾ cup boiling water. Add ½ cup cold water. Set aside. Bake cake according to directions on box. Cool cake 20 to 25 minutes. Poke holes in cake with large fork. Pour gelatin over entire cake. Refrigerate. For topping, mix remaining ingredients and beat 3 to 8 minutes, or until stiff. Ice cake with topping. Refrigerate cake until ready to serve. May also substitute lime gelatin for strawberry and lemon cake mix for marble cake mix. Serves 10.

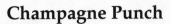

Champagne Punch

1	(6-ounce) can frozen lemonade concentrate, thawed	1	(750 ml) bottle champagne, chilled
2	(6-ounce) cans frozen pineapple juice concentrate, thawed	1	(750 ml) bottle white wine, chilled
4 ½	cups water	1	(2-ounce) package whole frozen strawberries, slightly thawed

Combine first three ingredients in punch bowl. Chill. Add wine and champagne just before serving. Float strawberries in punch. Yield: 18 ½-cup servings.

Pink Punch For Ladies

1	quart cranberry juice cocktail, chilled	1	(15 ½-ounce) can crushed pineapple, chilled
1	quart pineapple juice, chilled	2	quarts ginger ale, chilled

Mix all ingredients and pour over ice ring in punch bowl. Rose petals may be sprinkled over punch as a garnish. Yield: 36 ½-cup servings.

ABCs of
Children's Parties

Wayside Inn Since 1797 - Middletown

Children young and old will surely enjoy discovering the past at nearby Bell Grove Plantation and Cedar Creek Battlefield in the Shenandoah Valley. Spend the day hiking, fishing and picnicking along Skyline Drive and the Shenandoah National Park before retiring to the historic Wayside Inn Since 1797 in Middletown. Originally a coachstop known as Wilkerson's Tavern, the Inn boasts 22 guest rooms, each decorated with fine period antiques, all available for purchase. The Wayside Inn is noted for its authentic regional cuisine. Treat the children to an exciting get-away weekend at the Wayside Inn.

ABCs of Children's Parties

Appetizers
A Child's Cheese Ball
Orange-Yogurt Dip for Fresh Fruit

Beverages
Merry Punch
Milkshake
Panda Punch
Purple Cow Shakes

Crafts and Favors
Astronaut Helmets
Candy Airplanes
Christmas Ornament Clay
Face Paint
Finger Paint
Ghost Tree Centerpiece
Heart Game/Valentines for Mom
   and Dad
Make Your Own Jewelry
Playdough
Soap Snow
Space Goop
Valentine Basket

Desserts
Christmas Cutout Cookies
Critter Cupcakes
Cupcakes-For-A-Crowd
Don't Cook Cookies
Friendship Cookies
Candy Cake
Monkey Cake
Peanut Butter Balls
Peanut Butter Bars
Peanut Butter Kisses
Peanut Butter Sandwich Cookies
Potato Chip Cookies
Satellite S'Mores
Sugar Cookies
Sweetheart Cookies

Entrees
Bambi Salad
Christmas Tree Peanut Butter and
   Jelly Sandwiches
Eggs in Bologna Cups
Jack-O-Lantern Pizzas
Toasty Hot Dog Roll-ups

Fruits and Vegetables
Bananas and Vanilla Wafers
Creamy Fruit Popsicles
Cucumber Circles
Holiday Snack Tree
Man-In-The-Moon Faces
Snack Tray for Zoo Party

Miscellaneous
Caramel Nut Popcorn
Chocolate Covered Worms
Fruit-Filled Ice Cream Cones
Jello Blox
Munchy Crunchy Granola
Peanut Butter Surprise Muffins
Popcorn Lollipops
Porcupine Balls
Pumpkin Cups

Any one or all of these "ABC" tips will make party-giving for children a fun and educational experience. Children learn faster and experiment more when they are involved in making the decisions. This is a good opportunity for children to learn manners and thoughtfulness and teach lifetime skills. Children's parties are as simple as ABC's for the Virginia Hostess:

A   Always have a theme.

B   Backyard parties are great for entertaining little ones!

C   Children love helping with a party.

D   Drawing and coloring with "take-home" crayons is a simple activity.

E   Easter egg hunts are fun, indoors or out.

F   Find out what kind of party your child wants.

G   Goodie bags make special treats to end the party.

H   Have a checklist, one for yourself and one for your child.

I   If prizes are given, be sure each child receives one.

J   Jack-O-Lanterns make a scary Halloween centerpiece.

K   Keep the menu simple.

L   Let everyone take a turn at games and win a prize!

M   Make your own invitations for a change!

N   Nachos are a slumber party treat.

O   Open presents after refreshments so that everyone has time to eat.

P   Plan to decorate your table and include a favor at each place setting.

Q   Quench your partygoers' thirsts with fruit juices instead of punch.

R   Refreshments are probably the most important item.

S   Simple decorations will add a festive atmosphere.

T   Transportation themes are fun for all (examples: ship, train, bus)!

U   Use paper plates, cups, and napkins for easy clean-up.

V   Valentine parties give a little "Spring" to Winter months.

W   When having a party, let it be a learning situation for your child.

X   X marks the spot for a treasure hunt party.

Y   You must consider location and the number of children to invite.

Z   Zoo themes are great for preschoolers.

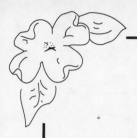

A MONSTER MASH

Let your elementary school age "monsters" help prepare the food and decorations for this party. The children will enjoy creating "monster faces" with washable face paint. Have your guests bring smocks or old t-shirts to protect clothing or provide t-shirts to paint as party favors.

Caramel Nut Popcorn

Peanut Butter Kisses

Candy Cake

Jack-O-Lantern Pizzas

Pumpkin Cups

Ghost Tree Centerpiece

Face Paint

Caramel Nut Popcorn

½	cup brown sugar	1	cup pecan halves, walnut
½	cup dark corn syrup		halves or peanuts
¼	cup butter	½	cup slivered almonds
½	teaspoon salt		
6	cups unsalted, popped popcorn (or 1 bag popped microwave popcorn)		

Preheat oven to 325 degrees. Butter a 15 ½x10 ½x1-inch jellyroll pan. Heat first four ingredients in a 3-quart saucepan over medium heat, stirring constantly until sugar is dissolved, about 5 minutes. Remove brown sugar mixture from heat; stir in popcorn and nuts until well coated. Spread in pan. Bake 15 minutes. Cool until slightly firm, about 5 to 7 minutes. Break up popcorn with a metal spatula. Let stand until firm, about 1 hour. Store in covered container. Yield: 8 cups.

Peanut Butter Kisses

½ cup butter or margarine
½ cup sugar
½ cup brown sugar
1 egg
1 teaspoon vanilla

½ cup peanut butter
1 ¾ cups flour
1 teaspoon baking soda
½ teaspoon salt
1 ½ bags chocolate kisses

Cream butter and sugars thoroughly. Add egg and vanilla; mix well. Mix in peanut butter. Add next three ingredients. Dough will be stiff. Roll into ¾-inch balls and roll in sugar. Place on ungreased cookie sheet. Bake at 375 degrees for 8 minutes. Remove from oven and place a kiss atop each cookie, pushing well into dough. Return to oven and bake another 2 to 5 minutes, until cookies are golden. Yield: 3 dozen.

Candy Cake

8 (1 7/8-ounce) caramel nougat in milk chocolate bars
½ cup butter or margarine
2 cups sugar
½ cup butter or margarine, softened
4 eggs

1 teaspoon vanilla
1 ¼ cups buttermilk
½ teaspoon baking soda
3 cups flour
1 cup chopped pecans
Milk Chocolate Frosting (recipe follows)

Melt candy bars and butter in saucepan over low heat, stirring constantly. Cool. Cream sugar and butter until light and fluffy. Add eggs, one at a time, beating well after each addition. Stir in vanilla. Combine buttermilk and soda; add to creamed mixture alternately with flour, beating well after each addition. Fold in candy bar mixture and pecans. Pour batter into a greased and floured 10-inch tube pan. Bake at 325 degrees for 1 hour and 20 minutes or until done. Frost cake and serve. Serves 10 to 12.

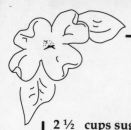

Milk Chocolate Frosting

2 ½   cups sugar
1   cup evaporated milk
½   cup butter or margarine,
       melted

1   (6-ounce) package semi-
       sweet chocolate pieces
1   cup marshmallow cream
       Milk

Combine first three ingredients in a heavy saucepan; cook over medium heat until small amount of mixture dropped in cold water forms a soft ball. Remove from heat; add chocolate pieces and marshmallow cream, stirring until melted. If necessary, add a small amount of milk to make it spreadable. Yield: 3 cups.

Jack-O-Lantern Pizzas

4   English muffins, split
1   tablespoon vegetable oil

8   ounces pizza sauce
8   slices mozzarella cheese

Cut muffins in half, brush each half with a little oil and broil until lightly browned. Spread 1 generous tablespoon pizza sauce on each muffin. Trim cheese into circles to fit muffin and cut out a Jack-O-Lantern face on each. Place one face on each muffin. Bake at 400 degrees until cheese melts, about 8 minutes. Yield: 8 pizzas.

Pumpkin Cups

Oranges
Fresh fruit, nuts or candy

Toothpicks

Cut off enough top of a navel orange so you can remove pulp. Once pulp is removed, drain for 10 minutes, then fill with fruit, nuts and candy. Put a toothpick in top of the "cap" which may be used as eating utensil. Scratch a face onto the orange and go over the "face" with a ball point pen so that features will stand out. Make one for each guest.

Ghost Tree Centerpiece

Small branch with several smaller limbs	Rubber bands
Clay flower pot	Black felt-tipped marker
Modeling clay	White string
Orange felt	Black rubber spiders
White facial tissues	(optional)

Mount branch in clay flower pot using modeling clay to hold it in place. Cover modeling clay with orange felt. Make four to six ghosts to hang on the tree. For each ghost, lay a white facial tissue on a flat surface. Roll a second tissue into a ball and lay it in the center of the first tissue. Wrap the first tissue around the wad to form a ghost shape and secure under the "head" with a rubber band. Draw a face on the ghost with the black marker. Make as many ghosts as desired. Tie the ghosts to the "tree" with white string. To make it extra scary, add black rubber spiders and commercial "cobwebs".

Face Paint

1	tablespoon solid shortening	1	teaspoon flour
			Food Coloring

In one section of a muffin tin, mix together shortening, flour and one drop of food coloring. Repeat step 1 with several colors in other sections of muffin tin. Use fingers to paint face. Wash off face paint with soap and warm water.

Decorations and Favors

Create an eerie atmosphere with easy games and favors. Your "spooks" will enjoy guessing the number of candy corn in a filled jar. You may reward all participants with a prize from a prize pumpkin. Offer trick-or-treat bags filled with candy for an easy and appropriate favor. Decorate the house with stringy cobwebs, white sheets and hanging spiders. Blindfold the children and lead them through a touch and feel spook house. To add to the frightening mood, fill shoe boxes with "yucky-touch" items such as cooked noodles, jello and pudding. BOO!!

OPEN HOUSE FOR THE HOLIDAYS

Children will enjoy hosting an open house for friends of all ages. With these tasty and easy-to-do recipes they will learn that planning and preparing for a party can be fun.

Merry Punch
Christmas Ornament Clay
Peanut Butter Bars
Christmas Cutout Cookies
A Child's Cheese Ball
Christmas Tree Peanut Butter and Jelly Sandwiches
Holiday Snack Tree

Merry Punch

1	(46-ounce) can pineapple juice, chilled	2	quarts carbonated lemon-lime drink, chilled
1	(46-ounce) can orange-grapefruit juice, chilled		

Mix all ingredients together in punch bowl. To keep punch cool as well as to make it more attractive, float a frozen fruit mold in the punch. Serves 25.

Christmas Ornament Clay

2	cups salt	1	cup cornstarch
⅔	cup water	½	cup cold water

Mix salt and water. Stir and boil. Add cornstarch and cold water. Stir until mixture thickens. Roll out dough and cut with cookie cutters. Use straw to make a hole at the top. Dry and decorate. Also can be used to make hand imprints. DO NOT EAT! These are great as favors for each child to take home at the end of the party.

78

Peanut Butter Bars

2	cups peanut butter	½	cup powdered milk crystals
½	cup brown sugar		
1	teaspoon vanilla	1	cup milk chocolate chips
2 ½	cups sifted confectioners' sugar	¼	cup butter
½	cup butter or margarine, melted		

Cream together first three ingredients until smooth. Add next three ingredients. Blend thoroughly. Press firmly into lightly buttered 8-inch square pan. For thinner bars, use larger pan. Melt together chocolate chips and remaining butter. Spread on top of peanut butter mixture. Chill until firm. Cut into squares. Store tightly covered in refrigerator. Yield: 20 bars.

Christmas Cutout Cookies

1	cup butter, softened	1	teaspoon baking soda
1	cup sugar	4	tablespoons milk
2	eggs	1	teaspoon vanilla
¼	teaspoon salt	4	cups flour

Cream first four ingredients. Dissolve soda in milk and add vanilla. Add milk mixture and flour alternately to butter mixture. Roll dough out to ⅜-inch thickness. Cut with appropriate cookie cutters. Decorate with sprinkles before baking or once cooled, ice and decorate. Bake at 350 degrees until brown. Yield: 3 dozen.

A Child's Cheese Ball

1	(8-ounce) package cream cheese, softened	2	tablespoons chopped green pepper
1	tablespoon chopped green onion	½	cup chopped walnuts or pecans
½	cup crushed pineapple, well-drained		

Add green onion, pineapple and green pepper to cream cheese. Mix well. Shape into a ball. Roll in nuts. Chill. Serve with assorted crackers and toasts.

Christmas Tree Peanut Butter and Jelly Sandwiches

Sandwich bread   Grape or strawberry jelly
Peanut butter

Using a cookie cutter, cut out Christmas trees from slices of whole wheat or white sandwich bread. Spread each slice with peanut butter. Spoon strawberry or grape jelly into pastry bag fitted with small round tip. Pipe jelly around borders of trees in thin line. Store in airtight container until ready to serve.

Holiday Snack Tree

1   12-inch to 16-inch cone-   Cherry tomatoes
    shaped Styrofoam form   Gherkin pickles
    Toothpicks   Radishes
    Cheese cubes   Parsley
    Green and black olives   Pineapple chunks

Spear individual cheeses, fruits and vegetables with a toothpick and decorate "tree". May substitute green and red cherries and diced fruit pieces for olives, radishes, cherry tomatoes and pickles. Fill in empty spaces with parsley. Finished tree makes a colorful centerpiece.

Decorations and Favors

With all of the hectic happenings during the holiday season, one never seems to have adequate time to pay attention to all party details. It's easy to add a festive touch to the party with the Holiday Snack Tree as a centerpiece. Make holiday cards by tracing cookie cutters on colored construction paper and have children decorate with crayons, glitter and tinsel. Send the young guests home with a holiday momento by providing ornament clay during the party and encouraging creative play. Happy Holidays!

SWEETHEART OF A SCHOOL PARTY

The grade school "room mother" will appreciate these healthy sweets and simple activities.

Sweetheart Cookies

Jello Blox

Popcorn Lollipops

Fruit-Filled Ice Cream Cones

Heart Game/Valentines for Mom and Dad

Valentine Basket

Sweetheart Cookies

¾	cup butter	1 ½	cups flour
½	cup sugar		Currant jelly
1	egg yolk		

Cream butter and sugar. Add egg yolk, then flour. Remove from mixer and knead into a ball. Chill in wax paper for several hours. When ready to bake, pinch off pieces of dough and roll into small balls. Place balls on greased cookie sheet. Press centers with a thimble and fill with a dab of jelly. Bake at 350 degrees for 20 minutes. Yield: 4 dozen.

Jello Blox

4	(3-ounce) packages flavored gelatin	4	envelopes unflavored gelatin
		4	cups boiling water

Mix above ingredients until dissolved and pour into 9x9-inch glass dish. Chill until firm. Cut into small squares or cut out with cookie cutter shapes that children can eat with their fingers. Yield: approximately 12 blox.

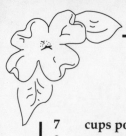

Popcorn Lollipops

7	cups popped popcorn	2	tablespoons butter
3	cups miniature marshmallows	¼ 8	teaspoon salt round lollipops

Put popcorn into large buttered bowl. Melt marshmallows, butter and salt in double boiler, stirring frequently, until mixture is smooth. Pour marshmallow mixture over popcorn. With buttered hands, mix thoroughly until all popcorn is coated, then quickly shape mixture around lollipops into 3 to 4-inch "balls". Yield: 8 lollipops.

Fruit-Filled Ice Cream Cones

Cake ice cream cones   Dried fruits and nuts
Fresh fruit chunks

For an easy and healthy snack, fill cake ice cream cones with chunks of fruit: pineapple, melon balls, grapes, apples, raisins, coconut, pears, etcetera. Children really enjoy these healthy, fun treats.

Heart Game/Valentines for Mom and Dad

Shoe Box   Pink and black
                                construction paper

Cover a shoe box with pink construction paper. Make a cut in the top of the box so a child's hand will fit inside. Cut pink and black hearts out of construction paper and place in the box. Have each child pick a heart from the box. If a black heart is chosen, the child is out of the game. Keep doing this until only one child is left with a pink heart. That child is the winner. After the game, the children write "Happy Valentine's Day, Mom and Dad" on the pink hearts.

Valentine Basket

Used envelopes (one per basket)
Doilies, crepe paper or
   construction paper

White craft glue
Candy hearts (optional)

Draw a heart in the corner of the envelope. Cut out the heart. Make a construction paper handle and glue or staple it to the top of the heart. Decorate the basket with doilies, crepe paper or construction paper hearts. Fill with candy hearts.

Decorations and Favors

In the middle of February in Virginia, bright reds and pinks are always a welcome sight! Decorate your table with colorful streamers, construction paper hearts, red hot candies and goody baskets lined with red or pink napkins. Hang a few red hearts from the ceiling. Provide the children with Valentines for Mom and Dad by organizing the Heart Game which uses construction paper hearts. Glitter pens are great for personalizing the valentines after the game. A perfect favor for the end of the party is a Valentine Basket to fill with candy hearts and other goodies. Have a sweet day!

RAIN, RAIN GO AWAY

Chase away those gloomy gray clouds with creative recipes and activities for all ages.

Monkey Cake

Don't Cook Cookies

Peanut Butter Balls

Sugar Cookies

Finger Paint

Playdough

Soap Snow

Monkey Cake

4	cans refrigerator biscuit dough (10 per can)	½	cup margarine, melted
1	cup sugar	1	cup raisins or chopped nuts (optional)
2	teaspoons cinnamon		

Cut each biscuit into quarters with scissors. Combine sugar and cinnamon. Shake biscuits a few at a time in the sugar mixture until coated. Place in greased bundt or tube pan. Add remaining sugar mixture to margarine. Pour over cake. Bake at 350 degrees for 40 to 45 minutes. Invert on plate to serve. Eat with fingers. Raisins or nuts may be included. Serves 12.

Don't Cook Cookies

1	cup honey	1	cup non-fat dry milk
1	cup peanut butter	1	cup raisins
1	cup oatmeal		

Mix all ingredients and form into cookies. Do not cook. Yield: 3 to 4 dozen.

84

Peanut Butter Balls

1	cup peanut butter	½	cup pecans (optional)
1	cup powdered milk	2	tablespoons margarine
½	cup raisins (optional)	8	graham crackers

Mix all ingredients except graham crackers and shape into small round bite-size balls. Roll in crushed graham crackers. Store in tightly covered container. Yield: 3 dozen.

Sugar Cookies

2	heaping cups sugar	1	teaspoon baking soda
1	cup butter	1	cup sour cream
2	eggs	1	teaspoon baking powder
1	teaspoon vanilla	5	cups flour

Cream together sugar and butter until fluffy. Beat eggs and blend in vanilla. Add to sugar mixture. Dissolve baking soda in sour cream. Sift baking powder and flour. Blend sour cream mixture and flour mixture with sugar mixture. Roll into logs and chill in waxed paper. Slice dough into 3⁄8-inch thickness and place on pan. Bake at 350 degrees for 10 minutes. Sprinkle with granulated sugar. Yield: 6 dozen.

Finger Paint

1	cup dry starch		Powdered tempera paint
½	cup water		Food coloring
1 ½	cups boiling water		
¾	cup powdered detergent soap		

Mix starch and cold water in a large glass bowl. Add hot water and stir rapidly. Add soap and stir until smooth. Add tempera paint and food coloring until you reach the desired color. Store in airtight container.

Playdough

1	cup salt	2	cups water
2	cups flour	2	tablespoons oil
2	teaspoons cream of tartar		Food coloring (optional)

Mix dry ingredients. Add food coloring to water if desired. Add wet ingredients, stir, and cook 3 to 5 minutes over medium heat until congealed. The dough will be a little sticky. Knead in remaining liquid. Store in airtight container.

Soap Snow

½   cup water   2   cups laundry soap flakes

Whip water and soap flakes with mixer, adding more soap or water as needed to resemble thick whipped cream. Use for frosting cardboard houses and making snowmen and snow balls. Dip hands in water before molding to avoid snow sticking to hands. Mixture dries to a porous texture and lasts for weeks.

Decorations and Favors

For those days when the rain just will not stop, find a cheerful, well-lit, casual room in your house for trying these creative activities. Arrange different centers so children may experiment with several "artistic" mediums. Perhaps the children would enjoy one major project, such as creating a city. Draw a city "map" on a large piece of paper or cardboard using fingerpaints. Frost small cardboard boxes with soap snow for houses, stores and other buildings and place them on the painted map. Make trees, flowers, people, cars, cats and dogs out of play dough. Give the city a creative name! If the city may be dismantled, send parts home with the children.

LET'S DRESS UP!

*Offer some fun to your young ladies while they experiment
with makeup, hair, and jewelry fashions. Invite each guest
to come to this party dressed in Mom's hat, jewelry
and clothes or as a favorite movie or rock star.*

Eggs in Bologna Cups

Orange-Yogurt Dip for Fresh Fruit

Purple Cow Shakes

Toasty Hot Dog Roll-ups

Potato Chip Cookies

Friendship Cookies

Make-Your-Own Jewelry

Eggs in Bologna Cups

2	teaspoons shortening	6	teaspoons milk
6	slices bologna, each about		Salt
	4 inches in diameter		Pepper
6	eggs		Paprika

Preheat oven to 375 degrees. Grease 6 muffin cups with melted shortening, using pastry brush. Melt 2 teaspoons shortening in skillet over low heat. Place 3 slices of bologna in skillet and fry until edges curl and centers puff. Lift each slice with tongs into a muffin cup and press into cup. Repeat with remaining bologna slices. Break 1 egg into center of each bologna slice to hold it down. Pour 1 teaspoon milk over each egg. Sprinkle eggs lightly with salt, pepper and paprika. Bake uncovered for 15 to 20 minutes or until eggs are set. Loosen each bologna cup with knife and lift to platter with spoon. Serves 6.

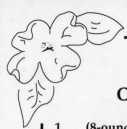

Orange-Yogurt Dip for Fresh Fruit

1	(8-ounce) carton lowfat plain yogurt	1	orange or 2 large tangerines, peeled, sectioned and seeded
2	tablespoons honey		
	Grated peel of ½ orange or tangerine	1	apple, sliced
		1	banana, sliced

In a small bowl, combine first three ingredients. Serve as a dip with fruit slices. Yield: 1 cup.

Purple Cow Shakes

1	(6-ounce) can frozen grape juice concentrate	1	cup milk
		2	cups vanilla ice cream

Pour first two ingredients into blender. Add ice cream. Cover and blend on high speed 30 seconds. Serve immediately! If a blender is not available, scoop ice cream into a 2-quart jar with remaining ingredients. Cover tightly and shake. Serves 4.

Toasty Hot Dog Roll-Ups

1	can crescent refrigerator rolls	8	hot dogs
		8	slices American cheese

Unroll crescent dough and separate each triangle. Place 1 hot dog and 1 slice of cheese on dough. Roll up. Place on greased cookie sheet. Bake at 350 degrees for 8 to 10 minutes or until golden brown. Serves 8.

Potato Chip Cookies

½	cup margarine	1	teaspoon vanilla
½	cup butter (you must use real butter)	1 ½	cups all-purpose flour
½	cup sugar	½	cup crushed potato chips
		½	cup chopped pecans

Cream together first four ingredients. Add flour. Mix well. Add crushed potato chips (not too fine) and pecans. Drop by spoonfuls onto lightly greased cookie sheet. Bake 10 to 12 minutes at 350 degrees until light brown. Cookies may be frozen. Yield: 3 dozen.

Friendship Cookies

1 ⅓	cups sugar	3	cups quick cooking	
⅓	cup cocoa		oatmeal	
½	cup butter, melted	1	teaspoon vanilla	
½	cup milk	½	cup nuts	

Using a 2-quart bowl, combine sugar and cocoa; stir until smooth. Add butter and milk. Microwave on high for 4 to 5 minutes or until a rolling boil is reached. Stir in remaining ingredients. Microwave on high 1 minute. Drop by teaspoonfuls onto waxed paper. Chill until set. May substitute either ½ cup crunchy peanut butter, ½ cup raisins or ½ cup coconut for cocoa. Yield: 2 to 3 dozen.

Make Your Own Jewelry

Colored toothpicks	Alphabet macaroni
Glue	Craft bar pin

Glue toothpicks (alternating colors) together and place on bar pin. Spell your name with alphabet macaroni and glue onto toothpicks. An alternative is to string macaroni or colored beads on fishing line or dental floss.

Decorations and Favors

The hostess Mom provides make-up, curlers, and nail polish to really make this dress-up fun and exciting. (Make sure you have soap, cold cream and towels for clean-up later!) A hostess with a little more time and space might arrange areas of the house as boutiques for jewelry, clothes, make-up and hair-styling. In addition to the dress-up items brought by the guests, find other fun dress-ups for the girls to try. Have a fashion show and take lots of Polaroid photographs. Lip gloss, nail polish and those Polaroid photographs make wonderful favors.

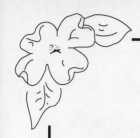

ZOO IT UP RIGHT!

*Toddlers and preschoolers will love the funny names of each
of these "critter" recipes. A Safari Animal Hunt is easy
to keep under control.*

Critter Cupcakes

Cupcakes-For-A-Crowd

Panda Punch

Snack Tray for Zoo Party

Bambi Salad

Critter Cupcakes

12 cupcakes baked in paper
   liners
1 ½ cups fluffy frosting
   Vanilla wafers, small
   (2-inch) cookies or
   (1 ½-inch) graham
   cracker squares

Gumdrops or jelly beans
Candy-coated chocolate
   candies, candy-coated
   chocolate-covered
   peanuts or candy of
   your choice
Red or black licorice whips

Frost each cupcake with about 2 tablespoons frosting. To make animals,
make a face of any animal (such as a mouse, bear, cat or raccoon) you
choose on top of each cupcake. Use any small cookie to stick into frosting
to make ears. To make nose, use a cookie for a snout or try a gumdrop or
jellybean. To make eyes, use small candies. To make mouth, use small
pieces of licorice whips. Yield: 12 cupcakes.

Cupcakes-For-A-Crowd

1	cake mix (any flavor)	¼	cup oil
1	(1 ½-ounce) package whipped topping mix	4	eggs
1	(3 ¾-ounce) package instant pudding (same flavor as cake)	1	can icing (same or different flavor) Sprinkles, candy-coated chocolate candies
1 ¼	cups water		or nuts

Combine first six ingredients in a large mixing bowl. Mix on high at least 3 minutes. Fill cupcake liners a little over ½ full. Bake at 350 degrees for 12 to 15 minutes. Cool and ice. Apply appropriate toppings to suit the age of the children. Yield: 36 cupcakes.

Panda Punch

1	quart package strawberry-flavored drink mix	1	(18-ounce) can pineapple juice
1	cup sugar	2	quarts ginger ale
1	quart water	1	(6-ounce) jar maraschino cherries
1	(12-ounce) can frozen orange juice		
1	(6-ounce) can frozen lemonade		

Dissolve drink mix and sugar in water. Add orange juice, lemonade and pineapple juice. If desired, freeze part of the punch in a ring mold to use in place of ice cubes. When ready to serve, add ginger ale and cherries. Serves 25.

Snack Tray for Zoo Party

Seedless grapes, red or green
American Cheese, cut up into bite-size pieces

Apples and pears, sliced into strips

Wash grapes and remove from stems. Arrange fruit and cheese on snack tray.

Bambi Salad

1	lettuce leaf		Mandarin orange segments
1	pear half	1	maraschino cherry
1	prune	1	raisin

Wash lettuce leaf and pat dry with paper towel. Place on salad plate. Place pear half, cut side down, on lettuce leaf. Cut prune in half lengthwise with scissors and take out pit. Place one prune half at large end of pear half for ear. With a teaspoon, scoop out a tiny hole in pear half for eye. Place 1 raisin in the hole. Cut cherry in half with scissors. Place one half at the top of narrow end of pear half for the nose. Use mandarin orange segments for the collar. Serves 1.

Decorations and Favors

Decorate for a Safari Animal Hunt by hiding stuffed animals or home-made construction paper animal cut-outs around the house. Together, the children go on a Safari, looking for the stuffed or paper animals. When they find an animal, they also find a basket or bag of prizes. Each child receives one prize for each "wild animal" found and saves his goodies in his "Safari" bag. Safari bags and hats might be made from brown lunch bags, grocery bags, or construction paper and decorated creatively before the "Hunt" begins.

ASTRONAUTS IN SPACE

Your young astronauts won't be "lost in space" testing delicious "galactic" treats and making a fun space helmet to take home.

Astronaut Helmets

Candy Airplanes

Satellite S'Mores

Space Goop

Man-In-The-Moon Faces

Peanut Butter Sandwich Cookies

Astronaut Helmets

Paper bags	**Crayons**
Aluminum foil	**Markers**
Pipe Cleaners	

For a fun activity, have each child make his/her own space helmet out of paper bags, tin foil, pipe cleaners, crayons, magic markers and paper towel tubes. Cut holes for the eyes, nose and mouth and tape various items to the bag to make these unique party favors.

Candy Airplanes

1	rubber band	1	stick of gum
1	stick peppermint	2	circle candies

Insert rubber band through both circle candies. Loop ends up over each end of stick of gum. Insert peppermint stick between circle candy and gum for body of plane. Plane may be used as a tree ornament or a toy, or disassembled and eaten!

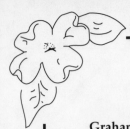

Satellite S'Mores

Graham crackers   Miniature marshmallows
Milk chocolate bars

Place graham crackers on a baking sheet. Cover each cracker with chocolate squares. Arrange marshmallows on top. Broil about 1 minute. Cover with another graham cracker to make a dessert sandwich.

Space Goop

| 1 | box graham crackers, broken into ¼ sections and placed on ungreased cookie sheet | 1 1 ¾ | cup butter or margarine cup firmly-packed brown sugar cup finely chopped nuts |

Heat the butter and sugar for 2 minutes or until sugar is dissolved. Pour over crackers. Top with nuts. Bake for 10 minutes at 325 degrees. This is great for an after school snack with milk. Serves 8.

Man-In-The-Moon Faces

Apples   Raisins
Peanut Butter

Have an adult cut an apple in half and remove the seeds. Each child spoons peanut butter into the pitted area of the apple half, then (still using a spoon) spreads peanut butter across the flat surface of the apple. Let children make a smiley face atop the peanut butter using raisins. Smile and eat.

Peanut Butter Sandwich Cookies

1 ½	cups sifted all-purpose flour	½	cup shortening
½	cup sugar	½	cup creamy peanut butter
½	teaspoon baking soda	¼	cup light corn syrup
¼	teaspoon salt	1	tablespoon milk
			Extra peanut butter

Sift dry ingredients together. Cut in shortening and peanut butter until mixture resembles coarse meal. Blend in corn syrup and milk. Shape into 2-inch roll; chill well. Slice ⅛ to ¼-inch thick. Place half the slices on ungreased cookie sheet; spread with ½ teaspoon peanut butter. Cover with remaining slices. Seal edges with fork. Bake at 350 degrees for 12 minutes. Cool. Yield: 2 dozen.

Decorations and Favors

The party room or the entry way may be decorated with stars and planets hanging from the ceiling. Cut out these heavenly bodies from aluminum foil, construction paper or fluorescent colored paper. Glitter will add some twinkle to the stars. Balloons inflated to different sizes can be the planets. Your guests will enjoy creating some celestial bodies, too, as party favors. For edible party favors, have star-shaped cookies baked and ready for decorating with icing and colored sugars. If the cookies are to be hung from the ceiling, make a hole in the top of each cookie with a large needle or cake tester while the cookies are still warm. Thread each child's decorated star with ribbon or silver string as a party favor. Send each child home with an astronaut "energy" pack containing dried fruits such as apricots, apples, pears and raisins.

SENSIBLE SNACKING

Any parent will appreciate a list of nutritious treats to choose for snacking. Introduce a new snack food to your child by making it into a game. For example, pick a color like green and have your child taste new foods that are the color green, such as broccoli, spinach and grapes.

Creamy Fruit Popsicles

Milkshake

Cucumber Circles

Bananas and Vanilla Wafers

Porcupine Balls

Creamy Fruit Popsicles

1	cup plain yogurt	½	cup chopped fresh fruit (apples, bananas, blueberries, peaches, pineapple, plums or pears)

Combine ingredients in a blender and whip one minute. Pour into popsicle molds or paper cups with popsicle sticks. Freeze. Serves 3.

Milkshake

½	cup fresh fruit (bananas or strawberries)	1	cup lowfat milk

Beat fruit with milk until smooth and creamy. Ice can be blended with the fruit and milk to make an icy drink, great for summertime. This is a good low-calorie snack. Serves 1.

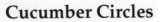

Cucumber Circles

Cucumber, sliced   **Processed cheese spread**

Spread cheese spread between 2 cucumber slices to make little sandwiches.

Bananas and Vanilla Wafers

Banana, sliced   **Peanut butter (optional)**
Vanilla wafers

Place a slice of banana, and peanut butter if desired, between 2 vanilla wafers.

Porcupine Balls

Waxed paper   **Peanut butter**
Table knife   **Crispy rice cereal**
Large marshmallows

Give each child a sheet of waxed paper. Pour cereal on paper. Have child spread peanut butter on a marshmallow with the knife. Roll in cereal. A yummy treat kids like to eat.

LUNCH BOX IDEAS

*Pack a new goody in your child's lunch box and you
will receive rave reviews.*

Chocolate Covered Worms

Munchy Crunchy Granola

Peanut Butter Surprise Muffins

Chocolate Covered Worms

1	(6-ounce) package chocolate chips	1	(3-ounce) can Chinese noodles
1	(6-ounce) package butterscotch chips	¼	cup chopped nuts

Melt chips in saucepan over low heat, stirring constantly. When melted, remove from heat and quickly stir in noodles and nuts. Drop by teaspoonfuls onto waxed paper. Chill. Keep refrigerated. Yield: 3 dozen.

Munchy Crunchy Granola

½	cup dried apples, apricots or mixed fruit, cut into small pieces	¼	cup sesame seeds
		¼	cup firmly packed brown sugar
1 ½	cups oats	¼	cup salad oil
1	cup golden raisins	2	tablespoons vanilla
1	(4-ounce) package toasted sunflower nuts	¼	teaspoon salt

Heat oven to 350 degrees. Spread fruit and remaining ingredients in ungreased jellyroll pan. Mix well. Bake for 10 minutes. Remove from oven and stir. Return to oven and bake an additional 10 minutes. Use granola as a topping for cereal or ice cream, serve in bowls for nibbles or pack in small plastic bags for snacks or lunch box treats. Store any leftover granola tightly covered in refrigerator. Yield: 4 cups.

Peanut Butter Surprise Muffins

¼	cup mashed banana (mash ripe banana with a fork)	½	cup sugar
¼	cup peanut butter	2	cups all-purpose flour
2	large eggs	1	teaspoon baking powder
⅓	cup vegetable oil	1	teaspoon baking soda
1	cup milk	1	cup chopped peanuts
			Jam or filling

Beat together first three ingredients in a medium-sized bowl until well blended and creamy. Add oil and milk and beat. Add dry ingredients. Beat. Stir in chopped peanuts. Grease and flour muffin tins. Fill each ⅓ full with batter. Spoon ½ teaspoon jam or other filling into the center of each muffin and top with additional batter, filling ⅔ full. Bake at 350 degrees for 15 minutes or until browned. Cool. To serve, frost with jam. Yield: 12 muffins.

PARTY THEME IDEAS

Fairy Tales and Cartoon Characters - Come dressed as your favorite character.

Treasure Hunt - Plan a treasure hunt for your swashbuckling pirates, indoors or outdoors.

Garden Hose Party - Invite friends over to splash in the sprinkler and play new games in the wading pool.

Sports - Tennis, Swimming, Soccer, Putt-Putt, Skating, Bowling - Rather than hosting the party in your home, take the children out for a treat.

Circus - Cracker Jacks, hot dogs, clown cones and animal crackers are perfect circus fare. Face painting and multi-colored balloons set the mood.

Western - Cowboy hats and red bandannas for children and decorations. Hunt for plastic cowboys and indians. Pan for gold using pennies in a sand box or wading pool.

50's Party - Poodle skirts and sweaters, burgers and milkshakes complement the sounds of 50's music.

Ballet Party - Make tutus, tiaras or magic wands to use in a recital at the end of the party, invite parents to come early and watch.

Olympics - Relay races, obstacle course and tossing games are perfect for outdoor fun. Have plenty of ribbons or medals for prizes. Decorate with flags and bunting.

Bicycle Party - Decorate bikes with multi color crepe paper, have a parade to a nearby park for a picnic.

Monster Mash - Let your elementary school age "monsters" help prepare the food and decorations for this party. The children will enjoy creating "monster faces" with washable face paint. Have your guests bring smocks or old t-shirts to protect clothing or provide t-shirts to paint as party favors (see page 74).

Dress Up Party - Offer some fun to your young ladies while they experiment with makeup, hair, and jewelry fashions. Invite each guest to come to this party dressed in Mom's hat, jewelry and clothes or as a favorite movie or rock star (see page 87).

Zoo It Up Right - Toddlers and preschoolers will love the funny names of each of these "critter" recipes. A Safari Animal Hunt is easy to keep under control (see page 90).

Astronauts In Space - Your young astronauts won't be "lost in space" testing delicious "galactic" treats and making a fun space helmet to take home (see page 93).

Splendor in the Grass

Richard C. Guy

Oatlands - Leesburg

Picnics are a family tradition during the summer months. Oatlands, the summer home of Mrs. William Corcoran Eustis of Washington, is the ideal setting to experience "splendor in the grass." Erected between 1799 and 1802, Oatlands House is renowned for its classic architecture. The portico's Corinthian columns, the drawing room's octagonal shape and the great hall are outstanding examples of its classic origins. Designed and built by George Carter, Oatlands House has never undergone any structural changes.

Surrounded by stone walls, Oatlands gardens contains a number of smaller areas enclosed by hedges of lilac, holly, and boxwood. Cedars, flowering trees and several fountains, including an 18th century fountain acquired in Paris, make this historic home a summer paradise.

Splendor in the Grass

Barbecues and picnics are a comfortable form of entertainment by which we can take advantage of an outdoor setting.

Appetizers
Shrimp Spread
Splashy Clam Dip

Beverages
Mint Julep

Breads
Jalapeno Cornbread
Parmesan French Bread
Virginia Ham Biscuits

Desserts
Butterscotch Brownies
Chocolate Sheet Cake
Fresh Coconut Pie
Homemade Ice Cream
Lemon Curd Tartlets
Pound Cake
Quick Lime Pie
Sherry Ice Cream Cake

Entrees
Barbecued Beef on Skewers
Gold Cup Barbecue Beef or Pork
Grilled Lemon-Mustard Chicken
Grilled Marinated Chicken
Grilled Sausage with Apples and
   Onions
Grilled Steak with Red Wine
   Marinade
Marinated Pork Kabobs
Salmon Pocket Sandwiches
Shrimp en Brochette
Steak Teriyaki
Steamed Spiced Crabs
Texas Barbecue Brisket

Miscellaneous
Individual Quiches
Marvelous Marinade

Salads
Broccoli Salad
Calico Rice Salad
Cold Beef Salad
Cucumber-Cottage Cheese Salad
Fresh Fruit Kabobs
Fruit Slaw with Honey Dressing
Hot Potato Salad
Pasta Salad
Pronto Pasta Salad
Stuffed Avocado Salad
Three Cabbage Slaw
Tomato-Cucumber Marinade

Vegetables
Baked Beans
Broccoli in Foil
Cool Carrots
Green Beans with Herbs
Grilled Corn with Bacon
Louisiana Sweet and Hot Beans
Pickled Carrots
Sweet Potato and Pineapple Kabobs

Food Safety

Keeping food safe to eat is a special challenge to the picnicker.

- Buy perishable foods last and refrigerate them immediately or put them in a cooler or insulated bag.
- Wash hands after contact with raw meat and poultry. Use clean utensils and plates for each product.
- Keep things cool in a. well insulated container with ice. Salads made with commercial mayonnaise are not as dangerous as once thought (because of their high acid levels) but they should be treated with care. Cold drinks will help keep things cool. When possible, place the cooler in the shade and keep the lid on.
- Put leftovers back in your cooler as soon as you finish eating. When possible, put your cooler in the passenger area of the car - it is much cooler than the trunk.

Packing a Successful Picnic

- Pack the basket in reverse order of unloading with tablecloth on top. Next, pack crushable food items such as chips and crackers. Wrap eating and cooking utensils in napkins and pack on top.
- Cover one end of your table with aluminum foil; prepare foods on it then use it to wrap dirty utensils.
- Pack a damp face cloth or moistened "baby wipes" to clean hands after the meal.

Table Decor

- Consider using a bright tablecloth with a dual purpose such as a bedspread, vinyl tablecloth or shower curtain.
- For windy days, tie corners of cloth in self knots or sew 2 or 3 drapery weights in the corners. You may want to sew a triangle shaped pocket on corners and then fill with rocks.
- Placemats can double as seat cushions.
- Place settings should be easy to carry. Paper picnic products are available in a wide range of colors and shapes.

Starting a Fire

Outdoor barbecuing is fun and easy when a few basic rules are followed. For a successful fire, you will need to use approximately 30 charcoal briquets per pound of meat or enough to cover your cook area with a single layer. After selecting a high quality charcoal, stack the briquets in a pyramid on the grate. Saturate with charcoal starter fluid. Never use gasoline or kerosene to start a fire as it gives your food an undesirable flavor. Let the starter fluid soak into the briquets for 5 minutes. Strike a match and hold it to the coals to light. If the fire will not light or is slow to catch, NEVER spray more fluid directly onto the charcoal. Rather, soak a few briquets with more lighter fluid in a tin and then add them to the grill. Finally, relight the grill. The fire is ready when the coal is 80 percent gray with ash and it glows red in the center. This takes approximately 30 minutes.

Spread the coals around the grate with long handled tongs. Place food on the grill and cook as indicated in your recipe. If a long cooking time is needed, it will be necessary to add more briquets to maintain the fire. Place 10 to 20 briquets at the outer edge of the fire and incorporate them into the center when they are ashen. Easier clean-up is achieved by rubbing the grill with cooking oil or spraying with an aerosol substitute before beginning to grill. For best results, have all ingredients to be barbecued at room temperature. To reduce loss of meat juices, use a spatula or tongs to turn meat rather than piercing with a fork.

Grilling with Wood Chips and Herbs

Once the standard fire making is mastered, experiment with adding wood chips and herbs for variety. Many stores have a selection of fruit and flavoring wood chips. It is also possible to sliver wood from fruit and nut trees right in your own backyard, just be sure that the wood is seasoned and dry rather than green. Regardless of the source, soak the wood for 20 minutes in water to allow the wood to smolder instead of burn. While the wood is soaking, prepare your fire as usual. After it is ready, add a few chips of wood every 20 - 30 minutes. Choose your wood from some of the traditional pairings.

Hickory - pork, poultry, fish, beef
Mesquite - fish, beef, lamb
Cherry - turkey, lamb, fish, chicken, duckling
Apple - pork, fish, turkey
Maple - turkey, ham

Another savory idea to add a subtle flavor to your food is to add herbs to your fire. Select whatever herb suits the particular recipe you are using. Use either fresh or dried herbs. The procedure is the same. Soak the herbs in water for at least 20 minutes. Shake or squeeze out excess water. Place directly on coals and add additional herbs every 30 minutes. The more herbs used, the more flavorful the results.

CHERRY BLOSSOM PICNIC

Each year in early April, the beautiful pink buds on the cherry trees begin to swell and Washingtonians know that summer is not far away. People from all over come to enjoy the glory of the trees and the shower of petals when the wind blows.

Steak Teriyaki
Cucumber-Cottage Cheese Salad
Pickled Carrots
Fresh Coconut Pie

Steak Teriyaki

1	sirloin steak, about 1-inch thick	⅓	cup grated onion
¼	cup water or white wine	¼	teaspoon dry mustard
½	cup soy sauce	2	tablespoons sugar
½	teaspoon ground ginger	⅛	teaspoon garlic powder

Cut sirloin steak into very thin slices, cutting across grain. Place steak strips in shallow dish. Combine remaining ingredients in a jar with tight-fitting lid. Pour over steak strips and marinate for several hours, turning occasionally. Drain steak; reserve marinade. Lace steak strips on skewers. Grill, turning to brown evenly, brushing occasionally with marinade until desired doneness, approximately 8 to 15 minutes. Serves 4 to 6.

Cucumber-Cottage Cheese Salad

1	(3 ¼-ounce) package lime-flavored gelatin	1	cup cottage cheese
1	cup hot water	2	tablespoons chopped green pepper
1	tablespoon vinegar	1	tablespoon shredded carrots
½	cup mayonnaise		
1	tablespoon minced onion		
1	medium cucumber, chopped, seeds removed		

Mix first five ingredients well. Allow to partially jell before adding remaining ingredients. Serves 4 to 6.

Pickled Carrots

3	(16-ounce) cans whole baby carrots, drained, 1 cup liquid reserved	2	teaspoons whole cloves
		3	tablespoons sugar
½	cup white vinegar	½	teaspoon dry mustard
		1 ½	teaspoons salt

Combine carrots, reserved carrot liquid, vinegar and remaining ingredients. Cover. Refrigerate overnight. Stir occasionally. Drain before serving. Serves 8.

Fresh Coconut Pie

1 ½	cups sugar	3	eggs, beaten
2	tablespoons flour	1	cup milk
1	fresh coconut, grated	½	cup butter, melted
1	teaspoon vanilla	1	(9-inch) pie shell, unbaked

Combine sugar and flour. Add next five ingredients. Pour into pie shell. Bake pie in a 450 degree oven for 10 to 15 minutes; reduce heat to 325 degrees for an additional 25 to 30 minutes, or until golden brown. Serves 6 to 8.

GOLD CUP

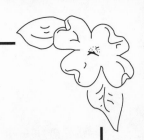

Virginia's premier social event of the spring is the Gold Cup Race. Some people go to watch the horses run and some people go to see and be seen, but everyone goes to enjoy a tailgate picnic. Gold Cuppers plan their tailgate picnics very carefully. Crystal glasses, silver trays and champagne buckets are common sights. Fresh flowers adorn every feast. This delicious menu will surely draw attention to your party! Invite friends to join you, bring your binoculars and don't be surprised if you see a celebrity.

Mint Julep

Gold Cup Barbecue Beef or Pork

Broccoli Salad

Cool Carrots

Baked Beans

Virginia Ham Biscuits

Lemon Curd Tartlets

Mint Julep

1	large bunch freshly cut mint	½	tumbler crushed ice
		2	jiggers bourbon
1	tablespoon sugar		

Crush part of mint with ice and sugar. Add bourbon. Place remaining mint in glass with more crushed ice. Yield: 1 serving.

Gold Cup Barbecue Beef or Pork

3 ½   pounds pork or beef
1   teaspoon dry mustard
3   tablespoons flour
⅛   teaspoon red pepper
¼   cup Worcestershire sauce
1   teaspoon salt

Dash pepper
1   large onion, chopped
2   cloves garlic, minced or 2
       teaspoons garlic powder
1   (14-ounce) bottle catsup

Cut meat into chunks; add water to cover. Boil until tender. Remove and shred meat. Measure broth from meat and add water to make 2 cups. Measure flour and add remaining ingredients to Worcestershire sauce. Mix well and add to liquid. Simmer for a couple of hours. Serves 8 to 10.

Broccoli Salad

2   bunches broccoli
1   small red onion, chopped
½   cup raisins
12   slices bacon, cooked and
       cut into small pieces

½   cup peanuts (optional)
1   cup mayonnaise
½   cup sugar
2   tablespoons vinegar

Use flowerets from broccoli; parboil until tender, drain well. Combine onion, raisins, bacon and peanuts with broccoli. Mix mayonnaise, sugar and vinegar. Pour dressing over broccoli mixture before serving and toss lightly to coat. Serves 6 to 8.

Cool Carrots

2   bunches carrots, peeled
       and thinly sliced
1   green pepper, finely
       chopped
1   (10-ounce) can tomato
       soup, undiluted

½   cup vegetable oil
⅔   cup sugar
1   teaspoon dry mustard
1   small jar pickled onions,
       drained, liquid reserved
       Vinegar

Add vinegar to reserved onion liquid to equal ¾ cup. Cook carrots for 10 minutes in salted water. Drain. Mix vinegar liquid and remaining ingredients together, bring to a boil and cook 5 minutes. Pour over carrots. Chill overnight. Will keep in refrigerator several days. Serves 8.

Baked Beans

1	large can pork and beans	1	cup brown sugar	
1	large can deviled ham		Several dashes catsup	
4	tablespoons mustard	2	small onions, sliced	

Mix first five ingredients together. Ingredients may be stored in refrigerator overnight. In a baking dish, layer bean mixture with onions alternately, ending with onions on top. Bake at 350 degrees for 45 minutes. To keep warm, wrap in several layers of newspaper before transferring to a basket for travel. Serves 6.

Virginia Ham Biscuits

½	cup finely chopped Smithfield Ham	2	teaspoons baking powder
		2	tablespoons shortening
2	cups flour	¾	cups whole milk

Preheat oven to 400 degrees. Sift flour and baking powder in a bowl. Mix with ham. Cut in shortening with knife until mixture has consistency of cornmeal. Add milk, handling as little as possible. Pat out with hands or roll on floured board. Cut out with biscuit cutter and bake on cookie sheet 6 to 8 minutes, or until brown. Yield: 12 to 15 biscuits.

Lemon Curd Tartlets

1 ½	cups sugar	1	teaspoon cornstarch
½	cup butter or margarine		Prepared pastry shells
½	cup lemon juice		Whipped topping or
	Grated rind of 3 lemons		meringue (optional)
6	eggs, slightly beaten		

Melt first four ingredients in top of double boiler. Beat eggs slightly and add to mixture. Cook until thick, about 5 minutes. Add cornstarch and blend well with whisk. Lemon curd will thicken as it cools. Just before serving pour into pastry shells and top with whipped topping or meringue. Yield: Filling for about 10 pastry shells.

A PICNIC EN ROUTE
TO THE CONCERT

You and your friends have tickets for a terrific concert at Wolf Trap. Do not let the traffic on the way to the theatre spoil your evening - enjoy a picnic en route and begin the fun early.

Cold Beef Salad

Salmon Pocket Sandwiches

Individual Quiches

Fresh Fruit Kabobs

Parmesan French Bread

Butterscotch Brownies

Cold Beef Salad

1	clove garlic	1	large tomato
½	teaspoon pepper	1	(14-ounce) jar artichoke
½	teaspoon sugar		hearts in brine, drained
1	tablespoon Dijon mustard	3	green onions, chopped
3	tablespoons red wine	2	tablespoons chopped
	vinegar		parsley
½	cup oil		
½	pound cold cooked roast beef or steak, sliced ¼-inch thick		

Crush garlic. Add next three ingredients; stir to make a paste. Blend in vinegar and whisk in oil. Cut roast beef and tomato into bite-size pieces. Quarter the artichoke hearts. Combine beef, tomato, artichoke, onions and parsley in a large bowl. Pour dressing over all and toss well. Chill for several hours or overnight to blend flavors. Serve with lettuce. Serves 4.

Salmon Pocket Sandwiches

1	(7 ½-ounce) can salmon	2	teaspoons minced parsley
2	tablespoons finely	2	(6-inch) whole wheat pita
	chopped green pepper		breads, halved
2	teaspoons finely chopped		Alfalfa sprouts or lettuce
	celery		Chopped almonds
2	teaspoons minced onion		(optional)
2	teaspoons mayonnaise		
2	teaspoons grated		
	lemon peel		

Drain salmon and flake. Combine with next six ingredients. Pack into covered refrigerator container and keep well chilled. When ready to serve, divide into four equal portions and pack into pita bread halves, garnish with alfalfa sprouts or lettuce. Sprinkle with chopped almonds. Variation: Combine salmon mixture with cooked elbow macaroni and serve as a salad without pita bread. Serves 4.

Individual Quiches

2	cups sifted flour	1	tablespoon grated
1 ½	teaspoons salt		Parmesan cheese
½	cup vegetable oil	¼	cup sautéed mushrooms
¼	cup water		or crabmeat
2	eggs, beaten	1	teaspoon salt
1 ½	cups cream		Pinch coriander

Preheat oven to 400 degrees. Mix flour and salt in a bowl. In measuring cup, pour oil and water, but do not mix together. Pour liquid all at once into flour. Stir lightly until mixed. Roll into balls. Shape into tiny tarts and bake about 5 minutes. Combine remaining ingredients. Remove pastry shells from oven. Lower heat to 325 degrees. Fill each tart with 1 tablespoon egg mixture. Bake filled tarts 15 minutes or until quiche has set. Keep them hot and toasty in an insulated container. Yield: 2 dozen.

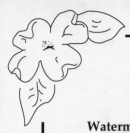

Fresh Fruit Kabobs

Watermelon
Cantaloupe
Strawberries
Fresh pineapple
Bananas

Seedless grapes, red
or green
Orange juice
Wooden skewers

Cut fruit into 1-inch cubes. Arrange in any colorful combination on wooden skewers. Drizzle with orange juice to keep fruit from discoloring. Chill until ready to serve.

Parmesan French Bread

1   tablespoon chopped chives
⅛   teaspoon garlic salt
¼   cup grated Parmesan
     cheese

1   loaf French bread, sliced
¾   cup butter, softened

Preheat oven to 375 degrees. Combine seasonings and cheese with butter, mixing well. Spread butter between bread slices. Wrap in foil. Bake for 20 minutes. For crispier bread, leave top of foil open. Serves 6.

Butterscotch Brownies

¼   cup butter
1   cup brown sugar
1   egg
1   teaspoon vanilla
½   cup flour
1   teaspoon baking powder

½   teaspoon salt
½   to 1 cup finely chopped
     nuts
¾   cup grated coconut
     (optional)

Preheat oven to 350 degrees. Melt butter in saucepan. Stir in brown sugar until dissolved. Cool slightly. Beat in egg and vanilla. Sift flour; resift with baking powder and salt. Stir into cooled butter mixture. Add nuts and grated coconut. Chopped dates and figs may be substituted for nuts. (Dust dates and figs with flour before adding). Pour batter into a greased 9x9-inch pan. Bake about 20 to 25 minutes. Cut into bars when cool. Yield: 16 2 ¼-inch brownies.

POOLSIDE PICNIC

The hot sun and the cool water of a pool provide a beautiful contrast for a summer picnic.

Splashy Clam Dip

Grilled Steak with Red Wine Marinade

Green Beans with Herbs

Pasta Salad

Sherry Ice Cream Cake

Splashy Clam Dip

1	(6 ¾-ounce) can minced clams, drained, juice reserved	2	teaspoons grated onion
		1	teaspoon Worcestershire sauce
1	(8-ounce) cream cheese, softened	3	drops hot pepper sauce
		2	teaspoons lemon juice
¼	teaspoon salt	1	teaspoon chopped parsley

Combine all ingredients except clam juice and blend. Gradually add about ¼ cup reserved juice and beat. Chill. Serve with crackers. Yield: 2 ½ cups.

Grilled Steak with Red Wine Marinade

	Steaks of your choice	¼	cup vegetable oil
1	cup red wine	1	tablespoon seasoned salt
1	teaspoon garlic juice	1	teaspoon salt
¼	cup soy sauce or teriyaki sauce	1	teaspoon oregano
		1	teaspoon pepper

Mix all ingredients. Marinate steaks 8 hours or overnight. Grill to desired doneness. Yield: 2 cups marinade.

Green Beans with Herbs

1	pound fresh green beans, cut into 1-inch pieces	2	teaspoons fresh basil or ½ teaspoon dried basil
3	tablespoons butter	½	cup chopped onion
¼	cup chopped celery	1	clove garlic, minced
2	teaspoons fresh rosemary or ½ teaspoon dried rosemary		

Cook or steam beans until almost tender. Stir in remaining ingredients. Cook covered about 5 minutes or until beans are tender. Serves 4.

Pasta Salad

1	pound medium bow-tie or shell pasta	1	cup fresh, grated Parmesan cheese
½	cup olive oil	½	cup sliced pimento
½	cup vegetable oil	1	bunch fresh broccoli, cut into flowerettes
½	cup white wine vinegar		
2 ½	teaspoons salt	½	cup toasted pine nuts or toasted slivered blanched almonds
1	teaspoon Dijon mustard		
½	teaspoon white pepper		

Cook pasta according to package directions; drain. Rinse with cold water; drain well. Set aside. In a pint jar with tight fitting lid, combine next seven ingredients. Cover and shake well. In large bowl combine pasta and pimento. Pour dressing over and toss gently. Cover and let stand at least 4 hours, tossing occasionally. May be made ahead to this point and refrigerated up to 24 hours. In large saucepan blanch broccoli in boiling, salted water 1 minute. Drain and cool. Add broccoli and ¼ cup nuts to pasta 30 minutes before serving and toss. Spoon into serving dish and sprinkle with remaining nuts. Let stand at room temperature until ready to serve. Yield: 12 cups.

Sherry Ice Cream Cake

1	angel food cake	2	egg yolks, beaten
1	quart vanilla ice cream,	½	cup butter
	softened	1	cup Sherry
1	cup sugar		

Early in day, split cake in half horizontally, packing well with ice cream. Fill in hole with ice cream and freeze. Cream butter and sugar well. Melt slowly over low heat. Add yolks a little at a time, stirring constantly. In a thin stream add Sherry. Continue stirring over low heat until sauce is well blended and thick. Cool. At beginning of meal, remove cake from freezer, and place in refrigerator. To serve pour sauce over cake, as much as it will absorb. Slice and serve. Remaining sauce may be served with cake. Serves 10 to 12.

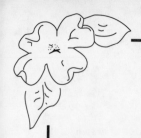

JULY 4TH PICNIC

Enjoy celebrating Independence Day with fireworks, outdoor concerts and this unique holiday menu.

Shrimp Spread

Grilled Lemon-Mustard Chicken

Marvelous Marinade

Pronto Pasta Salad

Chocolate Sheet Cake

Homemade Ice Cream

Shrimp Spread

1 pound medium shrimp, cooked, shelled and cut in half	Juice of ½ lemon
	1 ½ teaspoons Worcestershire sauce
½ cup mayonnaise	1 small clove garlic, minced,
1 (8-ounce) package cream cheese, softened	or ¼ teaspoon garlic powder
3 tablespoons catsup	Seasoned salt to taste
½ cup finely chopped onion	Pepper to taste
½ cup finely chopped celery	Dill weed to taste

Combine all ingredients except dill weed. Chill. Sprinkle lightly with dill weed before serving. Serve with mild crackers. Yield: 3 cups.

Grilled Lemon-Mustard Chicken

½	cup lemon juice	¾	teaspoon salt
¼	cup Dijon mustard	¼	teaspoon coarsely ground
¼	cup finely chopped fresh		pepper
	herbs, any combination:	8	chicken breasts, skinned
	thyme, rosemary, basil,		and boned
	oregano, parsley		
1	tablespoon finely chopped		
	lemon zest		

Combine all ingredients except chicken breasts and mix well. (If fresh herbs are not available, use 4 teaspoons of dried herbs.) In large non-metallic shallow dish arrange chicken pieces and cover with marinade. Refrigerate 2 to 4 hours. Prepare grill. Grill chicken breasts 10 minutes on each side or until done. Serves 6 to 8.

Marvelous Marinade

1 ½	cups vegetable oil	¾	cup soy sauce
¼	cup Worcestershire sauce	2	teaspoons salt
½	cup wine vinegar	1	tablespoon seasoned
⅓	cup lemon juice		pepper
2	cloves garlic, crushed	1 ½	teaspoons parsley flakes
3	tablespoons bourbon	2	teaspoons dry mustard
	(optional)		

Mix all ingredients together. Use to marinate any meat or poultry. Yield: 3 cups.

Pronto Pasta Salad

1	pound pasta shells	½	to ¾ cup red wine vinegar
¼	pound salami, diced	1	(4-ounce) can pitted black
¼	pound pepperoni, diced		olives, diced
¼	pound ham, diced	1	small onion, chopped
1	medium green pepper,	1	(8-ounce) package
	chopped		provolone cheese, diced
½	to ¾ cup vegetable oil		

Cook pasta shells according to package directions and allow to cool. Mix all remaining ingredients together and chill before serving. Serves 6 to 8.

Chocolate Sheet Cake

2	cups flour	1	teaspoon vanilla extract
2	cups sugar	½	cup margarine
½	cup margarine	4	tablespoons cocoa
½	cup shortening	6	tablespoons milk
1	cup water	1	(16-ounce) box
4	tablespoons cocoa		confectioners' sugar
2	eggs	1	teaspoon vanilla extract
½	cup buttermilk	1	cup chopped nuts
1	teaspoon baking soda		

Preheat oven to 350 degrees. Grease a 12x15-inch cake pan. Combine flour and sugar in large bowl. Mix next four ingredients in saucepan and let come to a rolling boil. Pour over sugar and flour mixture. Add next four ingredients and beat well. Pour into cake pan and bake for 20 minutes. For frosting combine margarine, cocoa, and milk and heat until melted. Pour over confectioners' sugar. Add vanilla. Beat well and add nuts. Let cake cool for about 5 minutes after baking before frosting. Serves 12 to 15.

Homemade Ice Cream

1	egg	2	cups scalded milk
1	tablespoon flour	2	cups Half and Half
1	cup sugar	1 ½	teaspoons vanilla
⅛	teaspoon salt		

Beat egg slightly. Mix in flour, sugar and salt. Add scalded milk gradually. Cook in double boiler over hot water until thickened, stirring frequently at first. If custard has a curdled appearance it will disappear during freezing. Chill the mixture. Add Half and Half and vanilla. Follow instructions for freezing ice cream depending on the type of ice cream freezer. Fruits and nuts may be added or served over ice cream. Yield: 1 ½ quarts or 8 to 10 servings.

PICNICKING AT THE BEACH

The sun is hot and the sand burns your feet, but after a day of volleyball and swimming in the ocean, a spicy beach picnic is in order. Build a bonfire on the beach or bring a portable hibachi.

Steamed Spiced Crabs

Shrimp En Brochette

Three Cabbage Slaw

Grilled Corn with Bacon

Calico Rice Salad

Steamed Spiced Crabs

Live crabs   Vinegar
Crab Seasoning

Put 1 to 2 inches of water in a large pot, add 2 to 3 tablespoons vinegar and bring water to a boil. Put crabs in boiling water and sprinkle with seasoning to taste. Steam crabs for 20 to 25 minutes.

Shrimp en Brochette

1 ½ pounds peeled jumbo   2   lemons, cut into wedges
     shrimp   Melted butter

Thread shrimp on skewers alternating every 1 or 2 shrimp with lemon wedges. Baste with melted butter. Grill about 5 minutes over hot grills, basting with butter; turn once. Serves 6.

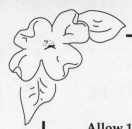

Three Cabbage Slaw

Allow 1 large handful of a combination of red cabbage, green cabbage, and bok choy (Chinese cabbage) per person.
1 scallion, cut into ½-inch pieces
2 cornichons

2 egg yolks
1 teaspoon celery seeds
1 tablespoon rice vinegar
1 tablespoon Dijon mustard
1 teaspoon salt
¾ cup vegetable oil
Salt and pepper to taste

With sharp knife (or shredder blade of food processor), shred the cabbages and put them in a salad bowl. To make dressing, chop scallion and cornichons in a blender. Add next five ingredients and blend well. With blender running, add oil, drop by drop, to make a thick mayonnaise. Toss dressing with shredded cabbages. Season with salt and pepper, if necessary, and chill until ready to use. Yield: 1 cup dressing.

Grilled Corn with Bacon

6 ears of corn
6 strips of bacon

Seasoned salt

Select corn that still has the husks on it. Strip husks back but not off; remove corn silks. Dust corn with seasoned salt and wrap a strip of bacon around ear of corn. Replace the husks and tie securely in place. Cook over charcoal for 15 to 25 minutes until done. Serves 6.

Calico Rice Salad

2 cups cooked rice
1 (8 ¾-ounce) can kidney beans, rinsed and drained
1 (8 ¾-ounce) can whole kernel corn, drained
3 green onions, sliced

¼ cup diced radish
¼ cup vegetable oil
¼ cup wine vinegar
1 tablespoon water
½ teaspoon curry powder

In large bowl, combine first five ingredients; set aside. In small bowl, combine remaining ingredients; beat until well blended. Pour over rice mixture; toss lightly. Chill several hours. Serves 4.

LABOR DAY POTLUCK PICNIC

*End the picnic season with a neighborhood gathering.
Set up the volleyball net, horseshoe pit and other yard games.
Assigning each family a side dish will ensure a good variety
of foods. We offer a wide variety of recipes but be sure
to include your personal favorites.*

Grilled Marinated Chicken

Barbecued Beef on Skewers

Hot Potato Salad

Louisiana Sweet and Hot Beans

Tomato-Cucumber Marinade

Fruit Slaw with Honey Dressing

Pound Cake

Grilled Marinated Chicken

6	frying chickens, cut into serving-sized pieces	1 ½	cups wine vinegar
½	cup vegetable oil	¼	cup salt
1 ½	tablespoons coarsely ground pepper	1 ½	tablespoons poultry seasoning
		1 ½	tablespoons garlic salt

Combine marinade ingredients. Pour over chicken and marinate overnight, basting frequently. Cook chicken for approximately 1 hour on a covered grill. Check for doneness. Serves 20 to 25.

Barbecued Beef on Skewers

1 cup finely chopped onion
1 ½ teaspoons minced garlic
3 tablespoons vegetable oil
1 cup water
¼ cup brown sugar
3 tablespoons soy sauce
2 tablespoons peanut butter
½ teaspoon ground ginger
Dash hot pepper sauce

1 ½ to 2 pounds flank steak cut
into ¼-inch slices or 2 to 3
pounds sirloin tip cut into
1 ½-inch cubes
Chopped green peppers,
small onions,
mushrooms and cherry
tomatoes (optional)

Sauté onion and garlic in oil. Add remaining ingredients except meat and cook until slightly thickened. Marinate meat 1 to 2 hours. Thread meat on skewers. Brush with marinade. Grill 10 to 15 minutes, basting with marinade. May alternate pieces of meat with vegetables on skewer before grilling. Serves 6 to 8.

Hot Potato Salad

3 slices bacon, drippings
reserved
2 tablespoons flour
½ onion, chopped
¼ cup vinegar
½ cup water
½ cup sugar

¼ teaspoon salt
¼ teaspoon pepper
3 cups diced cooked
potatoes
2 teaspoons parsley flakes
¼ teaspoon celery salt

Fry bacon until crisp. Remove bacon and drain on paper towel. Add flour to drippings. Cook briefly. Add onion. Cook until tender. Add next five ingredients. Heat. Add potatoes, parsley, celery salt and crumbled bacon. Heat. Serve warm. Serves 6.

Louisiana Sweet & Hot Beans

1	small onion, diced	1	cup brown sugar
5	strips of bacon	⅛	to ¼ teaspoon red pepper
1	(24-ounce) can old fashioned baked beans		

Fry bacon until tender. Add onion, cook until browned. Add remaining ingredients. Simmer 10 to 15 minutes covered on top of stove. Serves 4.

Tomato-Cucumber Marinade

2	medium tomatoes, sliced	½	cup vegetable oil
1	medium cucumber, peeled and thinly sliced	¼	cup wine vinegar
½	medium onion, thinly sliced and separated into rings	1	teaspoon dried basil, crushed
		1	teaspoon tarragon, crushed
		⅛	teaspoon pepper

Layer tomatoes, cucumber, and onion in shallow glass dish. Combine remaining ingredients; pour over vegetables. Cover and refrigerate for 5 to 24 hours. Serve as is or drain and arrange vegetables in lettuce lined bowl. This dish is especially attractive when one red and one yellow tomato is used. Serves 6.

Fruit Slaw with Honey Dressing

1	small onion, thinly sliced	1	cup sliced celery
2	cups shredded green cabbage	2	large red apples, unpeeled and cubed
2	cups coarsely torn spinach leaves	½	to 1 cup coarsely broken pecans or walnuts
2	cups red grapes, halved and seeded		Honey Dressing (recipe follows)

Combine first seven ingredients in large bowl. Set aside. Prepare dressing. Pour dressing over salad, toss gently. Cover and chill 1 to 2 hours. Add 2 cups cooked diced chicken or shrimp for main dish salad. Serves 8.

Honey Dressing

½	cup sour cream	⅛	teaspoon salt
3	tablespoons mayonnaise	¼	cup water (more for
3	tablespoons honey		thinner consistency)
1	tablespoon lemon juice		Dash pepper

Combine all ingredients to make dressing. Yield: 1 cup.

Pound Cake

3	cups sugar	3	cups all-purpose flour
1	cup butter	1	cup milk
¼	cup vegetable oil	1	teaspoon vanilla extract
6	eggs	1	teaspoon almond extract

Cream sugar and butter. Add oil. Beat well. Add eggs one at a time. Add flour and milk alternately. Blend well. Add vanilla and almond extracts. Pour into prepared bundt pan and set temperature to 325 degrees. Bake for 1 hour and 30 minutes. Serves 12.

INDIAN SUMMER FIESTA

Set the fiesta table with a bright tablecloth and terra cotta stoneware. A paper maché pinata stuffed with gifts and candy serves as a table decoration and party game. After dinner, suspend it from a branch and let each guest swing a sturdy stick at the pinata while blindfolded.

Jalapeño Cornbread

Texas Barbecue Brisket

Stuffed Avocado Salad

Quick Lime Pie

Jalapeño Cornbread

1 ½	cups yellow cornmeal	3	eggs, lightly beaten
3	teaspoons baking powder	½	cup vegetable oil
½	teaspoon salt	1	cup sour cream
1	cup grated Longhorn cheese	1	(8 ½-ounce) can cream style corn or 3 ears fresh corn, cut and scraped from cob
1	cup grated onion		
5	large jalapeños, finely chopped		

Preheat oven to 400 degrees. Grease a 9x13-inch baking pan. Mix together first three ingredients. Stir in cheese, onion and jalapenos. Add remaining ingredients; mix well. Bake for 20 to 30 minutes or until a straw comes out clean. May also be baked in mini muffin tins for 10 to 15 minutes in a 400 degree oven.

Texas Barbecue Brisket

1	(6 to 7 pound) beef brisket, first cut	½	(3.5-ounce) bottle liquid smoke
	Garlic salt	½	(18-ounce) bottle barbecue
	Salt and pepper to taste		sauce
	Celery salt		

In a 9x13-inch pan, place brisket fat side down. Sprinkle with salts and pepper. Pour liqiud smoke over all of brisket. Cover tightly with aluminum foil. Bake 5 hours in 275 degree oven. Remove foil, pour barbecue sauce over top of meat and cook uncovered another hour. Remove from oven and let cool before slicing.

Stuffed Avocado Salad

3	fresh avocados		Dash ground cardamon
¼	cup lemon juice		Dash Worcestershire sauce
1	(4-ounce) can green chilies, drained and seeded	1	(3-ounce) package cream cheese, softened
1	medium onion, peeled and quartered	1	small head lettuce, shredded
¼	teaspoon garlic salt	2	medium tomatoes, peeled,
	Dash red pepper sauce		seeded, and chopped

Cut avocados in half. Scoop out and reserve pulp, leaving shell intact. Mix next seven ingredients in blender. Add cream cheese and avocado pulp and blend until smooth. Spoon cheese mixture into shells. Arrange on 6 lettuce lined plates. Garnish with chopped tomato. Serves 6.

Quick Lime Pie

½	pint whipping cream, whipped	⅛	teaspoon grated lime rind
1	(14-ounce) can sweetened condensed milk	1	(9-inch) graham cracker crust
½	cup lime juice		Lime twists

Fold whipped cream into sweetened condensed milk. Add lime juice and rind. Stir until smooth and thickened. Spoon into crust. Freeze pie until almost firm, or freeze until firm and let stand at room temperature until slightly thawed. Garnish with lime twists. Serves 8.

COOKING OVER COALS

Food prepared over a fire or on a grill tastes better because of its charcoal flavor.

Grilled Sausage with Apples and Onions

Marinated Pork Kabobs

Sweet Potato and Pineapple Kabobs

Broccoli-in-Foil

Grilled Sausage with Apples and Onions

1	pound smoked sausage, cut into 1-inch cubes	2	Red Delicious apples, cored and quartered
2	small onions, skinned and quartered	2	tablespoons apple jelly
		1	tablespoon butter

Thread sausage, apples and onions on skewers. Combine jelly and butter; heat until melted. Brush glaze on sausage, apples and onions. Grill over moderately hot briquets 10 to 15 minutes or until cooked, basting with butter glaze and turning frequently. Serves 4.

Marinated Pork Kabobs

3	pounds boneless pork shoulder, cut into 2-inch cubes	2	tablespoons fresh lemon juice
½	cup vegetable oil	2	garlic cloves, minced
1	bay leaf, crumbled	1	tablespoon minced fresh sage or 1 teaspoon dried sage
⅓	cup dry Sherry		
2	teaspoons soy sauce	1 ½	teaspoons thyme or ½ teaspoon dried thyme
2	teaspoons honey		

Mix marinade in ceramic or glass bowl. Add meat and toss to coat. Let stand for 2 hours. Skewer meat with vegetables and cook on hot grill. Serves 6.

Sweet Potato and Pineapple Kabobs

6   fresh sweet potatoes   Butter or margarine
    Pineapple cubes

Parboil sweet potatoes. Cool, remove peelings, and cut into cubes. Alternate on skewers with fresh or canned pineapple cubes. Brush with melted butter or bacon drippings. Grill over hot coals until browned, 20 to 30 minutes. (Note - canned potatoes are too tender to skewer.) Variation: Wrap bacon strips around potatoes and secure with toothpicks. Arrange on skewers. Serves 6.

Broccoli-in-Foil

1   (16-ounce) package frozen   1   sheet heavy duty
    broccoli   aluminum foil
1   teaspoon salt   1   tablespoon butter or
1   tablespoon water   margarine

Remove broccoli from package and place in foil. Add water, butter and salt. Wrap broccoli as follows: Bring 2 sides of aluminum foil evenly together at top. Fold the two edges together until tight on food. Fold each end several times towards food until tight. Part of the ends can be left unfolded to form handles. Place foil package directly on coals on the grill. Cook for about 15 to 20 minutes. Turn occasionally. Serves 6.

Virginia Heritage

R. Guy

Prince William County Courthouse - Manassas

Virginia's heritage is well represented by the Prince William County Courthouse. Built of native brownstone and brick, it sits at the intersection of Grant and Lee Avenues and served the county from 1894 to 1984.

In July, 1911, the Courthouse was the backdrop for the Peace Jubilee. Organized by George C. Round, the jubilee was a festival to commemorate the 50th anniversary of the Battle of First Manassas, also known as the Battle of Bull Run. Attending were one thousand veterans who gathered to meet old friends and shake hands with those whom they met before in combat. President Taft and Governor Mann addressed those in attendance. In keeping with the southern tradition of hospitality, a "Love Feast of the Blues and Grays" luncheon was served free to all veterans.

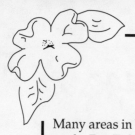

Virginia Heritage

Many areas in Virginia are known for their special commodities: Chesapeake Bay/Tidewater for seafood, Hanover for vegetables, Southside for peanuts and hams and Western Piedmont for vineyards, orchards and berry farms. Virginia's bounty provides any hostess with such a variety of foodstuff that any meal is a culinary delight.

Beverages
Mimosas

Breads
Buttermilk Ham Biscuits
Buttermilk Cornbread
Plantation Spoon Bread
Potato Rolls
Sally Lunn

Desserts
Bananas Foster
Cidered-up Pound Cake
Fresh Apple Cake
Peach Cobbler
Pineapple Cake

Entrees
Apple Smothered Pork Chops
Baked Virginia Ham with Wine
   Sauce
Cheddar Quiche
Grilled Stuffed Red Snapper
Roast Wild Duck with Wild Game
   Sauce
Stuffed Chicken with Apple Glaze
Virginia Crab Cakes

Fruits and Salads
Cucumber Salad
Fruit Compote
Tomato-Artichoke Aspic
Spiced Peaches

Soups
Crab or Shrimp Soup
Peanut Soup

Vegetables
Almond Asparagus
Baked Grated Carrots
Baked Vidalia Onions
Carrot-Sweet Potato Puff
Fresh Stuffed Mushrooms
Green Beans Almondine
Green Bean and Corn Casserole
Green Beans Vinaigrette
Wild Rice
Zucchini and Yellow Squash
   Casserole

SHENANDOAH BREAKFAST

This hearty eye-opener offers a variety of tastes, textures, and colors to your table.

Mimosas

Buttermilk Ham Biscuits

Cheddar Quiche

Almond Asparagus

Tomato-Artichoke Aspic

Fruit Compote

Mimosas

2	(12-ounce) cans frozen orange juice concentrate, thawed and divided	6	cups extra dry champagne, chilled
1	(16-ounce) jar Maraschino cherries with stems, drained		Mint sprigs

Prepare 1 can orange juice concentrate according to can directions. Pour into ice cube trays. Place a cherry in each cube; freeze 8 hours or overnight. Prepare remaining can orange juice concentrate according to can directions. Stir in champagne just before serving. Add ice cubes. Garnish with mint sprigs. Yield: 3 quarts.

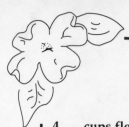

Buttermilk Ham Biscuits

4	cups flour	1	tablespoon sugar
2	tablespoons baking powder	⅔	cup butter, softened
1	teaspoon baking soda	1 ½	cups buttermilk
¾	teaspoon salt		Melted margarine
			Sliced Virginia Ham

Preheat oven to 450 degrees. Combine dry ingredients. Cut in butter. Add buttermilk. Stir until moistened. On lightly floured board, knead 4 to 5 times. Cut biscuits 1-inch thick with a cookie cutter and put on lightly greased cookie sheet. Brush tops with margarine and bake for 10 to 15 minutes. Slice biscuits in half, butter and add thinly sliced ham. These may be made ahead and frozen. Yield: 24 biscuits.

Cheddar Quiche

¾	pound bulk sausage, medium-hot	2	eggs, beaten
½	cup thinly sliced onion	1	cup evaporated milk
⅓	cup chopped green pepper	1	tablespoon parsley flakes
½	cup shredded sharp Cheddar cheese	¾	teaspoon seasoned salt
		¼	teaspoon garlic salt
1	tablespoon flour	¾	teaspoon pepper
		1	(8-inch) pie shell, unbaked

Preheat oven to 375 degrees. Fry sausage and drain. Set aside. Sauté onions and green pepper until tender. In bowl, combine cheese and flour. Stir in sausage, green pepper and onion. Spread in an unbaked pie shell. Mix remaining ingredients and pour into shell. Place quiche on cookie sheet and bake until browned and set, about 45 minutes. Serves 6 to 8.

Almond Asparagus

2	pounds fresh asparagus	1	cup blanched, slivered almonds, toasted
4	tablespoons butter or margarine		Salt and pepper
2	tablespoons lemon juice		

Wash asparagus. Cut into 1-inch diagonal slices. Melt butter in skillet. Add asparagus and sauté 3 to 4 minutes. Cover skillet and steam about 2 minutes or until tender but crisp. Toss asparagus with lemon juice and almonds. Salt and pepper to taste. Serve warm. Serves 8.

Tomato-Artichoke Aspic

4	cups cocktail vegetable juice, divided	1	(12-ounce) carton small curd cottage cheese
2	(3-ounce) packages lemon-flavored gelatin	2	cups mayonnaise
1	teaspoon Worcestershire sauce	½	cup capers
			Bibb lettuce
1	(14-ounce) can artichoke hearts, drained and halved	1	(2-ounce) jar black caviar
3	green onions with tops, cut into 1-inch pieces	8	to 9 lemon slices, halved (optional)
1	(8-ounce) package cream cheese, cut into 1-inch pieces		

Bring 2 cups vegetable juice to a boil in a medium saucepan; remove from heat and add gelatin, stirring until dissolved. Stir in remaining 2 cups juice and Worcestershire sauce. Pour 2 cups gelatin mixture into an oiled 11-cup ring mold. Let remaining juice mixture stand at room temperature. Chill mixture in mold until the consistency of unbeaten egg white. Press artichoke halves into thickened mixture around outside of mold; chill until gelatin is firm. Position knife blade in food processor bowl. Add green onions. Top with cover and process, pulsing 5 or 6 times until onions are chopped. Add cream cheese and cottage cheese; process 15 seconds or until smooth. Spread cheese mixture evenly over chilled aspic, spreading to edge of mold. Gently pour remaining gelatin mixture over cheese layer; chill until gelatin is firm. Combine mayonnaise and capers; mix well. Chill until serving time. Run a thin metal spatula between ring mold and aspic all the way around; unmold onto serving platter. Surround aspic with Bibb lettuce leaves. Place half of caper mayonnaise in a small serving bowl; place in center of aspic mold. Place a heaping tablespoon of caviar onto center of caper mayonnaise. Gently press lemon slices around outside of aspic mold, if desired. Serve remaining caper mayonnaise topped with remaining caviar in a separate bowl. Serves 14.

Fruit Compote

1   (16-ounce) can pear
    halves, undrained
    and chopped
1   (15 ¼-ounce) can
    pineapple chunks,
    undrained
1   (10-ounce) package
    frozen strawberries,
    thawed and undrained

1   (8 ¾-ounce) can fruit
    cocktail, undrained
2   bananas, sliced
2   apples, peeled, cored
    and cubed
½   cup Maraschino cherries
1   (3 ½-ounce) package
    instant vanilla
    pudding mix

Combine fruit; blend. Stir in pudding mix. Cover; refrigerate 8 hours or overnight. Serve with a slotted spoon. Serves 8.

VIRGINIA BANQUET

Virginia's heritage is rich in history, hospitality and home cooking. This Virginia banquet will convey Old Dominion hospitality to your guests.

Baked Virginia Ham with Wine Sauce
Green Beans Almondine
Carrot-Sweet Potato Puff
Spiced Peaches
Potato Rolls
Plantation Spoon Bread
Cidered-Up Pound Cake

Baked Virginia Ham

1	(12 to 15 pound) country ham	¾	cup firmly packed brown sugar
	Whole cloves		Fresh parsley sprigs (optional)
2	cups orange juice, divided		

Place ham in a very large container. Cover with cold water and soak overnight. Remove ham from water and drain. Scrub ham thoroughly with a stiff brush and rinse well with cold water. Replace ham in container and cover with fresh cold water. Bring to a boil. Cover. Reduce heat and simmer 1 hour. Drain off water. Cover ham with fresh cold water. Cover and simmer an additional 4 to 5 hours, allowing 25 minutes per pound. Turn ham occasionally during cooking time. Cool. Carefully remove ham from water. Remove skin. Place ham, fat side up, on a cutting board. Score fat in a diamond design and stud with whole cloves. Place ham, fat side up, in a shallow roasting pan. Combine 1 cup orange juice and sugar. Coat exposed portion of ham with orange juice mixture. Bake uncovered at 325 degrees for 30 minutes. Baste frequently with remaining orange juice. Transfer to serving platter; garnish with parsley. Serves 24.

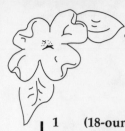

Wine Sauce

1	(18-ounce) jar apple jelly	½	teaspoon ground ginger
½	cup Port wine		Pinch pepper
¼	teaspoon onion juice		

Combine all ingredients in a small saucepan. Cook until boiling. Remove from heat. Skim off foam with a metal spoon. Serve with sliced ham. Yield: approximately 1 ¼ cups.

Green Beans Almondine

4	cups fresh green beans	¼	cup butter or margarine
1	cup blanched almonds, toasted or ½ cup sliced almonds, toasted	½	teaspoon dried whole oregano

Wash beans and bring to boil in 4 quarts salted water. Lower heat and simmer covered for 20 to 30 minutes or until tender. Drain. Sauté almonds in butter until lightly browned. Add almonds and oregano to cooked green beans and toss well. Serves 8.

Carrot-Sweet Potato Puff

¼	cup chopped onion	1	(3-ounce) package cream cheese, softened
2	tablespoons butter		
2	(18-ounce) cans sweet potatoes, drained	2	eggs
		1	teaspoon salt
1	(16-ounce) can diced carrots, drained	¼	teaspoon nutmeg
		⅛	teaspoon pepper

Sauté onion in butter until tender but not brown. Beat together sweet potatoes and carrots until smooth. Add onions and remaining ingredients; beat until fluffy. Spoon into a buttered 2-quart baking dish. Bake uncovered at 325 degrees for 45 minutes until hot or cover and chill. Uncover and bake at 325 degrees for 1 hour. Serves 8.

Spiced Peaches

2   (29-ounce) cans peach   4   3-inch cinnamon sticks
    halves in heavy syrup   1 ⅓ cups sugar
2   teaspoons whole cloves   1   cup vinegar

Drain peach halves, reserving syrup. Combine syrup with remaining ingredients in a medium saucepan. Bring to a boil, cover, and simmer 5 minutes. Remove from heat; add peach halves and cool completely. Refrigerate in an airtight glass container overnight. Flavor of peaches becomes stronger when stored several days. Serves 8.

Potato Rolls

3   medium potatoes   1 ½ cups potato water, cooled
½   cup sugar   1   teaspoon salt
⅔   cup shortening   5   cups flour
2   eggs   Butter, melted
1   package active dry yeast

Peel potatoes and boil until tender. Remove potatoes, reserving water, and mash. In a large bowl, cream sugar and shortening together. Add eggs and beat well. Mix in 1 cup warm mashed potatoes. In another bowl, dissolve yeast in measured potato water. Combine potato water and salt and mix well. Add flour and yeast water alternately to potato mixture. Knead well. Unrisen dough may be stored in refrigerator for 5 days. Pinch off dough as needed. Form dough into desired shape and let rise on a greased cookie sheet or in muffin tins for about 2 ½ hours. Bake at 425 degrees for 12 minutes, brushing tops with melted butter half way through cooking time. Yield: 4 dozen.

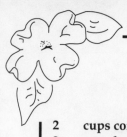

Plantation Spoon Bread

2	cups cornmeal	¼	cup butter or margarine, melted
2	cups boiling water		
1 ½	cups milk	3	eggs, separated, at room temperature
1	teaspoon salt		

Combine cornmeal and water; stir until well blended. Mixture will be thick. Stir in milk, salt and butter. Beat egg yolks until thick and lemon colored; stir into cornmeal mixture. Beat egg whites until stiff but not dry. Gently fold into cornmeal mixture. Pour into a lightly greased 1 ½-quart casserole. Bake at 350 degrees for 40 minutes or until a knife inserted in center of bread comes out clean. Serves 8.

Cidered-Up Pound Cake

3 ¼	cups all-purpose flour	½	cup shortening
½	teaspoon salt	3 ¼	cups sugar
¾	teaspoon ground cinnamon	6	eggs
½	teaspoon baking powder	1	teaspoon vanilla extract
½	teaspoon allspice	1	cup apple cider
½	teaspoon nutmeg		Caramel Glaze
1	cup butter, softened		(recipe follows)

Combine first six ingredients. Set aside. Cream butter, shortening and sugar until light and fluffy. Add eggs, one at a time, beating well after each addition. Add dry ingredients alternately with cider and vanilla. Spoon batter into greased and floured 10-inch tube pan. Bake at 325 degrees for 1 ½ hours. Cool 15 minutes. Remove from pan and top with Caramel Glaze. Serves 10 to 12.

Caramel Glaze

½	cup sugar	1 ½	tablespoons light corn syrup
¼	teaspoon baking soda		
¼	cup butter	¼	teaspoon vanilla extract
¼	cup buttermilk		

Combine all ingredients in a saucepan over medium heat. Boil 10 minutes. Yield: 1 cup.

TASTE OF THE TIDEWATER

Virginia's shoreline shelters a vast bounty of fish and shellfish. For the tastiest menu, select recipes that use the fresh catch of the day.

Crab or Shrimp Soup

Grilled Stuffed Red Snapper

Virginia Crab Cakes

Cucumber Salad

Green Beans Vinaigrette

Buttermilk Cornbread

Fresh Apple Cake

Crab or Shrimp Soup

¾	cup butter or margarine	1	tablespoon seafood seasoning
1	cup flour		
2	cups chicken broth	2	quarts Half and Half
2	cups milk	¼	cup sherry
¼	teaspoon pepper	1	pound crabmeat (carefully picked for shells)
1	tablespoon Worcestershire sauce		Salt to taste
2	tablespoons chives		
1	teaspoon parsley flakes		

In a soup kettle, make a white sauce by melting butter; add flour and chicken broth alternately, stirring constantly with a whisk. Add milk, all seasonings and Half and Half. As it heats, stir with whisk to remove lumps. Add sherry and crabmeat. Heat, but do not boil. For shrimp soup, follow same directions but omit crabmeat. Add 3 tablespoons tomato paste and 2 pounds shrimp cut into bite-size pieces. Serves 8.

Grilled Stuffed Red Snapper

6	slices bread	⅛	teaspoon thyme
1	cup beef or fish stock	¼	teaspoon hot sauce
¼	cup minced celery	1	egg, lightly beaten
¼	cup finely chopped green onion	1	teaspoon salt, divided
		¼	teaspoon white pepper
2	tablespoons butter	1	(4 to 6 pound) dressed
2	tablespoons chopped parsley		red snapper
			Basting Sauce
1	(6 ½-ounce) can white crabmeat		(recipe follows)
2	tablespoons fresh chopped tomato, or tomato catsup		

Soak bread in cold beef or fish stock; squeeze dry, and reserve liquid. Set aside. Sauté celery and onion in butter over low heat. Add bread, reserved liquid and next six ingredients. Stir to mix well adding ½ teaspoon salt. Sprinkle fish inside and out with remaining salt and pepper. Stuff cavity with bread mixture; skewer opening closed. Place fish in a wire grilling basket; grill over hot coals 15 minutes on each side or until fish flakes easily when tested with a fork. Baste frequently with Basting Sauce. Serves 6.

Basting Sauce

3	tablespoons butter, melted	¼	teaspoon hot sauce
1	teaspoon salt	¾	cup vegetable oil
3	tablespoons lemon juice		
3	tablespoons Worcestershire sauce		

Blend first five ingredients in a small bowl. Add oil a little at a time and blend well. Yield: about 1 cup.

Virginia Crab Cakes

1	pound crabmeat	2	slices bread, crumbled
1	egg		Salt and pepper to taste
1	tablespoon mayonnaise		
1	tablespoon prepared mustard		

Mix all ingredients. Shape into patties. Fry in deep fat until golden brown. Serves 6.

Cucumber Salad

4	medium cucumbers	1	teaspoon tarragon
	Salt	1/8	teaspoon white pepper
1	cup heavy cream, whipped	1	or 2 tablespoons sherry
1	teaspoon chopped chives		wine vinegar

Peel cucumbers; cut in half lengthwise and remove seeds. Cut into 1/2-inch slices. Sprinkle with salt and refrigerate. Combine whipped cream and spices. Add 1 tablespoon sherry wine vinegar and taste; add remaining tablespoon gradually, tasting as you add. Chill dressing. When ready to serve, drain cucumbers and add to dressing. Serves 6.

Green Beans Vinaigrette

3/4	pound fresh green beans	1	tablespoon red wine vinegar
1/3	cup chopped green onion		
2	tablespoons fresh snipped parsley	1	teaspoon Dijon mustard
2	cloves garlic, minced, or 1/4 teaspoon garlic powder	3	tablespoons olive oil or cooking oil
			Salt and pepper

Wash and trim beans. Cook beans and onions, covered, in small amount of boiling salted water 5 to 6 minutes or until crisp-tender. Drain vegetables well. Combine next four ingredients. Gradually add oil, stirring with whisk or fork. Add dash salt and pepper. Stir until well blended. Pour over green beans and heat through or refrigerate and serve cold. Serves 6.

Buttermilk Cornbread

1	cup cornmeal	2	cups buttermilk
1	cup all-purpose flour	2	eggs, beaten
2	teaspoons baking powder	2	tablespoons bacon
1	teaspoon salt		drippings or shortening,
1	teaspoon baking soda		melted

Combine first four ingredients. Mix well. Dissolve soda in buttermilk. Add buttermilk mixture, eggs and bacon drippings to dry ingredients; stir just until moistened. Pour batter into a greased 9-inch cast-iron skillet. Bake at 450 degrees for 20 minutes or until browned. Cut into wedges and serve hot. Serves 8.

Fresh Apple Cake

2	cups sugar	3	cups flour
1 ½	cups vegetable oil	1 ¼	teaspoons baking soda
2	teaspoons vanilla extract	1	teaspoon cinnamon
2	eggs, beaten	½	teaspoon nutmeg
	Juice of ½ lemon	3	cups chopped apples
1	teaspoon salt	1 ½	cups pecans

Combine first five ingredients and beat well. Combine next five ingredients and add to previous mixture. Beat well. Add apples and pecans and mix by hand. Pour into a greased bundt pan and bake for 1 ½ hours at 325 degrees. Serves 12.

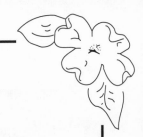

GAME NIGHT

Wild game is available to many Virginians. Often, men enjoy taking on or sharing the responsibility of cooking. Make Game Night a feast you won't want to miss!

Fresh Stuffed Mushrooms

Roast Wild Duck with Wild Game Sauce

Wild Rice

Green Bean and Corn Casserole

Baked Vidalia Onions

Bananas Foster

Peach Cobbler

Fresh Stuffed Mushrooms

1	pound fresh mushrooms	½	teaspoon thyme
1	tablespoon lemon juice	2	ounces Monterey Jack cheese, shredded
½	teaspoon herb seasoned salt, divided	½	tablespoon ground nutmeg
2	tablespoons chopped onion	3	tablespoons chopped chives
1	clove garlic, chopped		

Wash mushrooms and break stems from caps, reserving stems. Put caps in a large skillet and season inside and out with ¼ teaspoon herb salt. Add water to fill skillet ¼ inch. Add lemon juice. Cover and cook slowly for about 5 minutes. Cool. Grate or chop mushroom stems. Place in small skillet with onions and garlic. Add thyme and remaining herb salt. Cover and cook on low heat until water has evaporated from mushrooms, about 5 minutes. Remove lid and cook until all moisture has evaporated, stirring occasionally. Add cheese and let cook until cheese is creamy. Add nutmeg and chives and stir until blended. Fill mushroom caps with stuffing mixture and reheat. Serve hot. Serves 8.

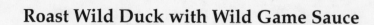

Roast Wild Duck with Wild Game Sauce

2	ducks, cut in half	1	tablespoon dry mustard
	Garlic, salt and pepper	½	tablespoon nutmeg
	to taste		Juice of 1 small lemon
1	cup chopped celery	2	cups water
1	large onion, chopped		Paprika
1	clove garlic, chopped		Wild Game Sauce
1	cup chili sauce		(recipe follows)
1	tablespoon Worcestershire		
	sauce		

Rub duck halves with garlic, salt and pepper. Place breast side down in roaster. Combine other ingredients except paprika. Pour over ducks. Bake covered at 325 degrees for 3 hours. When ducks are tender, turn breast side up and sprinkle with paprika. Bake uncovered until brown. Serves up to 16.

Wild Game Sauce

1	(10 to 13-ounce) jar currant	1	(11-ounce) can mandarin
	jelly		oranges, drained
½	cup Port wine	⅛	teaspoon nutmeg
2 ½	tablespoons horseradish		Salt and pepper to taste

In medium saucepan melt jelly. Bring to boil. Mix remaining ingredients and add to jelly. Serve hot with game. Yield: about 3 cups.

Wild Rice

1	medium onion, chopped	1	cup brown rice
1	(2 ¼-ounce) package	1	(4-ounce) can mushrooms
	slivered almonds or pecans	2	cups bouillon (2 cubes
½	cup butter		dissolved in 2 cups water)
1	cup wild rice		

Melt butter and sauté onions and nuts in a casserole dish. Add rice, mushrooms and bouillon. Bring to a boil. Cover and bake in a 350 degree oven for 1 hour. Stir and serve. Serves 6 to 8.

Green Bean and Corn Casserole

1	(12-ounce) can Mexican-style corn, drained	1	(10 ¾-ounce) can cream of celery soup, undiluted
1	(16-ounce) can French-cut green beans, drained	¼	teaspoon white pepper
½	cup diced celery	¼	cup butter or margarine, melted
½	cup diced onion	½	cup slivered almonds
½	cup shredded sharp Cheddar cheese	1	cup herb-seasoned stuffing mix
½	cup commercial sour cream		

Combine first eight ingredients in a medium bowl. Stir well. Spoon mixture into a lightly greased 8-inch square baking dish. Combine remaining ingredients in a small bowl. Toss gently. Sprinkle over casserole. Bake uncovered at 350 degrees for 45 minutes. Serves 6.

Baked Vidalia Onions

4	large vidalia onions	1	teaspoon salt
4	tablespoons butter or margarine	⅛	teaspoon pepper
			Parmesan cheese

Trim and peel each onion. Cut each onion as if quartering, but do not cut all the way through. Press 1 tablespoon of butter or margarine into each onion. Sprinkle with salt and pepper followed by a generous amount of cheese. Wrap each onion in aluminum foil. Bake at 400 degrees for one hour. Serves 4.

Bananas Foster

¾	cup unsweetened apple juice	2	teaspoons cornstarch
2	dashes apple pie spice	2	tablespoons rum
3	medium-size ripe bananas, peeled	⅛	teaspoon maple flavoring
		⅛	teaspoon butter flavoring
		3	cups vanilla ice cream

Combine apple juice and apple pie spice in a large skillet. Cut each banana in half crosswise, and slice in half lengthwise. Add bananas to juice mixture. Cook over medium heat just until bananas are heated, basting often with juice. Combine next four ingredients. Add to banana mixture. Bring to a boil. Boil 1 minute, stirring constantly. Serve hot over vanilla ice cream. Serves 6.

Peach Cobbler

6	tablespoons margarine	¾	cup milk
2	cups sugar, divided	2	cups peaches
¾	cup all-purpose flour		Dash salt
2	teaspoons baking powder		

Melt butter in a 2-quart baking dish. Combine 1 cup sugar, flour, salt and baking powder. Add milk and stir. Pour batter into dish. Do not stir. Combine peaches and 1 cup sugar. Spoon over batter. Do not stir. Bake at 350 degrees for 1 hour. Serves 6 to 8.

SOUTHSIDE SUPPER

Serve up these traditional Virginia specialties.

Peanut Soup

Stuffed Chicken with Apple Glaze

Apple Smothered Pork Chops

Zucchini and Yellow Squash Casserole

Baked Grated Carrots

Sally Lunn Bread

Pineapple Cake

Peanut Soup

¼	cup butter	½	pound peanut butter
¼	cup diced onion	1 ½	teaspoons celery salt
1	stalk celery, diced	½	teaspoon salt
1 ½	tablespoons flour	½	tablespoon lemon juice
4	cups chicken broth or stock, heated	¼	cup ground peanuts

Melt butter in skillet and sauté onion and celery until translucent. Add flour and mix well. Add hot chicken stock and cook for 30 minutes. Remove from stove, strain and add remaining ingredients except ground peanuts. Just before serving, sprinkle soup with ground peanuts. Serves 10.

Stuffed Chicken with Apple Glaze

1	box stuffing mix	¼	teaspoon pepper
1	cup grated apple	2	tablespoons cooking oil
½	teaspoon lemon peel	1	chicken
¼	cup raisins		Apple Glaze
¼	cup celery		(recipe follows)
½	teaspoon salt		

Prepare stuffing mix according to box directions. Add next four ingredients to prepared stuffing. Wash and dry chicken inside and out. Stuff cavity with prepared stuffing. Rub outside of chicken with oil. Season with salt and pepper. Bake covered for 1 hour at 375 degrees. Brush with glaze and cook for 30 minutes longer. Serves 4 to 6.

Apple Glaze

| ½ | cup apple jelly | ½ | teaspoon ground |
| 1 | tablespoon lemon juice | | cinnamon |

Mix all ingredients and simmer for 3 minutes. Yield: ½ cup.

Apple Smothered Pork Chops

6	pork chops	3	tablespoons molasses
2	teaspoons salt, divided	3	tablespoons flour
1 ½	teaspoons sage, divided	1	cup hot water
	Vegetable oil	1	tablespoon cider vinegar
3	tart apples, peeled, cored	⅓	cup raisins
	and sliced ¼-inch thick		

Season each chop with ¼ teaspoon salt and ¼ teaspoon sage. In skillet, brown chops on both sides in a small amount of vegetable oil. Place chops in a shallow baking dish; reserve drippings. Arrange apples on chops. Pour molasses over apples and chops. Sprinkle flour over drippings in skillet. Cook until brown, stirring occasionally. Slowly add water, stirring constantly to keep smooth. Bring to a boil. Stir in cider vinegar, ½ teaspoon salt and raisins. Pour over apples and chops. Cover and bake at 350 degrees for 1 hour. Serves 4.

Zucchini and Yellow Squash Casserole

2	zucchini squash, sliced ¼-inch thick	2	tomatoes, thinly sliced
2	yellow squash, sliced ¼-inch thick	1	tablespoon butter
	Salt and pepper to taste		Fine bread crumbs
5	slices American cheese	1	to 2 tablespoons water, if desired

Layer squash in buttered casserole. Salt and pepper to taste. Place a layer of cheese on squash followed by a layer of tomatoes. Salt and pepper to taste. Top with pats of butter and sprinkle with bread crumbs. Bake in a covered casserole dish at 400 degrees for 1 hour. Serves 6.

Baked Grated Carrots

3	cups grated carrots	1	tablespoon lemon juice
2	tablespoons margarine, melted	2	tablespoons dry sherry
		1	tablespoon chopped chives

Place grated carrots in a casserole dish. Pour melted margarine, lemon juice and sherry over carrots. Sprinkle with chives. Cover. Bake at 350 degrees for 30 minutes. Serves 6.

Sally Lunn Bread

2	cups scalded milk	1	yeast cake or 1 package dry yeast
⅔	cup shortening		
2	teaspoons salt	3	eggs, beaten
¼	cup sugar	6	cups flour

Preheat oven to 350 degrees. Scald milk, add shortening, salt and sugar. When lukewarm, add yeast and eggs. Stir in flour and beat until smooth. Cover bowl and let rise until double in bulk. Push down and spoon into greased tube or bundt pan. Cover and let rise again (30 to 40 minutes). Bake 45 to 50 minutes. Serves 6 to 8.

Pineapple Cake

½	cup shortening	¼	teaspoon baking soda
1 ½	cups sugar	1	cup buttermilk
2	eggs	1	teaspoon vanilla extract
2	cups all-purpose flour		Pineapple Frosting
2	teaspoons baking powder		(recipe follows)

Cream shortening in a medium mixing bowl. Gradually add sugar, beating well. Add eggs, one at a time, beating well after each addition. Combine next three ingredients. Add to creamed mixture, alternately with buttermilk, beginning and ending with flour mixture. Stir in vanilla. Pour batter into 2 greased and floured 8-inch round cake pans. Bake at 350 degrees for 35 minutes or until a wooden pick inserted in center comes out clean. Cool in pans 10 minutes. Remove layers from pans and cool completely. Spread Pineapple Frosting between layers and on top of cake. Serves 8 to 10.

Pineapple Frosting

1	cup evaporated milk	1	teaspoon vanilla extract
1	cup sugar	1	(20-ounce) can crushed
3	egg yolks		pineapple, drained
½	cup butter or margarine		

Combine first four ingredients in a heavy saucepan. Cook over medium heat, stirring constantly, until mixture thickens. Stir in vanilla and pineapple mixing well. Cool completely before frosting cake. Yield: 3 ½ cups.

Casual Classics

Watt House - Richmond

Constructed in the early 19th century, Watt House was the center of the defensive position held by the northern army. The house served as headquarters for Union General Fitz-John Porter and as a hospital during the battle of Gaines-Mill in 1862.

Mrs. Sarah Watt, mistress of the house, was evacuated to a neighboring home before the battle began. She never returned to Watt house, having died at age 77 while staying with a neighbor.

The Watt House is not open to the public, but is maintained by the Richmond National Battlefield Park.

Casual Classics

Select several recipes from this chapter and create your own classic menu.

Appetizers
Bleu Cheese Puffs
Bread Dip da Dip
Clams Oregano
Crab Spread on English Muffins
Drunken Weiners
Party Rye Canapes

Breads
Beer Bread
Herb Bread
Open Faced English Muffin
   Sandwiches

Desserts
Apple Cake
Easy Coconut Cake
Mexican Wedding Cakes
Millie's Dilly
Strawberry Nut Cake
Turtle Cake
Watergate Cake

Entrees
Apricot Glazed Cornish Hens
Barbados Beef Stew
Beef Stroganoff
Chicken Fruit Salad
Deviled Swiss Steak
Goulash
Sausage in Polish Sauce
King Ranch Chicken
Pseudo Sauerbraten
Shrimp and Crabmeat Casserole
Sour Cream Lasagne
Stuffed Peppers

Soups
Barley Soup
Crab Soup
Egg Drop Soup
Minestrone

Vegetables and Salads
Broccoli Casserole
Corn Pudding
Spaghetti Salad

APPETIZERS

Bleu Cheese Puffs

Bread Dip da Dip

Clams Oregano

Crab Spread on English Muffins

Drunken Weiners

Party Rye Canapés

Bleu Cheese Puffs

½	cup butter, melted	1	(10-ounce) can refrigerator
3	ounces bleu cheese		buttermilk biscuits

Crumble cheese into butter. Cut each biscuit into quarters. Arrange on pan according to package directions. Pour cheese mixture over top of biscuits. Bake at 375 degrees for 8 minutes or until puffs are golden brown. Yield: 32 puffs.

Bread Dip Da Dip

1	cup mayonnaise		Dash garlic salt
1	cup sour cream		Dash hot pepper sauce
¼	cup dried parsley	2	loaves bread (cheese, rye
3	tablespoons dried minced		or pumpernickel)
	onion		

Mix together first six ingredients the day before serving. Refrigerate overnight. Cut one loaf of bread into bite-size squares. Set aside. Scoop out middle of remaining loaf and cut into squares. Stuff hollowed out loaf with dip. Place bread squares around loaf for dipping. Serves 8 to 10.

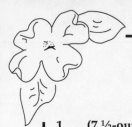

Clams Oregano

1	(7 ½-ounce) can chopped clams	1	tablespoon chopped fresh parsley
1	cup seasoned bread crumbs	2	teaspoons lemon juice
¼	teaspoon garlic powder	¼	teaspoon oregano

Drain clams, reserving liquid. Divide clams equally among 18 serving shells. Mix reserved liquid and remaining ingredients together. Divide breadcrumb mixture equally among clams and pat firmly to set. Bake at 350 degrees for 10 minutes or under broiler for 1 to 2 minutes. Yield: 1 ½ dozen.

Crab Spread on English Muffins

1	(5-ounce) jar Cheddar cheese spread	½	teaspoon seasoned salt
½	cup butter	1	teaspoon dried parsley
2	teaspoons mayonnaise	2	cups fresh crabmeat, cleaned for shells
½	teaspoon garlic powder	4	English muffins

Mix together all ingredients except muffins. Separate muffins into halves. Spread crab mixture onto each half. Cut each half into quarters. Place on cookie sheet and freeze for at least 40 minutes before cooking. Once frozen, these may be stored in zip lock bags in freezer for several weeks. When ready to serve, broil for 5 to 8 minutes or until golden brown. Yield: 32 appetizers.

Drunken Weiners

¾	cup bourbon	1 ½	cups catsup
1	cup brown sugar	1	package cocktail weiners

Combine first three ingredients in large casserole. Cook weiners in sauce. Serve with toothpicks or cocktail forks. These are better made one day ahead. Serves 10.

Party Rye Canapés

½   cup Parmesan cheese
2   tablespoons wine
½   cup mayonnaise

Dash Worcestershire sauce
Garlic powder to taste
Loaf party rye bread

Combine all ingredients except bread. Spread on rye rounds. Sprinkle with additional Parmesan cheese. Broil until bubbly. Serve warm. Serves 15.

BREADS

Beer Bread

Herb Bread

Open Faced English Muffin Sandwiches

Beer Bread

3	cups self-rising flour (or 3 cups all-purpose flour plus 4 ½ teaspoons baking powder and 1 ½ teaspoons salt)	3	tablespoons sugar
		1	(12-ounce) can beer, at room temperature

Preheat oven to 350 degrees. Mix all ingredients in a mixing bowl. Beat 10 times by hand. Bake 1 hour in greased loaf pan. May spread top with butter when warm. Slices better when cool. Yield: 1 loaf.

Herb Bread

1	tablespoon dried parsley flakes	½	cup butter, softened
¼	teaspoon dried dill		French or Italian bread, sliced but not through bottom crust
¼	teaspoon oregano		
1	clove garlic, minced		Grated Parmesan cheese

Preheat oven to 350 degrees. Combine first four ingredients. Spread butter on bread slices and sprinkle each slice with herb mixture. Sprinkle cheese over top of loaf. Warm bread in oven until top of loaf is golden brown. Yield: 1 loaf.

Open Faced English Muffin Sandwiches

English muffins
Dijon mustard
Muenster cheese

Ham slices
Pineapple slices

Separate English muffins and place on baking sheet. Spread each with Dijon mustard. Layer with cheese, ham and pineapple. Broil until cheese melts.

DESSERTS

Apple Cake

Easy Coconut Cake

Mexican Wedding Cakes

Millie's Dilly

Strawberry Nut Cake

Turtle Cake

Watergate Cake

Apple Cake

2	cups sugar	2	teaspoons cinnamon
4	cups sliced apples	2	teaspoons vanilla
2	cups flour	2	eggs, beaten
1 ½	teaspoons baking soda	1	cup cooking oil
1	teaspoon salt	1	cup chopped nuts

Sprinkle sugar over apples. Sift dry ingredients together twice. Add mixture to apples. Add remaining ingredients to apple mixture and stir only until well mixed. Pour into a 13x9-inch pan. Bake at 350 degrees for 45 to 50 minutes. Serves 12.

Easy Coconut Cake

1	white cake mix	2	cups sugar
2	(12-ounce) packages frozen coconut	1	(9-ounce) carton frozen whipped topping, thawed
2	cups sour cream		

Prepare cake mix according to package directions. Bake in two 8 or 9-inch cake pans. When cake is cool, split layers with thread to make 4 layers. Mix together coconut, sour cream and sugar. Set aside ½ cup of this mixture. Spread remaining mixture over cake layers. Assemble cake. Mix reserved ½ cup coconut mixture with whipped topping. Spread over cake top and around sides. Refrigerate, covered, for at least 24 hours or up to 3 days before serving. Serves 10.

Mexican Wedding Cakes

1	cup butter	2	cups sifted flour
¾	cup sifted confectioners'	1	cup finely chopped nuts
	sugar		Confectioners' sugar,
1	teaspoon vanilla		sifted

Cream together first three ingredients. With a spoon, mix in flour. Add nuts. Shape dough into ¾-inch balls, rolling in palm of hand. Place ½ inch apart on an ungreased cookie sheet. Bake in a 300 degree oven for 25 to 30 minutes or until cookies are creamy color. Remove to rack. While warm, roll in a little confectioners' sugar. Cool completely. Roll again in confectioners' sugar. Store in tightly covered containers. Yield: 3 ½ dozen.

Millie's Dilly

1	cup flour	1	(3-ounce) package instant
1	cup chopped pecans		chocolate pudding
½	cup butter or margarine,	1	(3-ounce) package instant
	softened		vanilla pudding
1	(8-ounce) package cream	2 ½	cups cold milk
	cheese, softened	1	teaspoon vanilla
1	cup confectioners' sugar		Chocolate Bar with
3	cups whipped topping,		almonds
	divided		

Mix together first three ingredients. Press into a greased 13x9-inch pan. Bake at 350 degrees for 20 minutes. Cool completely before adding next layer. Cream together cream cheese, confectioners' sugar and one cup whipped topping. Spread onto cooled crust. Refrigerate for 10 minutes. Mix puddings, milk and vanilla. Before it thickens, pour onto cream cheese layer. Refrigerate and let set up (about 15 minutes). Spread remaining whipped topping on top of pudding layer. Grate chocolate bar over top. This dessert must be kept refrigerated. Serves 12.

Strawberry Nut Cake

1	white cake mix	4	eggs
1	(3-ounce package)	1	cup coconut
	strawberry gelatin	1	cup chopped nuts
1	cup vegetable oil		Strawberry Frosting
1	cup frozen strawberries		(recipe follows)
¼	cup milk		

Preheat oven to 350 degrees. Mix all ingredients together and beat on medium speed for 2 minutes. Pour batter into a 9x13-inch greased and floured pan. Bake for 45 minutes. Cool. Top with frosting. Serves 12.

Strawberry Frosting

1	(16-ounce) box	½	cup strawberries
	confectioners' sugar	½	cup chopped nuts
½	cup margarine, softened	½	cup coconut

Mix all ingredients together and spread on cake. Yield: Frosting for 9x13-inch cake.

Turtle Cake

1	German chocolate cake	½	cup evaporated milk
	mix	¾	cup butter
1	(14-ounce) package	1	cup pecans
	caramels	1	cup chocolate chips

Preheat oven to 350 degrees. Prepare cake mix according to package directions. Pour half of batter into a greased 9x13-inch pan. Bake for 15 minutes. In top of double boiler over hot water, melt together caramels, milk and butter. Pour caramel mixture over baked cake. Sprinkle pecans and chocolate chips over caramel mixture. Spread on remaining batter and bake an additional 25 to 30 minutes. If desired, you may sprinkle ½ cup pecans over top of cake before returning to oven. Serves 12.

Watergate Cake

1	(3-ounce) package instant pistachio pudding	1	cup oil
		1	cup club soda
1	white cake mix	½	cup chopped walnuts
3	eggs		Watergate Frosting (recipe follows)

Beat all ingredients together. Pour into a greased and floured 9x13-inch pan. Bake at 350 degrees for 30 to 40 minutes. Cool completely. Frost. Serves 12.

Watergate Frosting

2	envelopes whipped topping mix	1 ¼	cups cold milk
1	(3-ounce) package instant pistachio pudding		

Mix together all ingredients. Beat well for 2 to 3 minutes. Spread on top of cooled cake. Sprinkle with nuts or coconut if desired. Yield: 1 ½ cups frosting.

ENTREES

Barbados Beef Stew

Apricot Glazed Cornish Hens

Beef Stroganoff

Chicken Fruit Salad

Deviled Swiss Steak

Goulash

King Ranch Chicken

Sausage in Polish Sauce

Pseudo Sauerbraten

Shrimp and Crabmeat Casserole

Sour Cream Lasagne

Stuffed Peppers

Barbados Beef Stew

3	pounds beef, cubed	¼	teaspoon pepper
3	tablespoons flour	⅓	cup cider vinegar
1	tablespoon fat	⅓	cup molasses
1	tomato, cubed	1	cup water
2	onions	6	carrots, chopped
1	teaspoon salt	½	cup raisins
1	teaspoon celery salt	½	teaspoon ginger

Coat beef with flour and brown in fat. Remove beef from pot. Set aside. Add next five ingredients to pot and bring to a boil. When mixture has come to a boil, add meat and remaining ingredients. Cook in slow oven at 275 degrees for 2 ½ hours or until meat is tender. Serve over rice. Serves 12.

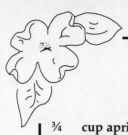

Apricot-Glazed Cornish Hens

¾   cup apricot preserves
2   teaspoons grated orange rind
2   tablespoons orange juice
4   (1 to 1 ¼-pound) Rock Cornish hens
¼   teaspoon paprika
½   cup cashews
2   tablespoons butter, melted
½   cup sliced green onions
2 ⅓ cups chicken broth
1   (6-ounce) package long grain and wild rice

Combine first three ingredients. Set aside. Remove giblets from hens. Rinse hens and pat dry. Close cavities, secure with wooden picks, truss and sprinkle with paprika. Place hens, breast side up in a lightly greased roasting pan. Bake at 350 degrees for 1 ¼ to 1 ½ hours. Baste frequently with about ½ cup apricot mixture during last 30 minutes. Sauté cashews in butter until golden. Drain and set aside, reserving butter in skillet. Sauté green onions in same skillet until tender. Add rice mix and prepare according to package directions, substituting chicken broth for water and omitting salt. When rice has cooked, stir in cashews. Arrange rice and hens on serving platter. Brush hens with remaining apricot mixture. Serves 4.

Beef Stroganoff

3   pounds round steak, ½-inch thick
¼   cup flour
¼   cup butter or margarine
1   large onion, thinly sliced
1   (10 ½-ounce) can consommé, undiluted
1   (10 ½-ounce) can tomato soup, undiluted
1   (4-ounce) can sliced mushrooms, drained
½   teaspoon salt
¼   teaspoon pepper
½   cup sour cream
    Hot cooked egg noodles

Partially freeze steak. Slice across grain into 2x¼-inch strips. Dredge steak in flour. Melt butter in large skillet. Add meat and onion. Cook until meat is browned. Stir in next five ingredients. Reduce heat to low. Cover and simmer 30 to 45 minutes or until meat is tender. Stir in sour cream and cook just until thoroughly heated. Serve over noodles. Serves 4.

Chicken Fruit Salad

4	cups chicken, cooked and diced	½	cup mayonnaise
1	cup chopped celery	½	cup sour cream
2	hard boiled eggs, chopped		Paprika
1	cup white grapes		Salt
1	cup mandarin oranges, well drained		Dry mustard
			Slivered almonds

Combine first seven ingredients. Mix well. Season with spices to taste. Arrange on serving platter and sprinkle with almonds. Serves 6.

Deviled Swiss Steak

¼	cup flour	¼	cup salad oil
2	teaspoons salt	1	tablespoon Worcestershire sauce
¼	teaspoon pepper		
1 ½	teaspoons dry mustard	1	(3-ounce) can mushroom caps, drained
1	(3-pound) round steak, 1 ½-inch thick		Butter

Combine first four ingredients. Sprinkle over meat and pound thin with mallet. Brown meat slowly on both sides in oil. Combine ½ cup water and Worcestershire sauce. Add to meat in skillet. Cover tightly and cook over very low heat for 1 ¾ to 2 hours, or until tender. Remove steak to a warm platter. Heat mushrooms in small amount of butter and serve over steak. Serves 6.

Goulash

½	cup solid shortening	4	tomatoes, peeled and
2	pounds veal or stew beef,		chopped
	cubed	3	pounds sauerkraut
2	pounds pork roast, cubed	4	teaspoons paprika
4	medium onions, chopped	2	pints sour cream, divided
3	green peppers, chopped		

Melt shortening in large skillet. Brown meat for about 2 minutes. Add next five ingredients to meat. Stir in 1 pint sour cream. Cover and bring to a boil. Reduce heat and simmer for 4 hours. Stir in remaining pint sour cream and return to a boil. Cook for 10 minutes, stirring occasionally. Serves 8.

King Ranch Chicken

1	large whole chicken	1	teaspoon chili powder
1	(10 ¾-ounce) can cream of	1	(16-ounce) can tomatoes
	mushroom soup,		with chilies
	undiluted	1	(12-count) package corn
1	(10 ¾-ounce) can cream of		tortillas
	celery soup, undiluted		Grated cheese (optional)
1	pound American cheese		

Boil chicken until it falls off the bone (approximately 1 hour). Reserve chicken stock. Bone and cut chicken into bite-size pieces. Melt soups and cheese together. Add chili powder and tomatoes. Dip tortillas, one at a time, into hot chicken stock to soften. Line bottom and sides of a large greased casserole dish with tortillas. Add a layer of chicken, ½ soup mixture and a layer of tortillas. Repeat layers ending with tortillas. Grated cheese may be added to the top. Bake at 325 degrees for 45 minutes. Serves 6.

Sausage in Polish Sauce

1	ring Polish Kielbasa sausage	1	tablespoon flour
2	cups beer	½	teaspoon Magee extract
2	cups water		Vinegar to taste
2	onions, sliced	1	teaspoon to 1 tablespoon
1	tablespoon butter		sugar

Simmer sausage and onion in beer and water for 20 minutes. Strain, reserving liquid. Set sausage aside. Melt butter. Blend in flour. Slowly add 1 cup of the reserved liquid. Stir until thoroughly blended. If sauce is too thick add more liquid. Add Magee extract, vinegar and sugar to taste. Slice sausage. Pour sauce over top. Serves 4.

Pseudo Sauerbraten

4	to 5 pound pot roast	1	bay leaf
¾	cup water	½	teaspoon coarsely ground black pepper
¾	cup vinegar	¾	cup chopped onion
2	teaspoons salt		Flour
3	tablespoons brown sugar	1	pound egg noodles, cooked
⅛	teaspoon ground cloves		
⅛	teaspoon allspice		
1	teaspoon ground ginger		

Brown meat in heavy kettle. Drain off fat. Add water, cover and simmer for 1 hour. Remove meat. Cut into ½ inch thick slices. Add remaining ingredients, except flour, to water in kettle. Mix well. Return meat to kettle. Cover and simmer 1 ½ hours or until tender. Strain and thicken gravy with flour. Serve over noodles. Serves 8.

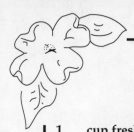

Shrimp & Crabmeat Casserole

1 cup fresh shrimp or (8-ounce) can shrimp	1 cup mayonnaise
1 cup crabmeat	1 cup chopped celery (optional)
1 cup chopped green pepper	1 cup stuffing mix, divided
1 cup chopped onion	

Mix all ingredients together using ¾ cup stuffing. Turn mixture into a greased casserole. Sprinkle remaining stuffing on top. Bake at 350 degrees for 45 minutes. Serves 6 to 8.

Sour Cream Lasagne

8 ounces lasagne noodles	¼ teaspoon garlic salt
1 pound ground beef	1 cup cottage cheese
2 (8-ounce) cans tomato sauce	1 cup sour cream
1 teaspoon salt	1 medium onion, chopped
½ teaspoon pepper	¾ cup shredded Cheddar cheese

Cook noodles according to package directions. Drain and cool on aluminum foil. Brown meat. Drain. Combine meat, tomato sauce and seasonings. Simmer 5 minutes. Combine next three ingredients. In a shallow casserole dish, layer ½ sauce, ½ noodles then ½ sour cream mixture. Repeat layers. Top with Cheddar cheese. Bake at 350 degrees for 30 minutes. Serves 6 to 8.

Stuffed Peppers

12 medium-size green peppers, hollowed	2 (8-ounce) cans tomato sauce
1 pound ground beef	¾ cup minute rice
1 cup chopped onions	¾ cup water
1 teaspoon salt	2 cups shredded Cheddar cheese
2 teaspoons chili powder	
½ teaspoon pepper	

Cook peppers in lightly salted water until just tender. Set aside. In large skillet, cook next five ingredients, mixing well. Add next four ingredients and simmer for 10 minutes. Fill green peppers with mixture. Place in baking pan and bake at 350 degrees for 15 minutes. Yield: 12 peppers.

SOUPS

Barley Soup

Egg Drop Soup

Crab Soup

Minestrone

Barley Soup

½	cup pearl barley	1	cup leeks, including 2 inches of green tops
1	pound ham hocks		
2 ½	quarts cold water	½	cup finely chopped onion
1	teaspoon salt	½	cup finely chopped celery
	Freshly ground pepper to taste	1	cup whipping cream
1	medium baking potato, peeled and finely chopped		

Combine first five ingredients in a 4 to 6-quart kettle. Bring water to a boil. Reduce heat and simmer for 45 minutes. Add next four ingredients and simmer 40 minutes longer. Remove ham hock and cut meat from bone. Add meat to soup, discarding bone. Add whipping cream. Heat soup for 2 to 3 minutes, making sure not to boil. Serves 6 to 8.

Egg Drop Soup

2	(14-ounce) cans chicken broth, fat skimmed off	4	tablespoons water
		2	eggs, slightly beaten
1	soup can water	1	tablespoon chopped scallions
2	tablespoons cornstarch		

Heat broth and can of water, covered, until boiling. Blend cornstarch and water. Add cornstarch mixture to broth, stirring well. Turn off heat. Add eggs, pouring in a light stream and stirring slowly. Add scallions. Serve immediately. Serves 4.

Crab Soup

½	cup plus 2 tablespoons butter or margarine	1	teaspoon parsley flakes
1 ⅓	cups flour	½	teaspoon pepper
2	(14-ounce) cans chicken broth	1	teaspoon chives
8	cups Half and Half	2	teaspoons Worcestershire sauce
1 ½	teaspoons seafood seasoning	1	pound crabmeat, cleaned for shell
		¼	cup sherry (optional)

Melt butter in soup kettle. Blend in flour and chicken broth, stirring until smooth. Add next six ingredients stirring slowly until thickened. Do not boil. Add crabmeat and sherry. Heat thoroughly. Serves 8.

Minestrone

½	pound sliced bacon	1	cup sliced carrots
3	tablespoons flour	1	cup chopped onion
1	(20-ounce) can kidney beans, undrained	1	cup chopped celery
10	cups beef broth	½	cup macaroni, uncooked
2	teaspoons crushed basil	½	cup cubed zucchini
1	teaspoon salt	½	pound mushrooms, sliced
1	(16-ounce) can tomatoes, drained	¼	cup grated Parmesan cheese
		¼	cup chopped fresh parsley

Fry bacon. Drain, reserving 2 tablespoons drippings. Crumble bacon and set aside. Stir flour in reserved drippings until smooth. Cook until light brown. Add beans, broth and seasonings. Bring to a boil. Add tomatoes, carrots and onion. Cook 10 minutes. Add celery and macaroni. Cook 10 minutes. Add remaining ingredients. Cook 5 minutes. Sprinkle with crumbled bacon. Serve with biscuits. Serves 8.

VEGETABLES AND SALADS

Broccoli Casserole

Spaghetti Salad

Corn Pudding

Spinach Casserole

24 Hour Salad

Broccoli Casserole

1	bag frozen chopped broccoli	1	cup mayonnaise
2	eggs, beaten	1	cup shredded cheese
1	onion, chopped		
1	(10 ¾-ounce) can cream of mushroom soup, undiluted		

Cook broccoli according to package directions. Drain well. Combine remaining ingredients. Mix well. Add broccoli to mixture and mix well. Turn into a buttered casserole dish. Dot with butter. Bake at 350 degrees for one hour. Serves 8.

Spaghetti Salad

1	pound thin spaghetti, cooked and drained	1	cucumber, thinly sliced
1	tomato, thinly sliced	½	cup sliced black olives (optional)
1	green or red pepper, thinly sliced	1	(8-ounce) bottle Italian salad dressing
1	Bermuda onion, thinly sliced	½	bottle tossed salad seasoning

Thoroughly mix together all ingredients. Chill overnight. Stir before serving. Serves 8.

Corn Pudding

2	cups sweet corn	2	eggs
¼	teaspoon salt	1	cup milk
4	tablespoons sugar		Butter
2	tablespoons flour		

Combine first four ingredients. Mix well. Beat in eggs. Add milk and stir. Pour into casserole. Dot with butter. Bake at 350 degrees for 30 minutes or until set. Serves 4.

Spinach Casserole

½	cup butter or margarine, softened	¼	cup lemon juice
1	(8-ounce) package cream cheese, softened	3	(10-ounce) packages frozen chopped spinach, cooked and drained
1	egg		Cheddar cheese, shredded
1	onion, diced		Salt and pepper to taste
1	tablespoon milk		

Cream together butter and cream cheese. Add next four ingredients. Mix well. Add salt and pepper to taste. Stir in spinach. Turn into casserole dish. Top with cheese. Cook at 350 degrees until bubbly. Serves 8.

24 Hour Salad

2	cups mayonnaise	1	cup sliced celery
2	tablespoons sugar	1	cup chopped green pepper
¼	cup milk	1	small onion, thinly sliced
	Pinch salt	10	strips bacon, cooked and crumbled
1	head iceberg lettuce, chopped	¾	cup shredded Cheddar cheese
1	(10-ounce) package frozen peas, thawed and drained		

Mix first four ingredients together and set aside. In a large salad bowl, layer next five ingredients. Spread on dressing and top with bacon and cheese. Cover tightly with plastic wrap and refrigerate for 24 hours. Toss well before serving. Fresh spinach may be substituted for lettuce, and fresh broccoli or cauliflower may be added, if desired. Serves 10 to 12.

After Five

Richard C. Guy ©

Michie Tavern - Charlottesville

Opened in 1765, Michie Tavern has been serving Virginians and her visitors ever since. The Michie family owned and operated this tavern for more than 150 years. Mrs. Martin Henderson bought it in the 1920's to house her antiques but moved it to its present site, close to Monticello, and reopened it as a tavern to capitalize on the tourist trade. Now owned by a group of local businessmen, it remains part of a restored village which also includes a smokehouse, springhouse, an ordinary, gristmill, and general store.

After Five

The traditional cocktail party or open house with a complete bar makes for a festive occasion. For many of us, it is the only way to entertain a large group at home. The traditional cocktail party is still the easiest, most inexpensive way to entertain elegantly.

With some ingenuity, the options for a cocktail party are endless; the setting and size of the group are up to you. Parties should still start after five p.m. - luckily it's always after five o'clock somewhere!

Hors d'Oeuvres
Baked Brie
Cheddar Wafers
Chili Quiche Appetizers
Crab Cocktail
Crêpes with Two Caviars
Eight Layer Taco Dip
French Market Bread
Fruited Cheese Ball
Garlic Shrimp
Ham and Cheese Rolls
Herbed Mushroom Rolls
Hot Artichoke Dip
Hot Crabmeat Dip
Parmesan Onion Canapes
Quesadillas
Sesame Seed Chicken
Shrimp Dip
Shrimp Tarts
Spicy Meatballs
Spinach Dip
Spinach Fondue
Strawberry-Cheese Ring
Stuffed Celery
Stuffed Mushrooms
Warm Pretzels with Sweet and Sour
   Mustard Sauce

Beverages and Punches for Bunches
Apricot Fruit Punch
Best-Ever Margaritas
Bourbon Punch
Christmas Rosé
Fruit Punch
Gin Punch
Lemonade
Champagne Punch
Sangria
Thirst Quencher's Punch
Whiskey Sour Slushies

Desserts
Apple or Pear Strudel
Chocolate Fondue
Dream Cheesecake
Flan

Entrees
Seafood Quiche
Shish-Kabobs
Taco Bar

Salad
German Potato Salad
Hearts of Palm Salad

Open House/Open Bar

The conventional cocktail party is fun and may be the first step in turning casual acquaintances into lasting friendships. Take this opportunity to mix different groups and to introduce new friends to long-time friends. You are free to mix and match drinks and hors d'oeuvres to suit your individual taste.

Preparations for a party are simplified by having a standard bar on hand at all times. The following basic bar may be used as a guideline for a cocktail party for 20 people.

> One bottle (750 ml) Vodka
>
> One bottle Scotch
>
> One bottle Bourbon
>
> One bottle Gin
>
> One bottle Rum
>
> One bottle Dry Vermouth
>
> Six bottles Wine - three white, two red, one sparkling
>
> One case of Beer - your choice
>
> One to six liter bottles each of Cola, Ginger Ale, Tonic Water
>
> One quart each of Tomato Juice and Orange Juice
>
> Three to six bottles Seltzer Water/Club Soda
>
> Limes, lemons, cocktail onions, olives and Maraschino cherries

Add to or subtract from the basic bar based on your guests' personal tastes. Many hosts, for example, may wish to add several bottles of white wine. A large punch bowl full of one of the tasty punches provided will allow the guests to serve themselves and add yet another means of socializing.

To determine the number of hors d'oeuvres needed, begin with the number of expected guests. For ten people, serve a minimum of four hors d'oeuvres, two cold and two hot. For each additional ten, add a cold and a hot hors d'oeuvre. For groups over fifty you may want to increase your proportions and introduce heavier finger foods such as deli platters and party rolls. Enjoy selecting your menu from some of our favorite hors d'oeuvres.

Basic Guide to Types and Serving Suggestions of Virginia Wines

WHITE WINES

Chardonnay (Shar-don-ay) Fruity wine, can have a taste of apples or citrus. Usually medium to full-bodied. A dry wine. Best served with poultry, seafood and pasta with white sauce.

Riesling (Reez-ling) Floral and fruity bouquet. Medium to full-bodied wine. Off-dry to semi-sweet. Best served with pork, seafood without a sauce, such as crab, fish and scallops, and desserts.

Gewurztraminer (Geh-vertz-tram-me-ner) Spicy and floral aromas. Light to medium-bodied. Off-dry to semi-sweet wine. Best served with ham, fish and desserts.

Sauvignon Blanc (So-vin-yawn-blonc) Scent of fresh herbs, cut grass or bell peppers. Light to medium-bodied. A dry wine. Best served with poultry, seafood without a sauce and pasta with red sauce.

Seyval Blanc (Say-voll-blonc) Scent of green apples or nectarines. Light to medium-bodied wine. Crisp and very dry. Best served with poultry and seafood.

Vidal Blanc (Vee-doll-blonc) Green apples and nectarine aromas and flavors. Light to medium-body wine. Off-dry to semi-sweet. Best served with pork chops or roasts and seafood without sauce.

RED WINES

Cabernet Sauvignon (Cab-er-nay So-Vin-yawn) Berry aromas and flavors. Medium to full-bodied wine. Tannic and dry. Best served with beef roasts or steaks, lamb, and pork chops or roasts.

Merlot (Merlow) Softer in flavor than Cabernet Sauvignon. Medium to full-bodied wine. Dry. Best served with lamb, ground beef, and red sauces.

Pinot Noir (Pe-no-Nwahr) Cherry aroma with rich flavors. Medium to light-bodied wine. Dry. Best served with ground beef, lamb and poultry.

Chambourcin (Sham-boor-san) Rich grape aroma and flavor. Full-bodied wine. Dry. Best served with ground beef.

SPECIALITY WINES

Blush and Rose Wines (Ro-za) Light pink table wine. Usually light and fruity.

Cabernet Blanc (Cab-er-nay Blonc) Made from the Cabernet Sauvignon. Light-bodied wine. Dry.

Brut (Broot) A sparkling blend of Chardonnay and Pinot Noir. Usually dry.

174

DIPS - HOT AND COLD

Crab Cocktail

Fruited Cheese Ball

Hot Artichoke Dip

Hot Crabmeat Dip

Shrimp Dip

Spinach Dip

Crab Cocktail

1	(8-ounce) package cream cheese	1	(12-ounce) jar cocktail sauce
1	pound fresh crabmeat	1	box crackers

Place cream cheese on plate. Crumble crab on top of cream cheese and pour cocktail sauce on top. Serve with crackers.

Fruited Cheese Ball

1	(6-ounce) package chopped dried fruits and raisins	1	cup shredded sharp Cheddar cheese
1	(8-ounce) package cream cheese, softened	1	tablespoon honey

Reserve 3 tablespoons of dried fruits and set aside. Combine remaining ingredients in a blender or food processor. Shape into a ball. Roll cheese ball in the reserved dried fruits. Serve with your favorite crackers.

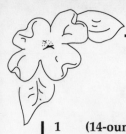

Hot Artichoke Dip

1	(14-ounce) can artichoke hearts, drained and chopped	1	cup mayonnaise
		1	cup Parmesan cheese
		1	clove garlic, minced

Combine ingredients and mix well. Lightly grease a 3-cup casserole dish. Spread mixture in dish and bake 20 minutes at 350 degrees. Serve with sesame or butter crackers. Yield: 2 ½ cups.

Hot Crabmeat Dip

1	(8-ounce) package cream cheese, softened	½	teaspoon horseradish
1	tablespoon milk	¼	teaspoon salt
8	ounces fresh crabmeat		Dash pepper
2	tablespoons finely chopped onion	⅓	cup sliced almonds, toasted

Mix all ingredients, except almonds. Spread in baking dish. Sprinkle with almonds. Bake at 375 degrees for 15 minutes. Serve with crackers. Yield: 2 cups.

Shrimp Dip

2	(8-ounce) packages cream cheese, softened	2	tablespoons grated onion
2	(6 ½-ounce) cans medium shrimp	2	tablespoons chopped parsley
3	tablespoons lemon juice	1	tablespoon horseradish
		2	drops bottled hot sauce

Mix cream cheese until smooth. Mash shrimp and add to cream cheese. Add remaining ingredients, mixing well. Shape into ball. Chill and serve with crackers. Yield: 4 cups.

Spinach Dip

1	(10-ounce) package frozen chopped spinach, thawed and drained	½	teaspoon herb-seasoned salt
⅔	cup mayonnaise	½	teaspoon dried oregano
⅔	cup sour cream	¼	teaspoon dill weed
½	cup chopped green onions	1	teaspoon lemon juice
1	(6-ounce) can water chestnuts, chopped	1	large red cabbage or 1 loaf round bread (for serving)

Combine all ingredients except cabbage or bread. Chill well. Trim core end of cabbage so that base is flat. Fold back some of the outer leaves. Cut a wide crosswise slice from the top, so that it is wide enough to remove ¼ of head. Remove enough inner leaves so that your shell is 1-inch thick. Rinse and drain. Spoon dip into cabbage shell and serve with crackers and vegetables. If using bread, slice 1-inch off top of loaf and cut into bite-size pieces. Reserve. Hollow out loaf, leaving a 1-inch thick shell. Cut hollowed out bread into bite-size pieces and serve with dip. Yield: 2 cups.

HEARTY HORS D'OEUVRES

Baked Brie

Cheddar Wafers

Chili Quiche Appetizers

Garlic Shrimp

Ham and Cheese Rolls

Herbed Mushroom Rolls

Parmesan Onion Canapés

Quesadillas

Sesame Seed Chicken

Spinach Fondue

Shrimp Tarts

Spicy Meatballs

Stuffed Celery

Stuffed Mushrooms

Baked Brie

4 ½	ounces Brie	1	tablespoon finely chopped parsley
1	tablespoon butter or margarine, softened	2	tablespoons slivered almonds
1	clove garlic, minced		

Preheat oven to 350 degrees. Cut crust off Brie and discard. Spread Brie with half the butter and half the garlic, then slice. Spread remaining butter and garlic in a small baking dish. Add parsley and almonds. Bake in oven until lightly browned, about 20 minutes. Add Brie to cover butter mixture and return to oven until cheese is melted and bubbling. Serve with chunks of sourdough French bread.

Cheddar Wafers

2	cups shredded Cheddar cheese	½	teaspoon salt
½	cup butter, softened	¼	teaspoon red pepper
1	cup flour	¾	cup chopped pecans

Cream cheese and butter. Sift flour, salt and pepper. Add to cheese mixture and mix well. Stir in nuts. Using a sheet of waxed paper, mold dough into a log. Chill several hours or overnight. Preheat oven to 375 degrees. Slice log thinly and bake on ungreased baking sheet 10 to 12 minutes or until wafers are lightly browned. Yield: 24 wafers.

Chili Quiche Appetizers

10	eggs	1	small can chopped chili peppers
½	cup flour		
1	teaspoon baking powder	1	pint small curd cottage cheese
1	teaspoon salt		
½	cup butter or margarine, melted	1	pound Monterey Jack cheese, shredded

Spray a 10x15x2-inch dish with cooking spray. Beat eggs. Mix in dry ingredients. Add butter, chilies and cheeses. Pour into baking dish. Bake at 400 degrees for 15 minutes, reduce heat to 350 degrees and bake an additional 40 minutes. Cool 10 minutes. Cut into bite-size pieces. Yield: 36 appetizers.

Garlic Shrimp

2	pounds raw shrimp	Garlic salt
½	cup butter or margarine	Paprika
	Juice of 2 lemons	

Peel and devein shrimp. Melt butter in large sheet pan with ½-inch sides. Add lemon juice. Place shrimp in pan and liberally sprinkle with garlic salt and paprika. Broil until shrimp are pink and firm (10 to 15 minutes). Serve warm with toothpicks. Serves 6.

Ham and Cheese Rolls

½	cup butter or margarine, softened	1	small onion, grated
2	teaspoons prepared mustard	1	package (20) party rolls
		¼	pound boiled ham, thinly sliced
2	tablespoons poppy seeds	1	(4-ounce) package Swiss cheese, sliced
2	teaspoons Worcestershire sauce		

Mix first five ingredients. Open rolls and spread mixture on both sides of roll. Fill with ham and cheese. Wrap rolls in foil and heat at 350 degrees until cheese melts, approximately 10 minutes. May be made ahead and frozen before baking. Yield: 20 sandwiches.

Herbed Mushroom Rolls

1	tablespoon minced shallot or green onions, white part only	1	(3 ½-ounce) package garlic and herb cream cheese
1	tablespoon butter or margarine	½	(17 ¼-ounce) package frozen puff pastry
¼	pound mushrooms, finely chopped	1	egg, mixed with 1 tablespoon water (egg wash)
1	teaspoon lemon juice		
1	tablespoon fresh or 1 teaspoon mixed dried herbs (any combination of dill, basil, tarragon or oregano)		

Preheat oven to 425 degrees. Sauté shallot or onion in butter until soft, about 5 minutes. Add mushrooms and lemon juice and cook until mushrooms are soft and juices are absorbed. Add herbs. Mix well and set aside to cool. Mix cream cheese with cooled mushrooms. Adjust seasonings to taste. Roll out puff pastry to 10x12-inch rectangle. Spread with filling and cut into fifteen 2x4 inch rectangles. Roll up each rectangle and brush with egg wash. Place seam side down on ungreased baking sheet. Bake until golden, about 15 minutes. Serve immediately. Yield: 15 rolls.

Parmesan Onion Canapés

1	cup mayonnaise	1	tablespoon milk
1	cup grated Parmesan cheese (fresh if available)	1	loaf cocktail rye bread, thinly sliced
½	cup finely chopped onion		

Mix ingredients together and spread on bread. Place on baking sheet and broil 2 to 3 minutes or until slightly bubbly and brown. Mixture will keep well in refrigerator in a tightly covered jar for about 2 weeks. Yield: 36 appetizers.

Quesadillas

10	large flour tortillas	1	(4-ounce) can chopped green chilies
1	(8-ounce) package cream cheese, room temperature	1	container frozen avocado dip, thawed
8	ounces Monterey Jack cheese, shredded		

Place 5 tortillas on a cookie sheet. Spread with cream cheese and sprinkle with Monterey Jack cheese and chiles. Cover with remaining tortillas. Bake at 350 degrees for 3 to 5 minutes (just enough to melt cheese and slightly crisp top of tortillas). Remove from oven. Cut each circle into 6 or 8 wedges, garnish with dip. Serve immediately. Yield: 30 to 40 wedges.

Sesame Seed Chicken

½	cup mayonnaise	2	pounds chicken, raw and cut into 2-inch strips
1	teaspoon dry mustard		Honey Dip
1	teaspoon instant minced onions		(recipe follows)
½	cup bread crumbs		
¼	cup sesame seeds		

Mix mayonnaise, mustard and minced onions together. Set aside. Mix bread crumbs and sesame seeds. Set aside. Coat chicken with mayonnaise mixture and roll in bread crumbs. Place on cookie sheet and bake at 375 degrees until brown (approximately 10 to 15 minutes). Serve hot with Honey Dip. Serves 6.

Honey Dip

1	cup mayonnaise	½	teaspoon parsley
2	tablespoons honey		

Combine ingredients and mix well.

Spinach Fondue

½	cup butter or margarine	1	(10-ounce) package frozen
1	small onion, chopped		chopped spinach, cooked
1	(10 ¾-ounce) can cream of		and drained
	mushroom soup,	¼	teaspoon garlic powder
	undiluted	¼	pound Cheddar cheese,
1	(8-ounce) can mushroom		shredded
	stems and pieces		Sherry

Sauté onion in butter for 5 minutes. Add remaining ingredients except Sherry. Simmer for 20 minutes. Before serving add a touch of Sherry. Serve in fondue pot with corn chips to dip. Yield: 4 cups.

Shrimp Tarts

1	(1 ½-pound) loaf thin	⅓	cup grated Parmesan
	sandwich bread		cheese
⅓	cup butter or margarine,	⅓	cup shredded Swiss cheese
	melted	¼	teaspoon Worcestershire
1	(4 ½-ounce) can tiny		sauce
	shrimp	⅛	teaspoon hot sauce
¾	cup mayonnaise		Paprika

Flatten bread with rolling pin. Cut out with 2 ½-inch floured cookie cutter and brush both sides with melted butter. Place in small muffin tins. Bake at 400 degrees for 8 to 10 minutes, until light brown. Rinse shrimp in cold water and drain well. Combine with remaining ingredients except paprika. Spoon shrimp mixture into shells and sprinkle with paprika. Bake at 400 degrees for 8 to 10 minutes until bubbly. Serves: 10.

Spicy Meatballs

1	pound ground beef or turkey	½	cup chili sauce
2	eggs, beaten	⅓	cup firmly packed brown sugar
⅛	teaspoon bottled hot sauce	3	tablespoons cider vinegar
¼	teaspoon pepper	2	tablespoons minced onion
½	teaspoon horseradish	1	tablespoon Worcestershire sauce
¼	teaspoon salt	½	teaspoon dry mustard
3	tablespoons finely chopped onion	¼	teaspoon pepper
¾	cup Italian bread crumbs	4	drops bottled hot sauce
½	cup catsup	1	tablespoon honey

Mix first eight ingredients well and shape into 1-inch balls. Sauté in skillet with 2 to 3 tablespoons melted butter until brown. Drain and set aside. Combine remaining ingredients in a large saucepan. Bring to a boil; simmer for 5 minutes. Add meatballs and simmer 10 more minutes. Serve in chafing dish and keep warm. Yield: 3 dozen.

Stuffed Celery

1	(8-ounce) package cream cheese, softened		Red pepper to taste
1	tablespoon plus 1 teaspoon whipping cream	1	bunch celery, washed, separated into stalks and cut into 4-inch pieces
½	teaspoon salt	⅓	cup finely chopped pecans

Combine first four ingredients in a small bowl. Beat well. Stuff celery with cream cheese mixture. Roll in pecans. Chill. Yield: 1 ½ dozen.

Stuffed Mushrooms

½	pound fresh mushrooms	¼	teaspoon oregano
½	cup butter	½	cup seasoned bread
½	cup minced onion		crumbs
2	tablespoons parsley	¼	cup Parmesan cheese
¾	teaspoon salt		

Remove mushroom stems from caps. Chop stems and sauté with next five ingredients until tender. Stir in bread crumbs and Parmesan cheese. Spoon mixture into mushroom caps. Broil for 8 minutes. Serve hot. Serves 4.

PUNCHES

Bourbon Punch
Christmas Rosé
Apricot Fruit Punch
Gin Punch
Champagne Punch
Fruit Punch
Thirst Quencher's Punch

Bourbon Punch

1	fifth bourbon		Red food coloring
1	(6-ounce) can fresh		(optional)
	lemon juice	3	quarts lemon-lime
1	(6-ounce) can frozen		carbonated drink
	orange juice concentrate	1	lemon, thinly sliced
1	(6-ounce) can frozen	1	orange, thinly sliced
	lemonade concentrate		

Chill all ingredients. Mix first four ingredients in punch bowl. Add a few drops of red food coloring, if desired. Add lemon-lime drink. Float ice ring. Add orange and lemon slices. Yield: 5 quarts.

Christmas Rosé

2	(750 ml) bottles California	1	pint flavored Italian Ice
	Rosé Wine, chilled		or sherbet
2	(6-ounce) cans frozen	1	pint club soda, chilled
	lemonade concentrate		

Combine all ingredients in punch bowl. Stir to mix. Yield: 3 quarts.

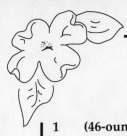

Apricot Fruit Punch

1 (46-ounce) can apricot juice   1 quart club soda, chilled
1 quart red fruit punch   Maraschino cherries
1 quart ginger ale, chilled

Mix together juices. Chill. Just before serving, add ginger ale and club soda. Garnish with cherries. Cherries may be frozen in ice cubes. Serve punch over ice. Yield: 4⅓ quarts.

Gin Punch

6 cups water   1 (8-ounce) jar Maraschino
2 cups sugar   cherries, undrained
1 (48-ounce) can pineapple   2 cups gin
   juice   1 (33.8-ounce) bottle ginger
1 (48-ounce) can grapefruit   ale, chilled
   juice

Combine water and sugar in a large saucepan. Bring to a boil and stir until dissolved. Cool. Combine sugar mixture, juices and cherries. Chill. Add gin and ginger ale just before serving. Yield: 6 ½ quarts.

Champagne Punch

2 (32-ounce) bottles   1 (6-ounce) can frozen
   cranberry juice, chilled   lemonade concentrate
1 (6-ounce) can frozen   1 pint brandy, chilled
   orange juice concentrate   2 (750 ml) bottles
1 (6-ounce) can frozen   champagne, chilled
   pineapple juice   Orange and lemon slices
   concentrate   Maraschino cherries

Mix all ingredients together in a punch bowl. Garnish with orange and lemon slices and cherries. Yield: 30 cups.

Fruit Punch

2	(3-ounce) boxes lemon or raspberry gelatin	2	(46-ounce) cans pineapple juice
2	cups boiling water	1	quart ginger ale, chilled
3	quarts water		
3	(6-ounce) cans frozen lemonade concentrate		

Dissolve gelatin in boiling water. Cool. Add remaining ingredients. Serve in punch bowl. Yield: 30 cups.

Thirst Quencher's Punch

1	(12-ounce) can frozen lemonade concentrate	1	liter ginger ale, chilled
1	(12-ounce) can frozen orange juice concentrate		Cherries, citrus fruit slices or mint sprigs

Prepare lemonade and orange juice according to package directions. When ready to serve, blend juices and ginger ale in punch bowl. Garnish with cherries, fruit slices and mint. Yield: 16 cups.

A MIDSUMMER BUFFET

This outdoor party is a breeze, especially when you prepare everything in advance. While your guests sip lemonade or whiskey sour slushies, have them assemble their own shish-kabobs to grill. Serve summer fruits swimming in a huge bowl of ice as a spectacular and scrumptious cap to the evening.

Shish-Kabobs

Lemonade

Whiskey Sour Slushies

French Market Bread

Dream Cheesecake

Shish-Kabobs

½	cup soy sauce	1	tablespoon chopped fresh parsley
¼	cup vegetable oil		
¼	cup tomato paste		Freshly ground pepper to taste
1	tablespoon fresh or 1 teaspoon dried oregano	2	pounds chicken cut into 1-inch chunks
2	cloves garlic, crushed		Cherry tomatoes, mushrooms, red and green peppers, green and yellow summer squash and onions
	Salt and pepper to taste		
2	pounds beef, cut into 1-inch chunks		
	Juice of 1 lemon		
½	cup olive oil		Cooked rice
1	clove garlic, peeled and minced		

Combine first six ingredients. Add beef and toss to coat. Marinate for a minimum of 4 hours. Combine next five ingredients. Add chicken and toss to coat. Marinate for at least 8 hours. (Marinated meats may be prepared the day before serving.) Cut vegetables into 1 inch pieces and arrange them on a large platter accompanied by the meats. Have your guests make their own shish-kabobs using skewers. Grill and serve on a bed of rice. Serves 10 to 12.

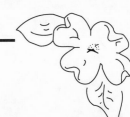

Lemonade

1	cup sugar	½	cup lemon juice
12	cups water		

In a medium saucepan bring sugar and 2 cups water to a boil. Cool. Add remaining water and lemon juice. Chill. To make a lemonade cocktail, add vodka or seltzer water to taste. Yield: 3 quarts.

Whiskey Sour Slushies

3	(6-ounce) cans frozen lemonade concentrate, thawed	4	cups water
		4	cups whiskey (bourbon)
1	(12-ounce) can frozen orange juice concentrate, thawed		

Mix all ingredients in large container and store in freezer until slushy. Garnish punch bowl with sliced oranges and cherries frozen in ice ring. When ready to serve, pour slush over ice ring. Yield: 2 ½ quarts.

French Market Bread

1	loaf French bread	¼	teaspoon dried thyme
½	cup butter, softened	¼	teaspoon paprika
¼	teaspoon salt		Dash garlic powder
¼	teaspoon dry mustard		

Preheat oven to 400 degrees. Slice bread into ½ inch slices. Combine remaining ingredients in bowl. Spread on both sides of bread. Wrap in aluminum foil and bake for 15 minutes. Serves 8.

Dream Cheesecake

1 ½ cups graham cracker crumbs (about 18 crackers)	1 teaspoon vanilla
2 cups sugar, divided	6 eggs
3 ½ tablespoons butter, melted	1 pint sour cream
4 (8-ounce) packages cream cheese, softened	2 teaspoons vanilla
	Fresh fruit, thinly sliced

Preheat oven to 350 degrees. Stir together graham cracker crumbs and 2 tablespoons sugar. Mix in butter thoroughly. Press mixture evenly into 9-inch deep dish glass pan. Beat cream cheese in large mixer bowl. Gradually add 1 ½ cups sugar, beating until fluffy. Add 1 teaspoon vanilla. Beat in eggs, one at a time. Pour over crumb mixture. Bake 50 minutes or until center is firm. Cool to room temperature. Mix together sour cream, 2 teaspoons vanilla and 6 tablespoons sugar. Pour over cheesecake and return to oven for 10 minutes. Chill at least 3 hours. Garnish with fresh fruit. Serves 12.

CINCO DE MAYO FIESTA

*Celebrate Mexico's Independence Day with
a South-of-the-Border social. Top off the evening
with a traditional Mexican dessert of flan. Ole!*

Eight Layer Taco Dip

Taco Bar

Best Ever Margaritas

Sangria

Flan

Eight Layer Taco Dip

1	cup sour cream	½	cup diced tomatoes
½	cup mayonnaise	½	cup shredded Cheddar
1	(1 ¼-ounce) package taco		cheese
	seasoning	½	cup chopped scallions
2	ripe avocados	½	cup chopped black olives
2	teaspoons lemon juice		Tortilla chips
1	can jalapeño bean dip		

Mix together first three ingredients. Mash avocados and mix in lemon juice. In a glass serving dish, layer bean dip, taco dip, avocado and remaining ingredients, except chips. Serve with tortilla chips. Yield: 6 cups.

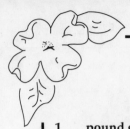

Taco Bar

1	pound ground beef or chicken		Taco shells
1	large onion, finely chopped		Cheddar and Monterey Jack cheeses, shredded
1	clove garlic, diced		Guacamole
2	small fresh chile peppers, diced		Diced tomatoes, onions, olives, peppers and lettuce
1	teaspoon cumin		Salsa
1	tablespoon fresh or 1 teaspoon dried cilantro		

In a large skillet, brown ground beef. Drain off fat. Add onion, garlic and chiles. Cook over medium heat for 5 to 10 minutes until onions are cooked but not brown. Add spices and enough water to cover. Lower heat to simmer and cook until all the water is absorbed. For chicken tacos, substitute 1 pound cooked shredded chicken for beef. Cook onions, garlic and chiles in water before adding chicken. Layer meat, cheese, guacamole and vegetables in taco shells. Top with salsa. Serves 6 to 8.

Best Ever Margaritas

6	ounces lime juice	1 ½	tablespoons sugar
4	ounces tequila		Crushed ice
2	ounces orange flavored liqueur		Lime wedges
1	ounce triple sec		Kosher salt

Pour first five ingredients into blender. Add ice to the top. Blend until smooth. Run lime wedge around rims of glasses. Put salt into bowl and dip rims into salt. Pour and enjoy! Serves 4.

Sangria

3	bottles dry red wine (approximately 9 cups)	1	quart club soda, chilled
½	cup orange juice	1	orange, sliced
½	cup orange liqueur	1	lemon, sliced
1	tablespoon sugar	1	peach, sliced
			Ice cubes

In a pitcher mix first three ingredients with sugar to taste. Chill overnight. Just before serving, add club soda and fresh fruit slices. Serve over ice or double recipe and serve from punch bowl. Serves 8.

Flan

1	cup sugar	⅔	cup sugar
2	(13-ounce) cans evaporated milk	1	tablespoon plus 1 teaspoon vanilla
6	eggs		

Preheat oven to 350 degrees. Heat 1 cup sugar in saucepan over low heat until melted and brown. Pour into large baking dish and allow syrup to harden. Beat together remaining ingredients and pour over hardened syrup. Put baking dish into a larger dish and pour hot water in larger dish almost to the top. Bake 45 minutes to 1 hour or until a knife inserted in custard comes out clean. Unmold. Serve warm or chilled. Serves 8.

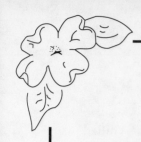

OKTOBERFEST

What better way to spend a crisp fall evening than at an Oktoberfest? Everyone brings a six pack of their favorite beer. Serve a variety of German sausages and sauerkraut to grill outside. If you don't wish to wait until autumn, May Day is another traditional Bavarian holiday to celebrate.

Warm Pretzels with Sweet and Sour Mustard Sauce

Bratwurst, Summer Sausage and Knockwurst

German Potato Salad

Sauerkraut

Apple or Pear Strudel

Variety of German Beers such as Becks or Lowenbrau

as well as German-process American beers such as

Samuel Adams

Warm Pretzels with Sweet and Sour Mustard Sauce

1	(14-ounce) can sweetened condensed milk	2	tablespoons Dijon mustard
¼	cup white wine vinegar	1	package frozen pretzels

Mix milk, vinegar and mustard together. Chill at least 4 hours. Adjust seasonings to taste. Cook pretzels according to package directions. Serve warm with dip. Yield: 2 cups dip.

German Potato Salad

4	pounds potatoes (approximately 6 large potatoes)	1	cup white wine vinegar
		½	cup mayonnaise
		¼	cup olive oil
1	large onion, finely chopped	1	tablespoon fresh or 1 teaspoon dried dill

Peel and dice potatoes. Boil until just tender, approximately 15 to 20 minutes. Let cool slightly. Toss potatoes with onions and vinegar. Let salad sit for one hour. Drain off vinegar; toss in mayonnaise, olive oil and dill. Serves 8 to 10.

Apple or Pear Strudel

1	package frozen phyllo dough, thawed	¼	cup chopped walnuts
		1	teaspoon cinnamon
½	cup butter, softened	4	apples, peeled and chopped
½	cup sugar		

Preheat oven to 350 degrees. Remove phyllo from package and quickly separate the dough in half. Working on a floured cloth, layer phyllo dough with butter brushed on each layer. Cover dough with plastic wrap or a damp cloth as you work to keep it from drying out. Mix remaining ingredients then spoon in a 3-inch strip along one side of phyllo dough, working to within 2 inches of edges. Using the cloth, gently roll dough in a jellyroll fashion. Tuck side under. Bake until golden brown, 35 to 40 minutes. For Pear Strudel, make the same as apple strudel except substitute 4 D'anjou pears for the apples. Serves 8.

A VALENTINE'S EVENING

Invite a few close friends to share an evening of delicious, romantic fun. Enhance the mood with touches of flowers, candlelight, chocolate and champagne.

Crepes with Two Caviars

Strawberry-Cheese Ring

Seafood Quiche

Hearts of Palm Salad

Chocolate Fondue

Crepes with Two Caviars

2 ¼	cups flour	4	hard boiled eggs, separated and diced
¾	teaspoon salt		
½	teaspoon baking powder	2	ounces black caviar
3	cups milk	2	ounces golden or red caviar
3	eggs		
2	tablespoons butter, melted		Fresh dill and lemon slices for garnish
1	cup sour cream		
1	red onion, finely chopped		

Sift flour, salt and baking powder twice. Add milk, eggs and butter. Beat until smooth. Heat a skillet over medium heat. Brush with butter. Pour ¼ cup batter into skillet, swirling batter to coat the skillet. Cook until light brown, turn and cook until crepe is light brown on both sides. Cooked crepes may be stacked but should be covered to prevent them from drying out. Arrange all ingredients on a large platter. Serve with warmed crepes. Yield: 16 crepes.

Strawberry-Cheese Ring

2   (8-ounce) packages sharp   ¼   teaspoon garlic salt
    Cheddar cheese   ¼   teaspoon pepper
1   small onion   Dash red pepper
1   cup pecans   Strawberry preserves
⅔   cup mayonnaise

Shred cheese in food processor. Add onion to processor and grate. Remove shredded cheese and onion from processor bowl and set aside. With knife blade, process pecans until finely chopped. Add mayonnaise and seasonings; pulse five or six times or until ingredients are blended. Stir mayonnaise mixture into cheese and onion, mixing well. Shape mixture into a ring on a serving platter. Chill several hours. Fill center of ring with strawberry preserves. Serve with crackers. Yield: 3 ¼ cups.

Seafood Quiche

1   (9-inch) pie shell, unbaked   1   teaspoon fresh or ¼
8   ounces shrimp, lobster or   teaspoon dried thyme
    crab, diced   Dash hot pepper sauce
¼   cup chopped pimento   ⅓   cup freshly grated
3   eggs   Parmesan cheese
1 ½ cups milk

Preheat oven to 375 degrees. Sprinkle seafood, then pimentos in bottom of pie shell. Beat together next four ingredients and pour into pie shell. Sprinkle with Parmesan cheese. Bake 35 to 40 minutes until custard is set. Let stand 10 minutes before serving. Serves 6.

Hearts of Palm Salad

1	(14-ounce) can hearts of palm Bibb lettuce	¼	cup Lemon French Dressing (recipe follows) Freshly ground pepper

Cut the larger pieces of palm in half or quarters, lengthwise. Place on the Bibb lettuce and add dressing. Dust top with a little pepper. Serves 4.

Lemon French Dressing

3	tablespoons lemon juice	¼	teaspoon sugar
½	teaspoon salt	¼	teaspoon dry mustard
⅛	teaspoon pepper	½	cup olive oil or salad oil

Combine all ingredients and mix well. Yield: ¾ cup.

Chocolate Fondue

1	(12-ounce) package semi-sweet chocolate morsels	Selection of fresh fruits such as strawberries, apples, bananas, tangerines, kiwi and pineapple
1	cup butter, softened Coffee liqueur, almond liqueur or orange liqueur	Pound cake

In fondue pot or in double boiler over low heat, melt chocolate and butter. Add liqueur to taste. Cut fruit and cake into bite-size pieces. Arrange prepared cake and fruit on large platter. Provide skewers or dessert forks for dipping. Yield: 2 ½ cups.

Grand and Elegant

© Richard C. Guy

Chatham Manor - Fredericksburg

Entertaining in a grand and elegant style was part of life at Chatham Manor. Located on the north bank of the Rappahannok River in Stafford County, this historic brick mansion was built by William Fitzhugh, Esquire, a member of the House of Burgesses, in 1769.

Documents indicate the Fitzhugh's lived in grand style and entertained an endless number of guests and relatives. During the Civil War, General Irvin McDowell made his headquarters at Chatham and was visited by President Lincoln. General Sumner of the Union Army used it as his headquarters during the Battle of Fredericksburg. After the battle, Clara Barton, of Red Cross fame, tended to the hundreds of wounded soldiers crowded into its twelve rooms. Despite the complete destruction of the gardens and trees, the old mansion survived the war and has since been restored to its former glory.

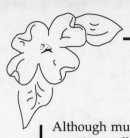

Grand and Elegant

Although much of our entertaining is casual, close friends and special occasions call for a more formal affair. Invitations, rather than a phone call, herald such an event. Elegant entertaining is a delightful way to mark a special moment!

Beverages
Brandied Coffee Nog
Brandied Peach Coffee
Coffee Delight
Fanciful Fruit Punch
Hot Peppermint Flip

Desserts
Black Russian Cake
Brandied Apples
Chocolate Almond Crème Roll
Chocolate Amaretto Mousse Pie
Chocolate Banana Meringue Torte
Chocolate Mousse Pie
Cocoa-Nut Layer Cake
Raspberry-Praline Souffle
Lemon Delight
New York Cheesecake
Piña Colada Cake
Pineapple-Cream Cheese Cake
Pineapple-Lemon Sherbet

Entrees
Baked Chicken Elegant
Beef Bourguignone
Chicken Breasts Mornay
Shrimp de Jonghe
Tuscan Meat Roll

Salads
Mandarin Orange Salad
Spinach Salad

Soups
Curried Carrot Soup

Vegetables
Asparagus Casserole
Bloody Mary Rice
Broccoli with Hollandaise Sauce
French Onion Rice
Ginger Carrots
Potatoes Au Gratin
Spinach Cheese Soufflé
Vegetable Medley
Wild Rice Casserole
Zucchini and Yellow Squash Medley

BUFFET FOR TWENTY FOUR

*A buffet supper is an ideal way to entertain
a large group in style.*

Tuscan Meat Roll

Broccoli with Hollandaise Sauce

Spinach Cheese Soufflé

Chocolate Amaretto Mousse Pie

Cocoa-Nut Layer Cake

Tuscan Meat Roll

6	eggs, slightly beaten	¾	cup sherry
1 ½	cups tomato juice	3	cloves garlic, minced
6	tablespoons chopped fresh parsley	6	pounds ground sirloin
½	tablespoon salt	1 ½	pounds thinly sliced ham
2 ¼	cups soft bread crumbs (Italian or French bread)	4 ½	cups shredded mozzarella cheese

Combine first seven ingredients. Add ground sirloin, mixing well. Divide meat, ham and cheese into thirds. On foil or waxed paper, pat one third meat mixture into a 12x10-inch rectangle. Repeat with the other ⅔. Place ⅓ of ham onto meat mixture, top with cheese, leaving ½ inch margin around edges. Repeat with remaining ingredients. Starting from the short end, roll the meat, using the foil or waxed paper to lift. Seal the edges and ends. Place the meat rolls in individual baking pans. Bake in a 350 degree oven for 1 hour 20 minutes. Cool for 10 minutes before slicing. Arrange on a serving tray garnished with fresh parsley. Serves 24.

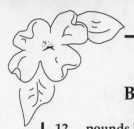

Broccoli with Hollandaise Sauce

12   pounds broccoli, trimmed   ½   cup lemon juice
1   cup butter   Salt to taste
6   egg yolks

Boil 12 cups of water. Blanch broccoli, 1 pound at a time, 3 to 4 minutes. Do not overcook. Keep broccoli in a covered dish in the oven at 200 degrees until ready to serve. Melt butter in top of double boiler over low heat. Whisk in egg yolks and lemon juice, stirring until sauce is thickened. Remove from heat and whisk for 1 minute. Arrange broccoli attractively on a serving dish, drizzle with hollandaise sauce. Serve additional hollandaise sauce on the side. Serves 24.

Spinach Cheese Soufflé

2   (8-ounce) packages cream   6   (10-ounce) packages frozen
     cheese, softened   chopped spinach, thawed
1   cup butter, softened   and squeezed dry
2   eggs   2   onions, finely diced
2   tablespoons milk   1   cup grated sharp Cheddar
½   cup lemon juice   cheese

Preheat oven to 350 degrees. Butter two large casseroles. Cream together cream cheese and butter. Add eggs, milk and lemon juice, beating until well blended. Mix in onion and spinach. Pour into casseroles. Top with grated cheese and bake 25 to 30 minutes or until cheese bubbles. Serves 24.

Chocolate Amaretto Mousse Pie

2   (1 ½-ounce) envelopes   ⅓   cup Amaretto
     whipped topping mix   1   (9-inch) deep dish pie
1 ½ cups milk   crust, baked and cooled
2   (4 ⅛-ounce) packages   1   (8-ounce) container frozen
     chocolate instant pudding   whipped topping, thawed
     and pie filling mix   Chocolate candy bar

Prepare topping mix according to package instructions. Add milk, pudding mix and Amaretto. Beat with electric mixer 2 minutes at high speed. Spoon mixture into pastry shell. Top with whipped topping. Chill 4 hours. When ready to serve, shave candy bar over topping. Serves 8.

Cocoa Nut Layer Cake

½ cup unsweetened cocoa
½ cup boiling water
1 ¾ cups unsifted all-purpose flour
1 teaspoon baking powder
1 teaspoon baking soda
⅛ teaspoon salt
½ cup butter or margarine, softened

2 cups granulated sugar
2 eggs
1 teaspoon vanilla extract
1 ⅓ cups buttermilk
½ cup finely chopped pistachio nuts or walnuts
1 cup heavy cream
Chocolate Frosting (recipe follows)

In small bowl, mix cocoa with boiling water. Cool completely. Preheat oven to 350 degrees. Grease and flour three 8-inch round cake pans. Sift flour, baking powder, soda and salt. In large bowl of electric mixer, combine the butter, sugar, eggs and vanilla. Beat at high speed until fluffy, about 5 minutes, occasionally scraping side of bowl and guiding mixture into beaters with rubber scraper. At low speed, blend in flour mixture (in fourths) alternately with buttermilk. Begin and end with flour mixture. Beat just until smooth. Measure 1 ⅔ cups batter into a small bowl. Stir in ½ cup chopped nuts. Pour into one prepared pan. Add cocoa mixture to remaining batter. Mix until smooth. Divide evenly between other pans. Bake 30 to 35 minutes, until cake tester inserted in center of cake comes out clean. Cool 10 minutes on rack. Remove from pans. Cool completely. Whip heavy cream until stiff. Refrigerate. To assemble cake, place one chocolate layer on cake plate, right side down. Spread with half of the whipped cream. Place the nut cake layer on next. Spread with rest of whipped cream. Top with remaining chocolate layer, right side up. With spatula, spread chocolate frosting on the sides and top. Garnish top edge of cake with coarsely chopped nuts. Serves 12.

Chocolate Frosting

⅓   cup light cream
⅓   cup butter or margarine
⅔   cup unsweetened cocoa
2 ⅔ cups sifted confectioners'
     sugar, divided

1   teaspoon light corn syrup
1   teaspoon vanilla extract
¼   cup coarsely chopped
     pistachio nuts or walnuts

In saucepan heat cream until bubbles form. Remove from heat. Add the hot cream to butter, cocoa, 1 ½ cups confectioners' sugar, corn syrup and vanilla. With portable mixer or wooden spoon, beat frosting until smooth. Add remaining confectioners' sugar, beating until smooth and thick enough to spread. Yield: 1 ½ cups.

EFFORTLESS BUFFET

*When planning a buffet supper select a simple menu
with make-ahead recipes. Arrange the buffet table attractively
and so that guests can easily serve themselves.*

Baked Chicken Elegant

Spinach Salad

French Onion Rice

Pineapple-Lemon Sherbet

Fanciful Fruit Punch

Baked Chicken Elegant

25	chicken breasts, skinned and boned	3	(10-ounce) cans cream of mushroom soup
25	slices bacon	3	packages dried chipped beef
3	cups sour cream		

Pound chicken breasts until they are ¼-inch thick. Roll breasts, then wrap with a slice of bacon. Mix together sour cream and soup. In 1 or 2 large casseroles, layer dried chipped beef, chicken breasts and sour cream mixture. Cover and bake in a 350 degree oven for 1 hour. Uncover and bake an additional hour. Serves 24.

Spinach Salad

3	pounds fresh spinach, washed and drained	2	cups sliced mushrooms
8	hard boiled eggs, chopped	2	cans Mandarin oranges, drained
1	pound fried bacon, crumbled		Spicy French Dressing (recipe follows)

Combine all ingredients. Toss with Spicy French Dressing. Serves 24.

Spicy French Dressing

1	cup vegetable oil	1	small onion, chopped
¼	cup vinegar	1	tablespoon Worcestershire
½	cup sugar		sauce
⅓	cup catsup	1	teaspoon salt

Combine oil and vinegar. Beat with electric mixer 3 to 5 minutes. Add remaining ingredients. Beat well. Yield: 2 cups.

French Onion Rice

4	(10 ½-ounce) cans French onion soup, undiluted	4	(8-ounce) cans sliced water chestnuts
1	cup butter or margarine, melted	4	cups uncooked long-grain rice
4	(4 ½-ounce) jars sliced mushrooms		

Combine soup and butter. Stir well. Drain mushrooms and water chestnuts, reserving liquid. Add enough water to reserved liquid to measure 2 ⅔ cups. Add mushrooms, water chestnuts, reserved liquid and rice to soup mixture. Stir well. Pour into two lightly greased 14x10x2-inch baking dishes. Cover and bake at 350 degrees for 1 hour and 10 minutes or until rice is tender and liquid is absorbed. Serves 24.

Pineapple Lemon Sherbet

6	pints lemon sherbet	3	fresh pineapples
6	tablespoons crème de menthe		Mint sprigs

Spoon three pints sherbet into chilled large-size bowl. Beat until smooth but not melted. Stir in crème de menthe. Spoon back into sherbet containers and refreeze overnight or until firm. Cut pineapples in half through top. Carefully cut meat away from rind, leaving a shell about ½-inch thick. Wrap and refrigerate shells. Remove core from pineapple. Place half the pineapple in a blender and purée until smooth. This should measure about 3 cups. Slice remaining pineapple thinly. Spoon remaining pints of sherbet into a large chilled bowl. Beat until soft but not melted. Stir in puréed pineapple. Spoon into 6-cup freezer container. Freeze overnight or until firm. Just before serving, arrange scoops of sherbets and sliced pineapple in chilled pineapple shells. Garnish with fresh mint. Serves 12.

Fanciful Fruit Punch

4	cups sugar	5	bananas
6	cups water	1	(46-ounce) can pineapple
	Juice of 2 lemons or 1		juice, chilled
	(6-ounce) can lemonade	2	quarts ginger ale,
	Juice of 5 oranges or 1		champagne or white wine,
	(6-ounce) can orange juice		chilled

Boil sugar and water until thick. Cool. Place lemon juice, orange juice and bananas in blender and purée. Add sugar mixture to fruit mixture and mix well. Pour into plastic containers and freeze well. An hour or so before party, remove from freezer and thaw until mushy. To this base add pineapple juice and up to 2 quarts of ginger ale, champagne or white wine according to taste. This is a convenient punch to make ahead and freeze. Garnish punch bowl with fruit slices or add fruit to punch base before freezing. Serves 20.

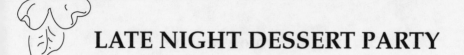

LATE NIGHT DESSERT PARTY

Whatever the event, accompany these tantalizing desserts with coffee, liqueurs and champagne to make a special affair.

Pineapple-Cream Cheesecake

Piña Colada Cake

Black Russian Cake

New York Cheesecake

Chocolate Mousse Pie

Coffee Delight

Raspberry-Praline Soufflé

Brandied Peach Coffee

Brandied Coffee Nog

Hot Peppermint Flip

Pineapple-Cream Cheesecake

2	cups flour	1	cup chopped nuts
2	cups sugar		(reserve for top)
2	eggs		Cream Cheese Frosting
2	teaspoons baking soda		(recipe follows)
1	(20-ounce) can crushed pineapple, undrained		

Mix all ingredients by hand. Pour into greased 13x9-inch pan. Bake 35 minutes at 350 degrees. Prepare frosting while cake is baking. Frost cake immediately while cake is still hot. Sprinkle with chopped nuts. Serves 12.

Cream Cheese Frosting

1	(8-ounce) package cream cheese, softened	¼	cup margarine, softened
1 ⅓	cups confectioners' sugar	1	teaspoon vanilla

In large bowl beat all ingredients until fluffy. Yield: 2 ½ cups.

Piña Colada Cake

½	cup rum	½	cup water
1	(4-ounce) package coconut cream instant pudding	1	cup flaked coconut (reserve for top)
1	box white cake mix		Piña Colada Frosting
4	eggs		(recipe follows)
¼	cup oil		

Blend all ingredients except coconut. Beat 4 minutes. Pour into two greased and floured cake pans. Bake in 350 degree oven for 25 to 30 minutes. (Do not undercook.) Cool 15 minutes. Remove from pans and cool on wire racks. Frost. Sprinkle with coconut. Keep refrigerated. Serves 12.

Piña Colada Frosting

1	(8-ounce) can crushed pineapple, undrained	⅓	cup rum
1	(4-ounce) package coconut cream instant pudding	9	ounces whipped topping

Beat first three ingredients. Fold in topping. Yield: 2 cups.

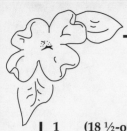

Black Russian Cake

1	(18 ½-ounce) package chocolate cake mix	¾	cup strong black coffee
½	cup vegetable oil	⅓	cup coffee liqueur
1	(4 ⅛-ounce) package instant chocolate pudding	⅓	cup chocolate liqueur
4	eggs, room temperature		Black Russian Topping (recipe follows)

Combine all ingredients in large bowl. Beat at medium speed for 4 minutes. Pour mixture into greased bundt pan or 10-inch tube pan. Bake at 350 degrees for 55 minutes. Use a toothpick to test for doneness. Allow cake to cool before removing from pan. Use a meat fork to punch holes in cake and spoon topping over. Serves 12.

Black Russian Topping

1	cup sifted confectioners' sugar	2	tablespoons coffee liqueur
2	tablespoons strong coffee	2	tablespoons chocolate liqueur

Combine all ingredients until mixture is smooth.

New York Cheesecake

1 ½	cups graham cracker crumbs	1	cup sugar
6	tablespoons sugar	5	eggs
6	tablespoons butter, melted	1	tablespoon lemon juice
3	(8-ounce) packages cream cheese, softened	1	teaspoon vanilla
		2	tablespoons cornstarch
		⅛	teaspoon salt (optional)

Mix first three ingredients. Press into 9-inch springform pan. (Note: Cake may be prepared without the crust.) Beat cream cheese until light and fluffy. Add sugar ¼ cup at a time, mixing well after each addition. Add eggs one at a time, beating 1 minute for each. Stir in remaining ingredients. Pour into pan (if no crust is used, butter pan). Bake at 350 degrees for approximately 1 hour. Cool on wire rack. Cover and chill 8 hours. May be garnished with fresh fruit or chocolate shavings. Serves 8.

Chocolate Mousse Pie

3	cups chocolate wafer cookies, crushed	2	cups whipping cream
½	cup unsalted butter, melted	6	tablespoons confectioners' sugar
1	pound semi-sweet chocolate	2	cups whipping cream
6	eggs, at room témperature, 4 separated		Sugar

Combine cookies and butter. Press into bottom and sides of a 10-inch springform pan. Refrigerate 10 minutes (or chill in freezer). Soften chocolate in top of double boiler over simmering water. Let cool to lukewarm (95 degrees). Add 2 whole eggs and mix well. Add yolks and mix until thoroughly blended. Whip cream with confectioners' sugar until soft peaks form. Beat egg whites until stiff but not dry. Stir small amount of cream and egg whites into chocolate mixture. Fold in remaining cream and egg whites. Turn mixture into crust, chill at least 6 hours, preferably overnight. Whip remaining 2 cups cream with confectioners' sugar to taste, until quite stiff. Loosen crust on all sides, using a sharp knife. Remove springform pan. Spread 1 ½ cups whipped cream over mousse. Pipe remaining cream into rosettes, decorating the top of the pie. Refrigerate until serving time. Serves 8 to 10.

Coffee Delight

	Freshly brewed coffee	¼	ounce bourbon
½	ounce coffee flavored liqueur		Whipped cream
½	ounce orange flavored liqueur		

Into tall Irish coffee mug, pour liqueurs and bourbon. Add coffee to fill. Garnish with fresh whipped cream. Serves 1.

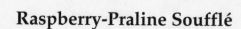

Raspberry-Praline Soufflé

2	teaspoons all-purpose flour	1	(12-ounce) package frozen raspberries, thawed
2 ⅓	cups sugar, divided	¼	teaspoon salt
¾	cup milk	1	cup heavy cream
2	eggs, separated		Raspberries and mint sprigs for garnish
1 ½	cups slivered blanched almonds		

Early in day: In saucepan, cook flour, ½ cup sugar and milk over medium heat until mixture boils and thickens, stirring constantly. In bowl, beat egg yolks. Stir in small amount of milk mixture. Slowly pour back into pan, stirring. Cook over low heat, stirring until thickened. Do not boil. Cover surface with plastic wrap. Chill. Grease cookie sheet. In skillet over medium heat, heat 1 ½ cups sugar until melted and golden. Stir in almonds. Immediately spread praline in a thin layer on cookie sheet. Cool. Crush praline with rolling pin. Press raspberries through sieve to remove seeds. When custard is cool, in small bowl, on high speed, beat egg whites and salt to soft peaks. Beat in ⅓ cup sugar, 1 tablespoon at a time, beating well after each addition, until sugar dissolves and whites are stiff. In large bowl with same beaters, beat cream at medium speed until soft peaks form. Fold custard and raspberry purée into cream; fold in beaten whites. Sprinkle ½ of praline on bottom of 8 x 3-inch springform pan. Keep remaining praline crisp in plastic bag. Spoon raspberry mixture over praline. Freeze soufflé at least 4 hours. Remove pan side. Reserve ¼ cup praline. Press remaining praline onto side of soufflé. If you wish, the soufflé may be removed from the pan with two pancake turners. Garnish with berries, reserved praline and mint. Serves 12.

Brandied Peach Coffee

¼	cup instant coffee powder	4	scoops peach ice cream
5	cups boiling water		Whipped cream
¼	cup peach brandy		Maraschino cherries

Pour boiling water over instant coffee stirring until dissolved. Divide equally among 4 (10-ounce) glasses. Stir in 1 tablespoon brandy and add 1 scoop ice cream to each glass. Top each glass with whipped cream and a cherry. Serves 4.

Brandied Coffee Nog

2	egg yolks, slightly beaten	⅓	cup brandy
1 ½	cups milk	¼	cup light corn syrup
1	cup Half and Half	¼	cup water
2	tablespoons light corn syrup	2	egg whites, at room temperature
1	tablespoon plus 1 teaspoon instant coffee powder		

Combine first five ingredients in a large saucepan. Cook over medium heat, stirring constantly until mixture thickens. Remove from heat. Stir in brandy. Set aside. Combine ¼ cup corn syrup and water in a small saucepan. Cook uncovered over high heat until boiling. Reduce heat and simmer 2 minutes. Beat egg whites until soft peaks form. Gradually add the hot syrup to egg whites, beating until stiff peaks form. Whisk egg whites into coffee mixture. Serve immediately. Yield: 6 cups.

Hot Peppermint Flip

1	egg	3	cups hot strong coffee
⅔	cup whipping cream		Whipped cream (optional)
1	tablespoon sugar		Peppermint sticks
½	cup peppermint schnapps		(optional)
½	cup brandy		

Combine first five ingredients in blender. Blend at high speed for 30 seconds. Pour half of mixture into a bowl. Set aside. Gradually add half of coffee to blender. Blend until frothy. Pour into individual cups. Repeat procedure with reserved mixture and coffee. Garnish each serving with whipped cream and a peppermint stick. Yield: 5 cups.

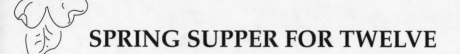

SPRING SUPPER FOR TWELVE

*Celebrate the introduction of spring with fresh flowers
and this light menu.*

Curried Carrot Soup

Chicken Breasts Mornay

Wild Rice Casserole

Asparagus Casserole

Mandarin Orange Salad

Chocolate Almond Crème Roll

Curried Carrot Soup

½	cup butter	2	(13 ¾-ounce) cans
2	cups chopped onion		condensed chicken broth
2	packages fresh carrots,	1 ½	teaspoons salt
	peeled and sliced (6 cups)	½	teaspoon pepper
2	teaspoons curry powder	2	cups light cream
2	thin strips lemon peel		

Sauté onion and carrots in butter for 5 minutes. Add curry powder and lemon peel and cook for 3 minutes. Pour broth into a 2 quart liquid measure and add water to make 2 quarts. Add to onion and carrots. Bring to a boil and simmer covered for 10 minutes. Remove; cool slightly. In blender, blend until smooth. Stir in seasonings. Add cream and heat. Do not boil. Serve warm or chilled. Serves 12.

Chicken Breasts Mornay

1 ½	cups finely chopped onion	6	whole chicken breasts, boned, skinned and halved
7	tablespoons butter or margarine, divided	½	cup white wine or apple juice
2	cups finely chopped mushrooms	¼	cup grated Parmesan cheese
1	tablespoon lemon juice		Mornay Sauce
½	teaspoon salt		(recipe follows)
¼	teaspoon pepper		
1	cup soft bread crumbs (2 slices)		

Sauté onion in 5 tablespoons butter in large skillet until tender, about 5 minutes. Add mushrooms, lemon juice, salt and pepper. Sauté, stirring constantly, until liquid has evaporated, about 5 minutes. Stir in bread crumbs; cool. Pound chicken breasts between sheets of wax paper to about ⅛-inch thickness. Place on work surface and divide mushroom mixture among chicken pieces. Roll up. Fasten with wooden picks. Heat remaining 2 tablespoons butter in large skillet. Brown chicken breasts, half at a time, on all sides, removing to a plate as they brown. Return all to skillet. Sprinkle with salt and pepper. Add wine, bring to a boil and lower heat. Simmer 20 minutes or just until tender. While chicken cooks, prepare Mornay sauce. Remove toothpicks from chicken and transfer to shallow baking dish. Boil cooking liquid to reduce to ½ cup if necessary. Pour liquid over chicken. Spoon Mornay sauce over chicken. Sprinkle chicken with Parmesan cheese. Bake in a preheated 400 degree oven for 15 minutes or until sauce is bubbly and top is browned. Garnish with parsley. This dish may be cooled, wrapped and frozen unbaked. To heat, remove baking dish from freezer to refrigerator in morning. Bake, covered in a preheated 400 degree oven for 30 minutes or until top is browned and chicken is heated through. Serves 12.

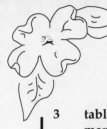

Mornay Sauce

3 tablespoons butter or margarine
4 tablespoons flour
1 (13 ¾-ounce) can chicken broth

1 cup light cream or milk
¾ cup shredded Swiss cheese

Melt butter in medium saucepan. Blend in flour. Cook 1 minute. Gradually stir in broth. Cook, stirring constantly, until sauce thickens and bubbles. Cook 2 minutes. Stir in cream and simmer, stirring constantly, on low heat for 5 minutes. Remove from heat and add cheese. Yield: 2 cups.

Wild Rice Casserole

1 cup chopped onion
1 cup chopped celery
3 tablespoons butter
1 (10-ounce) can cream of chicken soup
1 soup can milk

¼ cup grated Parmesan cheese
4 cups cooked long grain and wild rice
Salt and pepper

Sauté onions and celery in butter. Add soup and can of milk to onions and celery. Simmer for about 1 minute. Add cheese, rice and seasoning. Bake 30 to 40 minutes in a moderate oven. May be made in advance. Serves 12.

Asparagus Casserole

3 to 4 pounds asparagus, fresh or frozen
1 (10-ounce) can cream of mushroom soup diluted with ½ cup milk

1 (10-ounce) package sharp Cheddar cheese, sliced
2 hard boiled eggs, sliced

Blanch asparagus in boiling water for 3 minutes. Drain. Place asparagus in bottom of 1 ½ or 2 quart casserole dish. Mix soup with milk and pour a small amount over asparagus. Spread ⅓ of the cheese on top. Make a second layer of asparagus. Add remaining cheese, then eggs. Cover with remaining soup mixture. Bake at 350 degrees for 30 to 45 minutes, or cover and microwave on high for 12 minutes. Let stand 3 to 4 minutes before serving. Serves 12.

Mandarin Orange Salad

1	head iceberg lettuce, chopped	2	(10 ½-ounce) cans mandarin oranges, drained (reserve 1 to 2 tablespoons for dressing)
1	head romaine lettuce, chopped		
2	(2-ounce) packages slivered almonds		Mandarin Dressing (recipe follows)

Toss above ingredients. Serves 12.

Mandarin Dressing

⅔	cup corn oil	Reserved mandarin orange juice
⅓	cup apple cider vinegar	
1	teaspoon sugar	Dash pepper
1	teaspoon minced parsley	Dash tarragon

Mix above ingredients until well blended. Shake and pour dressing over salad just before serving. Yield: 1 cup.

Chocolate Almond Crème Roll

4	eggs, separated	½	cup pulverized blanched
¾	cups sugar, divided		almonds
1	teaspoon vanilla extract	1	cup confectioners' sugar,
2	tablespoons water		divided
½	cup all-purpose flour	1 ½	cups whipping cream,
¼	cup cocoa		divided
1	teaspoon baking powder	½	teaspoon almond extract
¼	teaspoon salt		Chocolate shavings

In small bowl, whip egg whites until foamy. Gradually beat in 8 table-spoons of sugar. Set aside. In large bowl, beat egg yolks until thick and lemon colored. Gradually beat in remaining sugar. Beat until very thick. Add vanilla and water. Stir together flour, cocoa, baking powder and salt. Fold into yolk mixture, then gently fold in whites. Grease a 15x10 inch jellyroll pan. Line with wax paper. Grease again. Pour cake mixture into pan, smoothing into corners. Bake at 350 degrees for 18 to 22 minutes or until top is dry when touched. Sprinkle ⅓ cup confectioners' sugar over tea towel. Turn baked cake out onto towel, removing waxed paper. Roll up. Place on rack to cool. Mix almonds with ⅓ cup confectioners' sugar. Beat 1 cup whipping cream; fold in almond mixture. Set aside. Beat remaining ½ cup whipping cream until stiff enough to hold a peak. Fold in ⅓ cup confectioners' sugar and almond extract. Keep cold until ready to frost cake, but do not hold more than 30 minutes. Unroll cooled cake. Remove towel. Spread with almond filling and roll up again. Frost just before seving. Sprinkle with chocolate shavings. You may serve with a scoop of ice cream. Serves 10.

V.I.P. DINNER, A.S.A.P.

When you are short on time and need an elegant meal for guests, this simple menu will impress all.

Shrimp de Jonghe

Bloody Mary Rice

Ginger Carrots

Vegetable Medley

Shrimp de Jonghe

½ cup margarine
4 cloves garlic, mashed
2 shallots, minced
½ cup sherry
1 tablespoon parsley
½ teaspoon salt
¼ teaspoon dried tarragon

Dash nutmeg
Dash thyme
¾ cup dry bread crumbs or stuffing mix
1 ½ pounds large raw shrimp, peeled and deveined

Combine margarine and garlic in 1 ½-quart casserole; microwave on high (100% power) for 2 minutes. Add shallots and cook on high 2 more minutes. Remove and discard garlic only. Stir in next six ingredients. Heat 20 seconds on high. Remove ¼ of seasoned margarine and stir into bread crumbs. Toss shrimp with remaining margarine mixture in casserole until well coated. Microwave on medium-high (70%) for 5 minutes. Stir. Sprinkle with bread crumb mixture. Microwave on medium-high (70%) until shrimp is pink and opaque, 1 to 4 minutes. Let stand 2 minutes before serving. Serves 6.

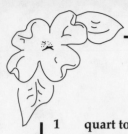

Bloody Mary Rice

1	quart tomato-vegetable juice	4	dashes hot pepper sauce
	Freshly ground pepper and salt to taste	½	teaspoon celery seed
		1	tablespoon horseradish
6	dashes Worcestershire sauce	2	cups wild or long grain and wild rice

Combine all ingredients except rice; mix well. Cook rice according to package directions, using juice mixture instead of water. You may substitute 3 ½ cups bottled bloody mary mix for juice mixture. Serves 6.

Ginger Carrots

5	medium carrots	¼	teaspoon ginger
1	tablespoon sugar	¼	cup orange juice
1	teaspoon cornstarch	2	teaspoons butter or margarine
¼	teaspoon salt		

Cook carrots until tender; drain. Combine next four ingredients in pan. Add orange juice and cook stirring constantly until mixture thickens. Boil 1 minute. Stir in butter and pour over carrots. Toss to coat evenly. Serves 6.

Vegetable Medley

1	bunch broccoli, cut into bite-size pieces	½	teaspoon salt
1	head cauliflower, cut into bite-size pieces	¼	teaspoon thyme
		8	to 10 cherry tomatoes, halved
3	zucchini, thinly sliced (unpeeled)	½	cup grated Parmesan cheese
3	tablespoons butter		

Arrange broccoli, cauliflower and zucchini in large round glass (microwaveable) dish or bowl. Cover with plastic wrap. Cook in microwave on high 9 to 11 minutes. Let stand 2 minutes with wrap on. Mix butter, garlic, salt and thyme. Melt 30 seconds on high. Add tomatoes to vegetables in baking dish. Top with butter mixture and grated cheese. Cook uncovered on high 1 to 2 minutes. Serves 6.

AN AUTUMN GATHERING FOR TWENTY-FOUR

Celebrate the bounty of fall harvest with dishes featuring beef, vegetables and fruit co-mingling with the savory spices and wine that bring autumn to mind.

Beef Bourguignone

Potatoes Au Gratin

Zucchini and Yellow Squash Medley

Brandied Apples

Chocolate-Banana Meringue Torte

Lemon Delight

Beef Bourguignone

¾	cup corn oil	¾	cup flour
8	pounds lean boneless stew beef, cubed	3	cups tomato puree
		6	cups dry red wine
2	onions, chopped (whole pearl onions may be substituted)	6	cups beef broth
		3	teaspoons thyme
		6	bay leaves
6	to 8 carrots, chopped	3	cups mushrooms (canned or fresh) sliced (optional)
2	to 3 celery stalks, chopped		

For added flavor, marinate beef in red wine. Reserve marinade for use in stew. Heat corn oil in skillet. Sauté cubed beef until nicely browned. Add onions, carrots and celery to skillet and sauté until just tender. Transfer all ingredients from skillet to stock pot. Blend in flour. Add remaining ingredients. Bring to a boil and reduce heat to simmer for 30 to 40 minutes. Remove bay leaves and add mushrooms. Serves 24.

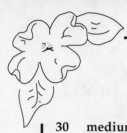

Potatoes au Gratin

30	medium potatoes, pared and sliced (about 10 pounds)	4	teaspoons dry mustard
		12	cups milk
1 ½	cups butter or margarine, divided	4	cups shredded Cheddar cheese
3	cups chopped onion	2	cups cracker crumbs
1	cup flour		Paprika
5	teaspoons salt		Pimento
4	teaspoons Worcestershire sauce		Parsley

Cook potatoes in boiling water until tender. Drain well. Melt 1 cup butter. Add onion. Sauté until tender. Blend in flour, salt, Worcestershire and dry mustard. Gradually stir in milk. Cook, stirring constantly, until sauce thickens; boil 1 minute. Remove from heat. Add cheese. Stir until melted. Place potatoes in 4 (11x7x1 ½-inch) baking dishes. Pour on cheese sauce. Sprinkle crumbs combined with ½ cup melted butter. Top with paprika. Bake in 350 degree oven 30 minutes or until golden. Garnish with parsley and thin pimento strips. Freeze baked or unbaked casseroles for later use. To serve: bake in 350 degree oven 45 minutes or until hot and bubbly. Serves 24.

Zucchini and Yellow Squash Medley

24	strips bacon	2	medium onions, thinly sliced
12	medium zucchini, sliced in ¼-inch rounds		
12	medium yellow squash, sliced in ¼-inch rounds		

Fry bacon in large dutch oven until crisp. Remove, drain and crumble. Set aside. Add remaining ingredients to dutch oven. Salt and pepper to taste. Cover and cook until just done, stirring occasionally. Do not overcook. Remove squash with slotted spoon into serving dish. Sprinkle with crumbled bacon. Serves 24.

Brandied Apples

8	large cooking apples	½	cup brandy
½	cup lemon juice	1	tablespoon grated lemon
⅓	cup butter or margarine		rind
⅔	cup firmly packed brown	⅓	cup brandy
	sugar		Vanilla ice cream
1	teaspoon cinnamon		

Peel and core apples. Cut into ½-inch wedges. Sprinkle with lemon juice. Melt butter in chafing dish, drain apples and stir into melted butter. Cook apples over medium heat stirring gently, about 3 minutes. Combine lemon rind, ½ cup brandy, brown sugar and cinnamon. Pour over apples. Cook 5 to 7 minutes. Heat ⅓ cup brandy. Pour over apples. Spoon apples into individual serving dishes. Serve hot or cold topped with vanilla ice cream. Serves 8.

Chocolate-Banana Meringue Torte

3	egg whites, room	3	tablespoons water
	temperature	3	cups whipping cream
1	cup sugar	¼	cup sugar
6	ounces semi-sweet	3	bananas, thinly sliced
	chocolate		

Preheat oven to 400 degrees. Butter and flour 3 10-inch springform pans. Beat egg whites in medium bowl on low for 1 minute, then on high until stiff, but not dry (about 30 seconds). Gradually beat in sugar until glossy (1 minute). Spoon into pans spreading to within ½-inch of edge. Put in oven and turn off. Let stand at least 8 hours or overnight without opening door. Melt chocolate with 3 tablespoons water in double boiler over hot water, stirring constantly; remove from water. Whip cream until soft peaks form. Add ¼ cup sugar. Beat until stiff, not dry. Place 1 meringue on plate. Arrange ½ of bananas on top. Spread ⅓ of chocolate and ¼ of cream on bananas. Top with second meringue. Press gently. Repeat with ⅓ chocolate and ¼ cream and remaining bananas. Top with third meringue. Frost top and sides with remaining cream. Drizzle top of torte with remaining chocolate. Refrigerate 2 hours before serving. Serves 10.

Lemon Delight

1	cup flour	1	(8-ounce) package cream cheese, softened
½	cup butter		
½	cup chopped pecans	2	(3 ½-ounce) packages instant lemon pudding mix
2	cups whipped topping, divided		
1	cup confectioners' sugar	3	cups milk

Combine first 3 ingredients by hand (knead with fingers). Turn into a 13x9-inch pan. Bake at 375 degrees for 15 minutes. Let cool. Beat one cup whipped topping with confectioners' sugar and cream cheese. Pour over cooled crust. Prepare pudding following package directions, using only 3 cups milk. Spread over second layer. Spread 1 cup whipped topping on top. Sprinkle with chopped pecans. Chill 4 hours. Serves 12.

Happy Holidays

Stone House - Manassas

The Stone House stands in the midst of the Manassas National Battlefield Park in Prince William County. Originally a tavern, Stone House offered comfortable refuge, especially to those travelling over the holidays. The sweet fragrance of freshly cut cedar decorated candlelit windows, offering a warm welcome to its guests. Constructed in 1828 of locally quarried sandstone, the Stone House was used as a Union field hospital during the 1st Battle of Manassas and as the headquarters of General Pope. The Stone House sits at the base of a hill known as a popular winter sledding location.

Happy Holidays

The holiday season is a time to preserve traditions and to share with family and friends. Happy Holidays presents ideas for gift giving as well as for entertaining from Thanksgiving through Christmas and into the New Year while maintaining the flavor of hospitality Virginia-style.

Beverages
Eggnog
Hot Cranberry Apple Cider
Spirited Eggnog
Wassail Bowl Punch
Wine Punch

Cookie Swap
Apricot Squares
Chocolate Caramel Layer Squares
Coconut Oatmeal Cookies
Crescent Cookies
Forgotten Cookies
Fruitcake Cookies
Lemon Custard Bars
Pecan Balls
Pumpkin Pie Squares
Seven Layer Cookies
Two-Minute Fudge

Desserts
Cheesy Dapper Apple Squares
Chocolate Chip Cinnamon Cake
Crème de Menthe Brownies
Holly Berry Cookies
Molded French Cream
Swedish Apple Pie

Entrees
Shrimp Creole
Spicy Marinated Beef Tenderloin

Holiday Gift Giving Ideas
Apple Cinnamon Muffins
Banana Bread
Black Walnut Pound Cake
Bouquet Garni
Chewy Fudge Brownies
Chocolate Turtles
Clay for Tree Ornaments, Homemade
Cranberry Chutney
Cranberry Cordial
Cream Cheese Icing

David's Bread and Butter Pickles
Dog Biscuits
Frypan Fruit Balls
Gingerbread with Lemon Sauce
Green Tomato Relish
Halfway Bars
Lemon Pecan Bread
Lemon Sauce
Rose Potpourri
Pumpkin Cake with Cream Cheese
    Icing
Spice Scent
Sugar Coated Nuts
Vanilla Extract, Homemade
Whole Wheat Carrot Banana Bread
Zucchini Bread
Zucchini Pickles

Hors d'oeuvres
Cauliflower Dip
Cheese Ball
Chicken Little Fingers with Easy
    Barbecue Sauce
Fresh Cooked Shrimp with Cocktail
    Sauce
Hot Bacon Appetizers
Petite Ham and Cheese Biscuits
Sausage Balls in Cheese Pastry
Zesty Meatballs

Miscellaneous
Evergreen Preservation
Holiday Scent
Olive Dressing
Party Mold
Raspberry Holiday Mold

Salads
Asparagus and English Pea Salad
Green Beans and Mushroom Salad

Vegetables
Nutty Yam Bake

Holiday Gift Giving

All of us enjoy receiving gifts of food during the holidays. Preparing homemade specialties is fun for the whole family. A gift from your kitchen is a warm and personal touch, whether you are remembering distant friends and relatives or thanking a child's teacher.

Packaging your culinary creation is as much fun as making it. Place cookies and candies in interesting baskets or tins lined with fabric. Glass containers display your dry mixes colorfully. Decorate with fresh greens, ribbons and assorted gift bags and boxes. Include any preparation instructions on the gift tag.

When sending gifts through the mail, consider their perishable nature and the practicality of shipping them. Candies, flavored popcorn and dry mixes are good choices for out-of-towners.

Since the winter holidays are exceptionally busy, "make-ahead" recipes are great, especially when they may be frozen. Fill your freezer and pantry early with these delights, so that gift-giving will be a pleasure.

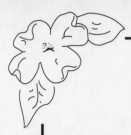

FLAVORFUL FAVORS

Sugar-Coated Nuts

Chocolate Turtles

Halfway Bars

Chewy Fudge Brownies

Frypan Fruit Balls

Sugar-Coated Nuts

12	ounces pecans	1	cup sugar
2	egg whites, beaten	½	cup butter, melted

Combine pecans and egg whites, stirring until coated. Stir in sugar, mixing well. Pour butter into jellyroll pan and spread nut mixture evenly over butter. Bake at 300 degrees for 30 minutes, stirring twice. Remove pecans from pan immediately. Cool on foil for 30 minutes. Store in covered container. Yield: 2 cups.

Chocolate Turtles

150	pecan halves (about 3 cups)	8	ounces semi-sweet chocolate
50	caramels, unwrapped		

Preheat oven to 300 degrees. On greased baking sheets arrange pecan halves in groups of 3, end to end, flat side down. Place a caramel on top of each cluster. Place in oven until caramels soften - about 5 to 8 minutes. Remove from oven and flatten caramels over pecans with a buttered spoon. Cool slightly. Melt chocolate in top of double boiler over simmering water. Dip turtles into chocolate and cool on waxed paper. Store in tightly-covered containers in a cool place. Yield: 50 chocolate turtles.

Halfway Bars

½	cup butter	1	cup flour
¼	cup brown sugar	½	teaspoon baking powder
¼	cup white sugar		Pinch salt
1	egg, separated	1	cup chocolate chips
½	teaspoon vanilla	½	cup brown sugar

Cream butter and sugars. Stir in egg yolk and vanilla. Add dry ingredients; batter will be stiff. Press into bottom of a buttered 8x8-inch pan. Sprinkle chocolate chips evenly on top. Beat egg white until stiff and add ½ cup brown sugar. Stir. Spread over chips. Bake at 350 degrees for 20 to 30 minutes. Yield: 24 squares.

Chewy Fudge Brownies

1	cup butter	¼	teaspoon salt
3	squares unsweetened chocolate	1	teaspoon vanilla
		1	cup flour
2	cups sugar	1	cup chopped nuts
4	eggs, beaten		

Melt butter and chocolate. Add sugar and eggs. Mix well with wooden spoon. Mix remaining ingredients. Add to chocolate mixture. Bake in 9x13-inch greased glass dish in 350 degree oven for 25 to 30 minutes. Yield: 24 brownies.

Frypan Fruit Balls

½	cup butter, melted	½	teaspoon vanilla
1	cup chopped dates	½	teaspoon almond extract
1	cup sugar	2	cups puffed rice cereal
2	eggs		Pinch salt
¼	cup chopped nuts		Coconut

Add butter to dates. Cream sugar and eggs. Add to dates. Cook over medium heat until thick, stirring constantly. Cool. Add remaining ingredients except coconut. Form into 1 ½-inch balls and roll in coconut. Store in airtight container and refrigerate. May be frozen; will keep for 1 month. Yield: 48 balls.

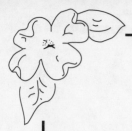

OVEN OFFERINGS

Apple-Cinnamon Muffins

Zucchini Bread

Gingerbread with Lemon Sauce

Banana Bread

Whole Wheat Carrot Banana Bread

Lemon-Pecan Bread

Pumpkin Cake with Cream Cheese Icing

Black Walnut Pound Cake

Apple-Cinnamon Muffins

2	cups flour	1	apple, shredded
2	tablespoons sugar	1	egg, lightly beaten
½	teaspoon cinnamon	1	cup milk
1	tablespoon baking powder	¼	cup vegetable oil
½	teaspoon salt		

Preheat oven to 400 degrees. Grease a 12-section muffin pan. In large bowl, mix dry ingredients with fork. In small bowl, combine egg with apple, milk and oil. Add egg mixture all at once to flour mixture. With spoon, stir just until flour is moistened (batter will be lumpy). Spoon batter into muffin cups. Bake 20 to 25 minutes until golden. Remove from pans immediately. May be frozen. Yield: 1 dozen.

Zucchini Bread

1	cup salad oil	¼	teaspoon baking powder
3	eggs, slightly beaten	1	teaspoon salt
2	cups sugar	3	teaspoons ground
2	cups grated raw zucchini		cinnamon
2	teaspoons vanilla	1	cup nuts
3	cups all-purpose flour	1	cup raisins
1	teaspoon baking soda		

Combine oil, eggs, sugar, zucchini and vanilla in a large mixing bowl. Blend well. Stir in dry ingredients. Do not beat. Stir in nuts and raisins. Spoon batter into 2 well-greased 8-inch loaf pans. Bake at 325 degrees for 1 ½ hours or until done. Yield: 2 loaves.

Gingerbread with Lemon Sauce

½	cup sugar	1	cup sour milk
½	cup butter	1	cup dark molasses
1	teaspoon ginger	2	cups flour
1	teaspoon cinnamon	1	teaspoon baking soda
½	teaspoon salt		Lemon Sauce
1	large egg		(recipe follows)

Combine sugar, butter, ginger, cinnamon and salt in a bowl. Add egg. Beat until fluffy. Add molasses and milk. Sift flour with soda and add to mixture. Bake at 325 degrees for one hour in a greased 9x9x2-inch pan. When cake is done, it will spring back to the touch. Include a jar of Lemon Sauce with this gift. Serves 8.

Lemon Sauce

⅓	cup sugar	½	teaspoon grated lemon rind
1	tablespoon cornstarch	1 ½	tablespoons fresh lemon
1	cup water		juice
3	tablespoons butter		Pinch salt

Mix sugar and cornstarch together in saucepan. Add water and cook, stirring constantly until mixture bubbles. Simmer gently for 3 to 5 minutes; remove from heat. Stir in remaining ingredients. Serve while hot with pudding or gingerbread. Yield: 1 ½ cups.

Banana Bread

1 ¼	cups flour	½	cup shortening
1	cup sugar	2	eggs
½	teaspoon salt	3	small, very ripe bananas,
1	teaspoon baking soda		mashed

Mix shortening with dry ingredients. Add eggs. Fold in mashed bananas. Pour into greased loaf pan. Bake at 350 degrees for 40 to 45 minutes. Yield: 1 loaf.

Whole Wheat Carrot Banana Bread

½	cup margarine, softened	½	teaspoon salt
1	cup firmly packed brown	½	teaspoon baking powder
	sugar	½	teaspoon cinnamon
2	eggs	1	cup mashed banana
1	cup all-purpose flour	1	cup shredded carrots
1	cup whole wheat flour	½	cup chopped walnuts
1	teaspoon baking soda		

Cream margarine and sugar. Beat in eggs. Sift together dry ingredients. Add dry ingredients alternately with bananas to sugar mixture, beating after each addition. Fold in carrots and nuts. Pour into 2 greased 8-inch loaf pans. Bake at 350 degrees for 40 to 50 minutes. Yield: 2 loaves.

Lemon-Pecan Bread

¾	cup butter or margarine,	¼	teaspoon salt
	softened	¾	cup buttermilk
1 ½	cups sugar	¾	cup chopped pecans
3	eggs	1	teaspoon grated lemon
2 ¼	cups all-purpose flour		rind
¼	teaspoon baking soda		

Cream butter and sugar. Add eggs, one at a time, beating well after each addition. Combine dry ingredients. Add to creamed mixture alternately with buttermilk, beginning and ending with flour mixture. Stir in pecans and lemon rind. Pour into a greased and floured 9x5x3-inch loaf pan. Bake at 350 degrees for 75 to 80 minutes or until a wooden pick inserted in center comes out clean. Cool in pan 10 minutes. Remove loaf from pan and cool completely. Yield: 1 loaf.

Pumpkin Cake with Cream Cheese Icing

2	cups sugar	2	teaspoons cinnamon
4	eggs	2	teaspoons baking soda
1	cup salad oil	½	teaspoon salt
2	cups pumpkin purée		Cream Cheese Icing
2	cups flour		(recipe follows)

Combine all ingredients in a large bowl. Turn into a greased and floured 9x13-inch pan. Bake in 350 degree oven for 35 minutes or more. Cool and ice with cream cheese icing. Serves 12.

Cream Cheese Icing

½	cup butter	2	teaspoons vanilla
1	(16-ounce) box confectioners' sugar	1	cup chopped nuts
1	(8-ounce) package cream cheese, softened		

Blend butter, sugar, cream cheese and vanilla in mixer and spread on top of cake. Sprinkle with nuts. Yield: 1 cup icing.

Black Walnut Pound Cake

1 ½	cups butter or margarine	1	teaspoon black walnut flavoring
1	(16-ounce) box confectioners' sugar, sifted	1	cup chopped black walnuts
6	eggs		
2	cups plus 2 tablespoons flour		

Cream butter and sugar. Add one egg at a time, beating thoroughly after each. Add flour gradually, mixing well. Add flavoring and nuts. Bake in a greased and floured tube pan at 350 degrees for 65 minutes. Remove from pan to cool on rack. Delicious if sliced thinly and served with vanilla ice cream between two slices, sandwich-style. Serves 12.

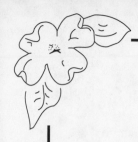

PICKLED PRESENTS

Cranberry Chutney

Zucchini Pickles

David's Bread and Butter Pickles

Green Tomato Relish

Cranberry Chutney

¼	cup snipped candied ginger	½	cup coarsely chopped toasted almonds
1	pound fresh cranberries	1	teaspoon grated onion
2 ¼	cups lemon juice	¼	teaspoon ground cloves
1	cup light raisins	1	cup water
2	teaspoons salt		

In large saucepan, combine all ingredients. Bring to a boil, stirring constantly. Simmer uncovered over low heat for 15 minutes, stirring occasionally. Pack in hot scalded jars and seal at once. Refrigerate. Yield: 2 ½ pints.

Zucchini Pickles

1	gallon zucchini, peeled	1	teaspoon salt
1	cup slacked lime	3	tablespoons pickling spices
1	quart plus 1 cup white vinegar	1	tablespoon round celery seed
4 ½	to 5 cups sugar		

Put zucchini and lime in enamel or stainless steel pan. Add water to cover and let set overnight. Drain and rinse well (2 or 3 times). Let sit in clear water for a couple of hours. Bring remaining ingredients to a boil. Add zucchini and heat through (15 to 20 minutes). Put in jars and seal. Yield: 7 pints.

David's Bread and Butter Pickles

4	quarts cucumbers, sliced ⅛-inch thick	5	cups sugar
8	small white onions, sliced ⅛-inch thick	5	cups white vinegar
		1 ½	teaspoons tumeric
2	green peppers, sliced	½	teaspoon ground cloves
½	cup salt	2	tablespoons mustard seed
		1	teaspoon celery seed

Wash and slice cucumbers, onions and peppers and mix together. Sprinkle salt over all and put into large non-corrodible pan. Cover with ice. Let stand 3 hours. Drain well. Mix remaining ingredients together and heat in large pot. When hot, add vegetables, stirring occasionally. Heat until scalded through, but do not boil. Pack quickly into hot jars and seal. Will keep a month or more. Serve chilled. Yield: 10 pints.

Green Tomato Relish

1	peck green tomatoes, chopped	2	pounds brown sugar
8	large green onions, chopped	2 ½	cups granulated sugar
		3	tablespoons pickling spice
½	cup salt	1 ½	quarts vinegar
8	large green peppers, chopped		

Combine tomatoes and onions. Sprinkle with salt and let sit overnight in an enamel pan. Rinse with cold water and drain well. Add remaining ingredients and cook for one hour over medium heat. Seal in sterilized jars. Yield: 16 pints.

MISCELLANEOUS MERRINESS

Bouquet Garni

Homemade Vanilla Extract

Homemade Clay for Tree Ornaments

Rose Potpourri

Cranberry Cordial

Spice Scent

Dog Biscuits

Bouquet Garni

2	tablespoons each of rosemary, parsley, thyme and marjoram	2	bay leaves, crushed
1	tablespoon each of oregano and peppercorns	¼	yard muslin, washed or cheese cloth
			Cotton string

Mix all herbs together. Cut muslin or cheese cloth into 5-inch squares. Fill each square with 2 tablespoons of herb mixture. Bring the four corners together to form a small bag, and tie with a piece of string. Use one bag as seasoning for soups or stews. To make a nice hostess gift, attach several bags to a wreath form and add a cluster of bay leaves and ribbon to make a bow. Yield: 4 bouquets.

Homemade Vanilla Extract

1	cup brandy	2	vanilla beans, cut into 1-inch pieces

Combine brandy and vanilla beans in a container with tight-fitting lid. Cover and let stand 3 months, shaking 3 times a week. Yield: 1 cup.

Homemade Clay for Tree Ornaments

1	cup corn starch	String, paint, clear shellac,
2	cups baking soda	saucepan, plate, damp
1 ½	cups cold water	cloth, knife or cookie
		cutter, brush

Mix corn starch and baking soda together thoroughly. Add cold water. Heat, stirring constantly, until mixture reaches a slightly moist, mashed potato consistency. Turn out on a plate and cover with a damp cloth. Knead when cooled. Roll out dough to a ¼ or ½-inch thickness and cut. Pierce a hole near the top for string. Let dry. Paint and let dry. Brush with shellac. Yield: 1 dozen 3-inch ornaments.

Rose Potpourri

1	pound Rose petals dried	1	ounce caraway seeds
	in shade or about 4 feet	1	ounce allspice
	from stove	¼	pound dried salt
1	ounce cloves		

Pound all ingredients together in a mortar or grind in a mill. Put compound in small cloth bags or let stand in an open dish. Yield: 6 cups potpourri.

Cranberry Cordial

1 ½	cups cranberry juice	2	cups vodka
1 ½	cups sugar		

In a saucepan, mix cranberry juice and sugar. Boil five minutes or until thick. Cool. Stir in vodka. Pour into bottles and let set at least one week. Chill until ready to serve. Enjoy as an aperitif or give as a holiday hostess gift. Yield: 5 cups cordial.

Spice Scent

Whole allspice	Lemon peel
Cinnamon sticks, cut up	Orange peel
Whole cloves	Whole rosemary

Combine 1 tablespoon of each ingredient together. Fill sachets or use for making pomanders.

Dog Biscuits

3 ½ cups unbleached all-purpose flour	4 teaspoons salt
2 cups whole-wheat flour	1 envelope active dry yeast
1 cup rye flour	¼ cup warm water
2 cups bulgur (cracked wheat)	3 cups chicken broth
1 cup cornmeal	1 egg, slightly beaten with 1 teaspoon milk
½ cup instant nonfat dry-milk powder	

Preheat oven to 300 degrees. Mix first seven ingredients with a wooden spoon in a large bowl. Dissolve yeast in warm water. Add to dry ingredients. Add chicken broth to flour mixture. Stir until dough forms. Roll out dough until it is ¼-inch thick. Using a large dog biscuit for model, cut out bone shapes from dough. Place on prepared cookie sheets. Brush dough with egg glaze. Bake bones for 45 minutes. Turn oven off. Biscuits should remain in oven overnight to harden. Yield: 30 large bones.

COOKIE SWAP PARTY

*A cookie swap party provides you with a delicious assortment
of homemade sweets. Invite ten to twelve friends to bring
one dozen cookies packaged for each of the other guests
plus a few extra cookies to sample at the party.
Attach a copy of the recipe to each package.*

Apricot Squares

Chocolate Caramel Layer Squares

Lemon Custard Bars

Pumpkin Pie Squares

Crescent Cookies

Coconut Oatmeal Cookies

Forgotten Cookies

Fruitcake Cookies

Seven Layer Cookies

Pecan Balls

Two Minute Fudge

Apricot Squares

1	cup butter, melted	1	teaspoon vanilla extract
1 ½	cups confectioners' sugar	1	cup ground walnuts, divided
2	egg yolks		
2	cups flour	1	pound apricot filling
2	teaspoons baking powder		

Add sugar to melted butter. Add remaining ingredients except apricots
and ¼ cup nuts. Beat. Put in greased 10x15-inch pan. Spread filling on
top. Sprinkle with nuts. Bake at 350 degrees for 20 to 25 minutes. Cool.
Sprinkle with confectioners' sugar. Yield: 24 squares.

Chocolate Caramel Layer Squares

1	(14-ounce) bag caramels	½	cup butter or margarine, softened
⅔	cup evaporated milk, divided	1	cup chopped nuts
1	(18 ½-ounce) box regular German chocolate cake mix	1	(6-ounce) package semi-sweet chocolate morsels

Combine caramels and ⅓ cup evaporated milk in top of double boiler; cook, stirring constantly, until caramels are completely melted. Remove double boiler from heat. Combine cake mix, remaining ⅓ cup milk and butter, mixing with electric mixer until dough holds together; stir in nuts. Press half of cake mixture into a greased 13x9x2-inch baking pan. Bake at 350 degrees for 6 minutes. Sprinkle chocolate morsels over crust. Pour caramel mixture over chocolate morsels, spreading evenly. Crumble remaining cake mixture over caramel mixture. Return pan to oven and bake 18 minutes; cool. Chill 30 minutes; cut into small bars. Bars will be soft and chewy inside. Yield: 5 dozen.

Lemon Custard Bars

2	cups plus 1 tablespoon flour	4	eggs, beaten
1	cup margarine, softened	2	cups sugar
½	cup confectioners' sugar	1	teaspoon baking powder
			Juice of 1 lemon

Combine 2 cups flour with margarine and confectioners' sugar in bowl, mixing well. Press into 9x13-inch baking dish. Bake at 350 degrees for 20 to 25 minutes. Combine remaining ingredients in bowl, beating well. Spread over crust. Bake for 20 to 25 minutes. Yield: 12 to 18 bars.

Pumpkin Pie Squares

1	cup sifted flour	1	(13-ounce) can evaporated
½	cup quick cooking rolled		milk
	oats	2	eggs
½	cup plus 2 tablespoons	¾	cup sugar
	firmly packed brown sugar	½	teaspoon salt
½	cup plus 2 tablespoons	1	teaspoon cinnamon
	butter, divided	½	teaspoon ground ginger
1	(16-ounce) can pumpkin,	¼	teaspoon ground cloves
	or 2 cups fresh pumpkin	½	cup chopped pecans

Combine flour, rolled oats, ½ cup brown sugar and ½ cup butter in mixing bowl. Mix until crumbly, using electric mixer on low speed. Press into ungreased 13x9x2-inch pan. Bake at 350 degrees for 15 minutes. Combine next eight ingredients in mixing bowl; beat well. Pour into crust. Bake at 350 degrees for 20 minutes. Combine pecans, remaining brown sugar and 2 tablespoons butter; sprinkle over pumpkin filling. Return to oven and bake 15 to 20 minutes or until filling is set. Cool in pan and cut into 2-inch squares. Yield: 2 dozen squares.

Crescent Cookies

1	cup flour	2	teaspoons vanilla
½	cup butter, softened	1	cup finely chopped pecans
2	heaping tablespoons		
	confectioners' sugar		

Mix all ingredients except sugar. Shape into crescents. Dough expands when cooked, so make small. Bake on greased cookie sheet in 325 degree oven for 12 to 18 minutes or until light brown. Roll in confectioners' sugar while still hot. Yield: 2 to 3 dozen.

Coconut Oatmeal Cookies

2	cups flour	1	cup shortening
1	cup sugar	2	eggs
1	teaspoon baking powder	½	teaspoon vanilla
1	teaspoon baking soda	1 ½	cups oats
½	teaspoon salt	1	cup nuts
1	cup brown sugar	1	cup coconut

Mix together flour, sugar, baking powder, soda and salt. Add sugar, shortening, eggs and vanilla; beat together. Stir in remaining ingredients. Form dough into small balls and roll in sugar. Bake at 350 degrees for 9 to 10 minutes. Yield: 5 dozen cookies.

Forgotten Cookies

2	egg whites	1	cup crushed walnuts,
⅔	cup sugar		optional
	Dash salt		
¾	cup miniature chocolate chips		

Beat egg whites until stiff. Add sugar and salt and beat. Fold in chips and nuts. Spoon onto foil-covered cookie sheet. Place in oven at 350 degrees for 1 minute. Turn off oven and leave in oven overnight. Yield: 2 to 3 dozen cookies.

Fruitcake Cookies

1 ½ cups all-purpose flour
½ teaspoon cloves
½ teaspoon cinnamon
½ teaspoon nutmeg
¼ teaspoon baking soda
¼ teaspoon salt
3 cups chopped pecans
½ pound candied pineapple, chopped
½ pound chopped dates
¼ pound candied red cherries, chopped
¼ pound candied green cherries, chopped
½ cup butter or margarine, softened
1 cup firmly packed brown sugar
2 eggs
⅓ cup white wine
1 ½ tablespoons milk

Combine first six ingredients in small bowl; set aside ½ cup of mixture. Combine pecans, pineapple, dates and cherries; mix well. Dredge fruit mixture in ½ cup reserved flour mixture. Cream butter in large mixing bowl; gradually add sugar, beating until fluffy. Add eggs, one at a time, beating well after each addition. Add dry ingredients alternately with wine and milk, beginning and ending with flour. Stir in fruit. Drop dough by level teaspoons onto greased cookie sheets. Bake at 325 degrees for 15 minutes or until golden. Cool on wire rack. Yield: 4 dozen.

Seven Layer Cookies

½ cup margarine, melted
1 ½ cups graham cracker crumbs
1 cup shredded coconut
1 (6-ounce) package semi-sweet chocolate (or mint) chips
1 (6-ounce) package butterscotch chips
1 cup chopped pecans
1 (14-ounce) can sweetened condensed milk

Melt margarine in 9x13-inch pan. Layer graham cracker crumbs, coconut, chocolate chips, butterscotch chips and nuts. Drizzle condensed milk over top. Bake at 350 degrees for 30 to 35 minutes. Cut while warm. Yield: 24 cookies.

Pecan Balls

½   cup butter, melted
2   tablespoons sugar
1   cup flour
1   teaspoon vanilla

Pinch salt
1   cup chopped pecans
    Confectioners' sugar

Combine ingredients together. Roll into 1 ½-inch balls. Bake for 20 minutes at 325 degrees. Roll in confectioners' sugar while still warm. Yield: 2 to 3 dozen.

Two Minute Fudge

1   (16-ounce) box
    confectioners' sugar
½   cup cocoa
¼   teaspoon salt

1   tablespoon vanilla extract
½   cup butter
¼   cup milk
1   cup chopped nuts

In a 1 ½-quart casserole, mix together sugar, cocoa, salt and vanilla until partially blended (mixture is too stiff to thoroughly blend in all of dry ingredients). Place butter on top in center of dish and add milk. Microwave on high 2 minutes, or until milk feels warm on bottom of dish. Stir vigorously until smooth. If all butter has not melted during cooking, it will as mixture is stirred. Blend in chopped nuts. Pour into well-buttered, 8x4x3-inch dish. Chill 1 hour in refrigerator or 20 to 30 minutes in freezer. Cut into squares. Yield: 36 squares.

OPEN HOUSE

Open your home for a relaxed gathering featuring spirited and spicy refreshments. Create a festive atmosphere with aromatic greens and potpourri.

Evergreen Preservation

Holiday Scent

Spirited Eggnog

Hot Cranberry Apple Cider

Wine Punch

Hot Bacon Appetizers

Sausage Balls in Cheese Pastry

Cauliflower Dip

Cheese Ball

Chicken Little Fingers with Easy Barbecue Sauce

Petite Ham and Cheese Biscuits

Zesty Meatballs

Cheesy Dapper Apple Squares

Fresh Cooked Shrimp with Cocktail Sauce

Crème de Menthe Brownies

Holly Berry Cookies

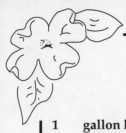

Evergreen Preservation

1	gallon hot water	2	cups light corn syrup
4	tablespoons micronized iron plant food	4	teaspoons bleach

Mix all ingredients together. Immerse greens in a large tub filled with mixture at least 24 hours before using.

Holiday Scent

3	(4-inch) cinnamon sticks	½	lemon, halved
3	bay leaves	½	orange, halved
¼	cup whole cloves	1	quart water

Combine all ingredients in tea kettle or saucepan. Bring to boil and reduce heat. Simmer as long as desired. Check container often and add water as needed. Mixture may be refrigerated for several days and reused. Not consumable.

Spirited Eggnog

6	eggs, separated	1	pint whipping cream
¾	cup sugar, divided	1	quart milk
½	teaspoon salt		Ice cream (optional)
1	pint whiskey		

Beat egg whites in large bowl until stiff. Add salt and fold in ¼ cup sugar. Whip cream. Beat egg yolks with ½ cup sugar. Add whiskey. (The whiskey cooks the yolks.) Fold in egg white mixture, whipped cream and milk. Transfer to bowl for serving and add ice cream to keep the eggnog cool. Serve with nutmeg on the side. Yield: 12 servings.

Hot Cranberry Apple Cider

2	quarts apple cider	4	(3-inch) cinnamon sticks
1 ½	quarts cranberry cocktail	1 ½	teaspoons whole cloves
¼	cup brown sugar	1	lemon, thinly sliced

Combine all ingredients in large kettle. Heat to boiling. Reduce heat and simmer 15 to 20 minutes. With slotted spoon, remove cinnamon, cloves and lemon slices. If desired, float fresh lemon slice in each cup. Yield: 3 ½ quarts.

Wine Punch

1	gallon Burgundy or rosé wine	1	(12-ounce) can apricot nectar
1	(6-ounce) can frozen lemonade, thawed and undiluted	2	(32-ounce) bottles lemon-lime carbonated beverage, chilled
1	(12-ounce) can frozen limeade, thawed and undiluted	1	(16-ounce) package frozen whole strawberries

Combine first four ingredients; chill. When ready to serve, pour chilled mixture into an ice-filled punch bowl. Pour in carbonated beverage and stir gently. Float strawberries on top. Yield: 2 gallons.

Hot Bacon Appetizers

½	pound bacon, cooked and crumbled	¼	cup butter or margarine, softened
¾	cup (6 ounces) shredded American cheese	2	teaspoons caraway seeds
		50	melba toast rounds

Combine first four ingredients, mixing well. Spread evenly on toast rounds. Place on baking sheet, and broil 2 minutes or until cheese melts. Serve hot. Yield: 50 appetizers.

Sausage Balls in Cheese Pastry

1	pound bulk pork sausage, mild or hot		1 ½	cups all-purpose flour
¾	cup dry bread crumbs		1	teaspoon paprika
⅓	cup chicken broth		2	cups (8-ounces) shredded sharp Cheddar cheese
⅛	teaspoon ground nutmeg		½	cup butter or margarine, softened
¼	teaspoon poultry seasoning			

Combine first five ingredients; mix well. Shape into 1-inch balls. Cook over low heat until done, turning to brown on all sides. Drain on paper towels. Combine next three ingredients. Cut in butter with pastry blender (mixture will be dry). Mix with hands until dough is smooth. Shape 1 tablespoon dough around each sausage ball, covering sausage completely. Place on greased baking sheets. May be prepared to this point and frozen. To serve, thaw and bake at 350 degrees for 15 to 20 minutes. Yield: 4 dozen.

Cauliflower Dip

1	cup mayonnaise		1	tablespoon ranch salad dressing
1	tablespoon curry powder			
1	tablespoon garlic salt		1	head cauliflower, washed and cut into flowerets
2	tablespoons grated onion			
1	tablespoon horseradish			

Mix first six ingredients well. Refrigerate for 2 hours before serving. Serve with fresh cauliflower. Yield: 1 cup.

Cheese Ball

2	cloves garlic	1	teaspoon curry
1	(8-ounce) package cream cheese, softened	10	teaspoons Sherry Chutney
1	cup shredded sharp Cheddar cheese	1	bunch green onions, chopped

Mince garlic in food processor. Add next four ingredients. Process until well blended. Form into a ball. Chill several hours. When ready to serve, pour chutney and chopped green onions on top. Better made ahead of time and frozen.

Chicken Little Fingers with Easy Barbecue Sauce

1	(12-ounce) jar orange marmalade	1	tablespoon Worcestershire sauce
1	(12-ounce) bottle chili sauce	1 ½	teaspoons celery seed
¼	cup vinegar	2	(16-ounce) packages chicken fingers

Combine all ingredients in a medium mixing bowl. Mix well. Serve with chicken fingers. Yield: 3 cups.

Petite Ham and Cheese Biscuits

1	(11-ounce) can refrigerated buttermilk biscuits	½	cup grated Parmesan cheese
1	(4 ½-ounce) can deviled ham		Lemon pepper marinade
¼	cup butter or margarine, melted		

Cut each biscuit into quarters; arrange evenly in two greased 8-inch round cake pans. Combine deviled ham and butter, mixing well. Spread on biscuit pieces. Spoon cheese on top; sprinkle lightly with lemon pepper marinade. Bake at 400 degrees for 12 to 15 minutes. Yield: 40 appetizers.

Zesty Meatballs

1 ½	pounds ground chuck	1	medium onion, chopped
¼	cup seasoned breadcrumbs	2	tablespoons all-purpose
1	medium onion, chopped		flour
2	teaspoons prepared	1 ½	cups beef broth
	horseradish	½	cup dry red wine
2	cloves garlic, crushed	2	tablespoons brown sugar
¾	cup tomato juice	2	tablespoons catsup
2	teaspoons salt	1	tablespoon lemon juice
¼	teaspoon pepper	3	gingersnaps, crumbled
2	tablespoons margarine		

Combine first eight ingredients, mixing well. Shape into 1-inch balls. Place in a 13x9x2-inch baking dish. Bake at 450 degrees for 20 minutes. Remove from oven and drain off excess fat. Heat margarine in large skillet. Sauté onion until tender. Blend in flour. Gradually add beef broth, stirring constantly. Add remaining ingredients. Cook over low heat 15 minutes. Add meatballs and simmer 15 minutes. Yield: 4 dozen.

Cheesy Dapper Apple Squares

1 ½	cups flour	1 ½	cups shredded Cheddar
1	cup brown sugar, firmly		cheese
	packed	2 ½	cups apples, peeled and
½	teaspoon baking soda		sliced, about 3 medium
¾	cup butter or margarine,	¾	cup sugar
	softened	½	cup chopped nuts
1 ½	cups graham cracker		
	crumbs, divided		

Combine flour, brown sugar, baking soda and margarine with ¼ cup graham cracker crumbs in large bowl. Mix until crumbly. Pat into ungreased 13x9-inch pan. Place cheese over crumbs. Stir together sugar and apples in medium-size bowl, then place over cheese. Sprinkle reserved graham cracker crumbs and chopped nuts over apples. Bake at 350 degrees for 35 to 40 minutes or until deep golden brown. Serve warm. May be made ahead of time and frozen. Yield: 48 squares.

Fresh Cooked Shrimp with Cocktail Sauce

1	cup chili sauce	3	tablespoons prepared
1	cup catsup		horseradish
⅓	cup lemon juice	6	drops hot sauce

Combine all ingredients, stirring well. Serve with fresh steamed shrimp. Yield: 2 ½ cups.

Crème de Menthe Brownies

1	cup sugar	1	teaspoon vanilla
1	cup butter plus 6	2	cups confectioners' sugar
	tablespoons butter,	2	tablespoons Crème de
	divided		Menthe
4	eggs, beaten	1	cup semi-sweet chocolate
1	cup flour		chips
1	(16-ounce) can chocolate		
	syrup		

Mix together 1 cup sugar, ½ cup butter, eggs, flour, chocolate syrup and vanilla; pour into greased 9x13-inch pan. Bake at 350 degrees for 30 minutes. Let cool. Cream ½ cup butter and combine with confectioners' sugar and Crème de Menthe. Spread over cake when cool. Melt together chocolate chips and remaining 6 tablespoons butter. Cool. Spread over frosting. Refrigerate. Yield: 2 to 3 dozen.

Holly Berry Cookies

¼	cup margarine	4	cups corn flakes
3	cups large marshmallows		"Red Hot" candies
1	teaspoon vanilla		
2	teaspoons green food		
	coloring		

Melt margarine and marshmallows over low heat. Add vanilla and food coloring. Mix well. Remove from heat and add corn flakes. Stir until well coated. Drop by spoonfuls onto waxed paper. Sprinkle with "red hots" while cornflake mixture is still warm. Allow to air dry several hours or overnight. Store in airtight container. Yield: 3 dozen.

TREE-TRIMMING SUPPER

*Enjoy this casual buffet while your guests partake
in the festivities of trimming the tree.*

Wassail Bowl Punch

Party Mold

Green Bean and Mushroom Salad

Shrimp Creole

Chocolate Chip-Cinnamon Cake

Wassail Bowl Punch

1	quart hot tea	2	cups orange juice
1	cup sugar	¾	cup lemon juice
1	(32-ounce) bottle cranberry juice cocktail	2	(3-inch) cinnamon sticks
		24	whole cloves, divided
1	(32-ounce) bottle apple juice		Orange slices

Combine hot tea and sugar in a large Dutch oven and stir in juices. Add
cinnamon and 12 whole cloves. Boil over medium heat 2 minutes.
Remove from heat and cool. Stud orange slices with remaining cloves.
Pour Wassail into punch bowl; float orange slices on top. Serves 24.

Party Mold

1	(8-ounce) plus 1 (3-ounce) package cream cheese, softened	½	cup golden raisins, chopped
½	cup butter or margarine, softened	⅓	cup chopped red Maraschino cherries
½	cup sour cream	⅓	cup chopped green Maraschino cherries
⅓	cup sugar		Grated rind of 2 lemons
1	teaspoon unflavored gelatin		Additional red and green cherries (optional)
¼	cup cold water		
1	cup chopped almonds, toasted		

Combine cream cheese and butter in a medium mixing bowl; beat until light and fluffy. Add sour cream and sugar, mixing well. Combine gelatin and cold water in small saucepan; cook over low heat, stirring constantly until gelatin dissolves. Add to cream cheese mixture, mixing well. Fold in almonds, raisins, chopped cherries and lemon rind. Lightly grease a 4-cup mold with mayonnaise; spoon mixture into mold. Cover and refrigerate overnight. Remove from refrigerator; let stand 20 minutes. Unmold onto a serving platter; garnish with red and green cherries. Serves 6 to 8.

Green Bean and Mushroom Salad

½	pound fresh green beans, trimmed and cut in half crosswise	1	hard-cooked egg white, thinly sliced
1	red onion, thinly sliced		Salt and pepper
½	pound mushrooms, sliced	1	head Romano lettuce, torn into pieces
1	large tomato, cut into thin wedges		Olive Dressing (recipe follows)

Cook green beans in boiling water just until they turn bright green. Rinse immediately under cold water and drain well. Place green beans, onion, mushrooms, tomato and egg white in salad bowl; toss with salt and pepper to taste. Add lettuce and olive dressing; toss well. Serves 8.

Olive Dressing

1	hard-cooked egg yolk	1	tablespoon olive juice
2	tablespoons red wine vinegar	3	large sprigs parsley
1	tablespoon lemon juice	1	clove garlic
1	tablespoon (1 ounce) pimento-stuffed green olives	½	teaspoon dried oregano
		½	cup vegetable oil
		⅓	cup olive oil

Process first eight ingredients in food processor or blender until well blended. Add oils, processing until smooth. Yield: 2 cups dressing.

Shrimp Creole

3	tablespoons vegetable oil	1	teaspoon Worcestershire sauce
2	large onions, diced		
½	cup diced green peppers	2	teaspoons parsley flakes
2	(28-ounce) cans stewed tomatoes, diced	½	teaspoon salt
1	teaspoon chives	½	teaspoon pepper
2	bay leaves	2	pounds shrimp, peeled
½	teaspoon celery seed	1	(6-ounce) can vegetable juice
1	teaspoon oregano		Flour (to thicken)
½	teaspoon garlic salt		

In large, heavy-bottomed saucepan, sauté onion and green peppers in oil. Add tomatoes and remaining ingredients except shrimp, vegetable juice and flour. Simmer slowly on low heat for about 1 hour. Thicken with vegetable juice and flour or cornstarch until desired consistency is reached. Add shrimp. Serve over rice. Serves 8.

Chocolate Chip-Cinnamon Cake

¾	cup butter	¼	teaspoon salt
1 ½	cups sugar	1	(12-ounce) bag chocolate
3	eggs		chips
1	pint sour cream	4	tablespoons cinnamon-
1	teaspoon vanilla		sugar (4 tablespoons sugar
3	cups flour		added to 1 teaspoon
1 ½	teaspoons baking soda		cinnamon)

Cream butter and sugar. Add next three ingredients. Sift in dry ingredients. Add 3 tablespoons cinnamon-sugar and ¾ bag chocolate chips. Mix well. Pour batter into greased and floured tube pan. Sprinkle with remaining cinnamon-sugar and chocolate chips. Bake in 350 degree oven for 1 hour or until done. Serves 12.

CHRISTMAS DINNER

Christmas dinner is the culinary highlight of the holiday season. Flickering candles, gleaming silver and a beautifully appointed table create an elegant setting for this celebrated dinner. The marinated beef tenderloin is an exceptional entree that makes this meal truly distinctive. Presented on a bed of watercress with jewel-like accents of red and green grapes, the tenderloin has a classic look that is well-suited for a Christmas feast.

Eggnog

Spicy Marinated Beef Tenderloin

Nutty Yam Bake

Asparagus and English Pea Salad

Raspberry Holiday Mold

Molded French Cream

Swedish Apple Pie

Eggnog

6	eggs	1	quart light cream
½	teaspoon salt		Nutmeg
1	cup sugar		
1	cup rum or 2 tablespoons rum flavoring		

In a large bowl, beat eggs until light and foamy. Add sugar and salt, beating until thick and lemon colored. Stir in rum and cream. Chill at least 3 hours. Sprinkle with nutmeg to taste just before serving. Serves 12.

Spicy Marinated Beef Tenderloin

4	cloves garlic, crushed	1	cup Port wine
1	teaspoon salt	1	teaspoon dried thyme
1	teaspoon pepper	1	bay leaf
½	teaspoon hot sauce	1	(5 to 6 pound) beef
1	cup soy sauce		tenderloin, trimmed
1	cup olive oil		

Combine first nine ingredients in a small bowl and mix well. Place tenderloin in large shallow dish. Pour wine mixture over top and cover tightly. Refrigerate overnight, turning occasionally. Drain off marinade and reserve. Place tenderloin on rack in baking pan and insert meat thermometer. Bake at 425 degrees 45 minutes to 1 hour, or until meat thermometer registers 140 degrees, basting occasionally with marinade. For medium-rare doneness, roast until internal temperature reaches 150 degrees. For medium doneness, roast to 169 degree internal temperature. Serves 12.

Nutty Yam Bake

3	large sweet potatoes or yams	2	eggs
		½	cup flour
1	cup sugar	½	cup sugar
¼	cup butter or margarine	¼	cup butter or margarine
1	teaspoon ground cinnamon	½	cup chopped walnuts
		½	teaspoon ground cinnamon
½	teaspoon ground allspice		Butter or margarine
¼	teaspoon ground nutmeg		
2	cups milk		

Cook sweet potatoes in boiling water until tender. Drain well. Skin and mash sweet potatoes while hot. Add next five ingredients. Beat in milk and eggs; whip well with mixer. Turn into greased 3-quart casserole. Combine next three ingredients and mix until crumbly. Mix in walnuts and cinnamon. Sprinkle over top of sweet potato mixture. Dot with butter. Bake in 375 degree oven 35 to 40 minutes. May be frozen after baking. Serves 6.

Asparagus and English Pea Salad

1	(0.7-ounce) package garlic salad dressing mix	1	(8 ½-ounce) can small early peas, drained
1	(15-ounce) can asparagus, drained	3	hard cooked eggs, chopped
			Shredded lettuce

Prepare salad dressing mix according to package directions. Set aside. Combine asparagus, peas and eggs. Pour dressing over mixture. Stir gently. Cover and chill several hours. Drain well. Serve on a bed of shredded lettuce. Serves 4.

Raspberry Holiday Mold

1	(20-ounce) can pineapple chunks	2	tablespoons lemon juice
2	(10-ounce) packages frozen raspberries, thawed	½	teaspoon salt
		1	cup chopped celery
2	(6-ounce) packages raspberry flavored gelatin	1	cup chopped walnuts
		1	(8-ounce) package cream cheese, softened
3 ½	cups boiling water	½	cup mayonnaise
1	teaspoon hot sauce		Finely chopped walnuts

Drain pineapple chunks and raspberries, reserving liquid. Press raspberries through a sieve or food mill and discard seeds. Dissolve gelatin in boiling water. Stir in pineapple juice, raspberry juice, lemon juice, hot sauce and salt. Chill until the consistency of unbeaten egg whites. Fold in pineapple, raspberry purée, celery and chopped walnuts. Pour gelatin mixture into a lightly oiled 10-cup ring mold. Chill until firm. Combine cream cheese and mayonnaise. Beat until smooth. Spoon into center of raspberry mold. Sprinkle with walnuts. Serves 16.

Molded French Cream

1	cup sour cream	½	teaspoon vanilla extract
1	cup whipping cream		Additional whipped cream
¾	cup superfine sugar		(optional)
1	envelope unflavored		Frosted green grapes
	gelatin		(optional)
¼	cup boiling water		
1	(8-ounce) package cream		
	cheese, softened		

Combine sour cream and whipping cream in a medium saucepan; beat at medium speed of electric mixer until blended. Gradually add sugar and beat well. Cook over low heat until warm. Dissolve gelatin in boiling water. Add to cream mixture and remove from heat. Beat cream cheese with an electric mixer until light and fluffy. Add cream mixture and vanilla, beating until smooth. Pour into a lightly oiled 4-cup mold. Chill until firm. Unmold on serving platter. Garnish with additional whipped cream and frosted grapes. (To frost grapes, dip in unbeaten egg white and then in sugar. Let dry in a cool place, but do not refrigerate.) Serves 8.

Swedish Apple Pie

¾	cup sugar	1	teaspoon vanilla
½	cup flour	1	cup sliced apples
1	teaspoon baking powder	½	cup nuts
¼	teaspoon salt	1	egg, well beaten
½	teaspoon cinnamon	1	(9-inch) unbaked pie shell

Mix dry ingredients. Combine next four ingredients and add to dry ingredients. Bake in pie plate in oven at 400 degrees for 5 minutes, then reduce heat to 350 degrees and bake an additional 25 minutes. Serves 6.

REFERENCES

Making Wine in Virginia

Virginia is the oldest wine-growing state. Efforts to grow vinifera vines began in Jamestown in 1609. Due to humid weather conditions and phylloxera, the efforts of early Virginia vineyards failed. Virginia vintners included Thomas Jefferson, who attempted to grow vinifera vines at Monticello for thirty years before turning to native grapes. The native grapes included Norton, Delaware, Catawba and Scuppernong.

It was not until the 1970's that experiments with vinifera vines were rejuvenated in Virginia. During this time chateau wineries began to flourish in central and northern parts of Virginia. Today, Virginia wines are produced from a wide variety of grapes including Chardonnay, White Riesling, Cabernet Sauvignon and Merlot.

Cooking with Wine

As a general guideline, dry white wines are more compatible with delicately flavored food such as chicken, fish, creamed soups and sauces, salads and desserts. With robust foods such as game, red meats, meat sauces and vegetable-based soups, dry red wines are most often used. Rosé wines go well with ham, some fowl, fruit and desserts.

Wines add a pleasing flavor to many kinds of food, but be careful not to overdo. If you want a subtle sauce, do not add more than two tablespoons of wine per cup of liquid. The exceptions are stews or broths.

Some foods are not compatible with wine at all. The chief enemy is vinegar. Other flavors which should be curtailed when wine is included in the recipe are curry, horseradish, hot peppers, excessive fats and oils and heavy chocolate.

Additional tips on cooking with wine:

Never boil wine. Bring it to a boiling point and then simmer it, but never actually boil the wine or the flavor will be boiled away.

Meat may be tenderized and the flavors of it improved by marinating in wine for a few hours prior to cooking. The marinating should be done in glass, porcelain or any material other than aluminum.

To prevent spoilage of leftover wine, add a few drops of olive oil to the bottle. The oil will float on the wine surface and keep air out of the wine. Another method of preserving leftover wine is to put the wine in a smaller container, which provides less contact with the air, close it tightly and store in a cool place.

Serving Wine

Every wine has its optimum serving temperature. Complex, robust red wines should be served between 57 to 61 degrees, uncomplicated red wines, rosé wines and complex white wines between 50 to 54 degrees, crisp and vigorous white wines from 46 to 50 degrees, and sweet white wines and champagne 43 degrees to 46 degrees.

Red wine may be presented directly from a cellar, or it may be cooled in cold water with a few ice cubes. White, rosé and all sparkling wines should be chilled in ice. These wines should be placed in an ice bucket which has a few cubes of ice in the bottom. Ice should then be packed around the bottle and the bucket should be filled with cold water. Chill for about 20 minutes, twirling the bottle occasionally to cool the wine evenly. Sparkling wine should be served in chilled glasses to reduce the amount of foam when it is poured.

Alternately, all wines may be cooled in the refrigerator; moistening the bottle with water will make the glass conduct heat better and speed the chilling process.

Wine is beautifully served in glasses that are simple, clear and un-adorned. Their capacity should allow for a normal portion to fill ⅓ of the glass, which leaves space for the bouquet. The exception is sparkling wines which should be served in a small glass ¾ full. The shape of the glass should have a stem long enough for a comfortable grip and a wide foot to provide a steady base.

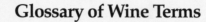

Glossary of Wine Terms

AROMA–The nose of a young wine, which will be primarily of fruit. With age, this becomes the bouquet.

BODY–The solidity of a wine, contributed by its basic elements, acidity, tannin and alcohol.

BOUQUET–The smell that develops in a wine during its evolution in the bottle. The term is also generally applied to a pleasant smell in any wine.

BRUT–Generally, the direct version of Champagne and other sparkling wines. Wines totally without dosage are known as brut zero, brut de brut and brut integrae.

CORKY–A fault caused by an improperly cured cork, which makes the affected wine emit a disagreeable smell.

COUPAGE–A blend; literally "cutting" one wine with another.

CRISP–Refreshing and relatively acid. Crispness is a desirable quality in light white wines that are drunk young.

DELICATE–A well-balanced light wine, with a pleasant but unassertive smell and taste. The term is also used to describe the fragile quality of good wine on the verge of decline.

DOSAGE–The sweetening of a sparkling wine, especially champagne, to cover natural high acidity.

DRY–Not sweet. A wine in which the sugar content has been fermented out.

EARTHY–A smell or taste reminiscent of soil.

FRUITY–Recalling fruits in its flavor. A variety of fruit odors and tastes, apart from the obvious one of grapes, may be discerned in wine–apple, apricot, black currant, blackberry, blueberry, cherry, citrus, peach, pear, plum, raspberry, or strawberry–as well as the heavy smell of cooked fruit.

FULL-BODIED–Fat or full of flavor, with all elements strongly defined.

LIGHT–Without much body, usually indicating a young wine that is ready to drink. Lightness is also a derogatory term applied to wine that does not live up to its expectations.

MELLOW–Mature and soft, with no edge of harshness.

NOSE–The smell of a wine.

OAK–The smell and taste of a wine that has been aged in new oak barrels.

ROBE–The colour and general aspect of a wine.

SOMMELIER–Wine waiter.

SPARKLING–The name given to wines that have been specially treated with carbon dioxide, which is released slowly in the form of tiny bubbles when the bottle is uncorked.

SWEET–A term applicable to wines in which the sugar content is either naturally high or has been increased by artificial sweetening.

TANNIN–One of the major elements in red wine, identifiable in tasting by the mouth-puckering effect it produces.

VINIFICATION–The wine-making process.

VINTAGE–Usually the year of harvest, can be used to denote the actual picking or the crop in general.

Vineyards	Wines Produced
CENTRAL VIRGINIA	
Autumn Hill Vineyards Route 1, Box 199C Standardsville, VA 22973 (804) 985-6100	Chardonnay, Riesling, Cabernet Sauvignon
Blenheim Wine Cellars, Ltd. Route 6, Box 75 Charlottesville, VA 22901	Chardonnay
Barboursville Vineyard P.O. Box 136 Barboursville, VA 22923 (703) 832-3824	Chardonnay, Riesling, Gewurztraminer, Pinot Noir Blanc, Cabernet Sauvignon Blanc, and Cabernet Sauvignon
Burnley Vineyards Route 1, Box 122 Barboursville, VA 22923 (703) 832-2828 (703) 832-3874	Chardonnay, Riesling, White, Blush, Claret
Chermont Winery, Inc. Route 1, Box 59 Esmont, VA 22937 (804) 286-2211	Chardonnay, Riesling, and Cabernet Sauvignon
Dominion Wine Cellars P.O. Box 1057 Culpeper, VA 22701 (703) 825-8772	White Riesling, Johannisburg Riesling, Chardonnay and Cabernet Sauvignon

Misty Mountain Vineyards, Inc.
SR 2, Box 458
Madison, VA 22727
(703) 923-4738

Chardonnay, Riesling, Seyval Blanc
Merlot, Cabernet Sauvignon, and
Virginia Chablis

Montdomaine Cellars
Route 6, Box 188A
Charlottesville, VA 22901
(804) 971-8947

White Riesling, Chardonnay, Cabernet
Blanc, Merlot, Cabernet Sauvignon

Simeon Vineyard, Ltd.
RFD 9, Box 293
Charlottesville, VA 22901
(804) 977-3502

Chardonnay, Cabernet Sauvignon

Stonewall Vineyard, Ltd.
Route 2, Box 107A
Concord, VA 24538
(804) 993-2185

Chardonnay, Cayuga White, Vin
Chochard, Claret, Vidal Blanc, Vidal
Blanc-Semi-Dry, Pyment (German-
Gluwein like)

EASTERN VIRGINIA

Accomack Vineyards
P.O. Box 38
Painter, VA 23420
(804) 442-2110

Chardonnay, Riesling, Old Dominion
White Table, Cabernet Sauvignon

Ingleside Plantation Vineyards
P.O. Box 1038
Oak Grove, VA 22443
(804) 224-8687

Chardonnay, Riesling, Chesapeake
Blanc, Williamsburg White, Virginia
Blush, Chesapeake Claret, Cabernet
Sauvignon Champagne, Wirtland
Rosé, Williamsburg Red

Williamsburg Winery, Ltd.
2638 Lake Powell Road
Williamsburg, VA 23185
(804) 229-0999

Chardonnay, Governor's White,
Plantation Blush, James River White,
Sir Christopher Wren White, Acte
12 Chardonnay, Vintage Reserve
Chardonnay, Merlot, Cabernet
Sauvignon

NORTHERN VIRGINIA

Farfelu Vineyard
Route 1, Box 23
Flint Hill, VA 22627
(703) 364-2930

Chardonnay, Cabernet Sauvignon

Hartwood Winery
345 Hartwood Road
Fredericksburg, VA 22405
(703) 752-4893

Chardonnay, Riesling, Seyval Blanc,
Rappahannock White, Rappahannock
Blush, Claret

Linden Vineyards
Route 1, Box 96
Linden, VA 22642
(703) 364-1997

Chardonnay, Seyval Blanc, Cabernet
Sauvignon, Cabernet Franc

Loudoun Valley Vineyards
RFD 1, Box 340
Waterford, VA 22190
(703) 882-3375

Chardonnay, Riesling, Blush,
Zinfandel

Meredyth Vineyards
P.O. Box 347
Middleburg, VA 22117
(703) 687-6277

Riesling, Seyval Blanc, Villard Blanc,
Premium Red, Delaware

Naked Mountain Vineyard
P.O. Box 131
Markham, VA 22643
(703) 364-1609

Chardonnay, Riesling, Sauvignon
Blanc, Claret

Oasis Vineyard
Highway 635, Box 116
Hume, VA 22639
(703) 635-7627

Chardonnay, Sauvignon Blanc,
Cabernet Sauvignon, Merlot,
Gewurztraminer, Cabernet Franc

Piedmont Vineyards & Winery
P.O. Box 286
Middleburg, VA 22117
(703) 687-5528

Chardonnay, Seyval Blanc,
Champagne

Swedenburg Winery
Middleburg, VA 22117
(703) 687-5219

Chardonnay, Riesling, Seyval Blanc,
Chantilly, Rhine Blush, Cabernet
Sauvignon, Sully Range

Tarara Vineyard
Route 4, Box 226
Leesburg, VA 22075
(703) 771-7100

Charval, Chardonnay, Cameo,
Renaissance, Cabernet

Willowcroft Farm Vineyards
Route 2, Box 174-A
Leesburg, VA 22075
(703) 777-8161

Chardonnay, Riesling, Seyval Blanc,
Cabernet Sauvignon, Cabernet Blanc

SHENANDOAH VALLEY

Deer Meadow Vineyard
Mountain Falls Route, Box 127-C
Winchester, VA 22601
(703) 877-1919

Chardonnay, Seyval Blanc, Golden
Blush, Merechal Foch, Red -
Chambourcin

265

Guilford Ridge Vineyard
Route 5, Box 148
Luray, VA 22835

Late Harvest Chelois, Paige Valley
Red, Paige Valley White

Shenandoah Vineyards
Route 2, Box 323
Edinburg, VA 22824
(703) 984-8699

Chardonnay (limited sales), Seyval
Blanc, Johannisberg Riesling, Blushing
Belle, Shenandoah Blanc, Vidal Blanc,
Shenandoah Rosé, Shenandoah Ruby

Winchester Winery
Mountain Falls Route, Box 188
Winchester, VA 22601
(703) 877-2200   (703) 877-1275

Riesling, Seyval Blanc, Winchester
White, Winchester Rosé, Vidal Blanc,
Red Chambourcin

SOUTHWEST VIRGINIA

Chateau Morrisette Winery, Inc.
P.O. Box 766
Meadows of Dan, VA 24120
(703) 593-2865

Chardonnay, White Riesling, Sweet
Mountain Laurel (dessert), Virginia
Blush, Cabernet Sauvignon, Merlot

Oakencroft Vineyard & Winery
Route 5, Box 438
Charlottesville, VA 22901
(804) 296-4188

Chardonnay, Seyval Blanc, Blush,
Cabernet Sauvignon

Prince Michel Vineyards
SR 4, Box 77
Leon, VA 22725
(703) 547-3709

Chardonnay & Barrel Select White
Burgundy Blush de Michel, Vavin
Nouveau

Rapidan River Vineyards
Route 4, Box 77
Leon, VA 22725

Chardonnay, Riesling, Pinot Noir
Champagne - "Sekt" - made from
Riesling wine Gewurztraminer

Rose Bower Vineyard & Winery
P.O. Box 126
Hampden Sydney, VA 23943
(804) 223-8209

Seyval Blanc, Marechal Foch, Vidal,
Chardonnay, Johannisberg Riesling,
Cabernet Sauvignon, Hampden Forest
Claret, Rose O'Grady, LeBateau
Rouge, LeBon Sauvage, Blushing Bride
Wedding Wine

Chateau Natural Vineyard
Route 4, Box 1535
Rocky Mount, VA 24151
(703) 483-0758

White Burgundy, Golden Green Eye,
Va. Villard Blanc, Born Wild, Rosé
Wild, Rosé Labrusca, Vintner's Choice,
Blackberry Wine, Red Table Wine

Freezing Timetable

Although some of these foods may be frozen longer, we found that many of them begin to deteriorate when kept longer than we suggest. Thawing and reheating times will vary according to size of item and temperature used for heating.

Food	Freezing Time	Comments
Cookies	2 to 3 months	Freeze 1 layer at a time on a baking sheet. When firm, wrap airtight in freezer wrap. Thaw, unwrapped, at room temperature.
Unbaked Dough	6 months	Drop cookies can be frozen on cookie tray. Removed and stored in airtight bag. Bake as needed. Can also shape dough into log, freeze, then slice slightly thawed dough and bake.
Meat, Fish & Poultry Dishes	1 to 6 months	Wrap cooked meat, fish and poultry dishes in freezer wrap; freeze 1 to 2 months. Wrap and freeze uncooked meats 3 to 6 months. All should be thawed, wrapped, in refrigerator, then used right away.
Breads & Coffee Cake	1 to 3 months	Cool baked goods before wrapping airtight in foil or freezer wrap. Freeze cakes up to 2 months and breads up to 3 months. Thaw in wrapper at room temperature.
Cakes	1 to 2 months	Freeze single-layer cakes or frosted layer cakes on a baking sheet. When firm, wrap airtight in freezer wrap. Thaw, unwrapped, at room temperature.
Dairy Products	6 to 9 months 1 to 3 months	Butter and Margarine Cheddar, Parmesan, American, Swiss, Muenster
Fruits–Fresh	6 to 12 months	Wash fruit. Remove seeds, peel. Cut up if desired. Place in airtight bags.
Pies	1 to 2 months	Wrap and freeze pastry shells, baked or unbaked, single or double-crust fruit pies. Bake while still frozen, but allow extra baking time. Avoid freezing cream or custard pies with meringue topping.
Vegetables–Fresh	8 to 10 months	Preparation varies. Follow recommended preparation technique for specific vegetables.

Foods That Do Not Freeze: Salad greens, uncooked tomatoes, cucumbers, cooked egg whites, mayonnaise, cake frostings made with egg whites, molded salads, cream cheese and cottage cheese.

Substitutions for Cooking

Item	Substitution
Baking Powder	1 t = ¼ t baking soda + ½ T cream of tartar, or ¼ t baking soda + ½ C buttermilk or sour milk (to replace ½ C liquid in recipe)
Butter	1 C = ⅛ C rendered fat + ½ t salt, or ⅞ C oil or 1 C hydrogenated fat + ½ t salt
Chocolate	1 oz. = 3 T cocoa + ½ T fat
Cocoa	3 T = 1 square chocolate (omit ½ T fat)
Cornstarch	1½ t cornstarch = 1 T flour
Eggs	1 whole = 2 yolks (in custard)
2 Large Eggs	3 small eggs
Flour, Cake	1 C = ⅞ C all-purpose flour (i.e. 2 T less)
Garlic powder	⅛ t = 1 clove garlic
Herbs	1 T fresh = 1 t dry
Honey	1 C = ¾ C sugar + ¼ C liquid
Milk, Whole	1 C = ½ C evaporated milk + ½ C water, or 4 T dry whole milk + ¾ C water, or 4 T nonfat dry milk
Milk, Buttermilk	1 C sweet milk, mixed with one of the following: 1 T vinegar, or 1 T lemon juice, or 1¾ t cream of tartar. Let stand 5 minutes.
Mustard	1 t dry = 1 T prepared
Sugar, Granulated	1 C = 1 C brown sugar, well packed 1 C = 2 C corn syrup (reduce required liquid) 1 C = 1½ C molasses (reduce required liquid)
Sour Cream	1 C = 1 C evaporated milk or 1 C plain yogurt or 1 C heavy cream plus 1 T vinegar
Tomato Juice	1 C = ½ C tomato sauce + ½ C water
Tapioca	1 T tapioca = 1½ T all-purpose flour

Table of Food Equivalents

	Food	Amount	Equivalent
Beverages	Coffee	2 T	1 serving
		2½ C	25 servings
		1 lb (5 C)	50 servings
	Coffee–instant	2 oz jar	125 servings
	Tea	1 lb	125 servings
Cereals	Flour		
	All-purpose	1 lb	4 C sifted
	Cake	1 lb	4½ C sifted
	Whole Wheat	1 lb	3½ to 4 C
	Macaroni	1 C raw	2 C cooked
	Noodles	1 C raw	2 C cooked
	Rice	1 C raw	3-4 C cooked
	Spaghetti	1 lb raw	7 C cooked
Crumbs	Bread, dry	1 slice	⅓ C fine, dry
	Crackers		
	Graham	15 crackers	1 C fine
	Saltine	22 crackers	1 C fine
Dairy Products and Eggs	Butter, Margarine	1 lb	2 C
	Cheese		
	Cottage	½ lb	1 C
	Cream	3 oz pkg	6 T
		8 oz pkg	1 C
	Grated, hard	¼ lb	1 C
	Cream, heavy	1 C	2 C whipped
	Milk		
	Condensed	15 oz can	1⅓ C
	Evaporated	6 oz can	⅔ C
	Eggs		
	Whole	4-6	1 C
	Whites	8-11	1 C
	Yolks	12-14	1 C
Fruit	Dried		
	Dates, pitted	1 lb (2½ C)	3 C chopped
	Raisins	1 lb	3 C
	Fresh		
	Apples	1 lb	3 C diced
	Avocado	1 medium	2 C cubed
	Bananas	1 lb (3)	2 C mashed
	Berries	1 pt	2 C
	Cherries	1 lb	2½ C pitted
	Grapefruit	1 medium	1¼ C pulp, ¾ C juice

	Food	Amount	Equivalent
Fruit, cont.	Lemon	1 medium	2-3 T juice, 1½ t rind
	Orange	1 medium	⅓ C juice, 2 T rind
	Pineapple	1 medium	2½ C cubed
	Rhubarb	6-8 stalks	3½ C diced, 2 C cooked
Nuts	Almonds		
	whole	6 oz	1 C
	slivered	1 lb	5⅔ C
	Coconut		
	grated	1 lb	5 C grated
		3½ oz	1 C
	Peanuts, shelled	1 lb	2½ C
	Pecans, shelled	1 lb	4 C
	Walnuts		
	in shell	1 lb	2½ C shelled
	chopped	4 oz	1 C
Sugar	Brown, packed	1 lb	2 C
	Confectioners'	1 lb	3½ C
	Granulated	1 lb	2 C
	Honey, Molasses and Syrup	1 lb	1½ C
	Non-caloric liquid sweetener	⅛ t	1 t sugar
	Chocolate Chips	6 oz	1 C
	unsweetened	8 oz	8 squares (1 oz)
Vegetables	Dried Beans and Peas	1 C raw	2¼ C cooked
	Fresh		
	Asparagus, cut	1 lb raw	2 C cooked
	Beans		
	Green or Wax	1 lb raw	3 C cooked
	Lima	1 lb	1 C shelled
	Broccoli	1 bunch	4-6 servings
	Cabbage	1 lb	4 C shredded, 2½ C cooked
	Carrots	1 lb (8-10)	3 C shredded, 2½ C chopped
	Cauliflower	2 lb head	3 C cooked
	Celery	8 branches	3 C cooked
	Corn	4 ears	1 C cut
	Eggplant	1 lb	2 C
	Mushrooms	1 lb (35-40)	5 C sliced, raw
		1 lb	2 C cooked, cut

Food	Amount	Equivalent
Vegetables, cont. Olives, stuffed	4 oz (48)	1 C sliced
Onions	1 medium	½ C chopped
Peas	1 lb	1 C cooked
Potatoes		
white	1 lb	2 C thinly sliced or 2 C cubed and cooked or 1¾ C mashed
sweet	1 lb	2 C
Spinach	1 lb	6 C raw, 1½-2 C cooked
Squash	2 lb	2 C cooked
Tomatoes	1 lb	1¾ C cooked

Food Quantities for 25 and 50 Servings

Food	25 Servings	50 Servings
Bread	50 slices or 3-lb loaves	100 slices or 6-lb loaves
Cheese (2 oz per serving)	3 lb	6 lb
Crackers	1½ lb	3 lb
Mayonnaise	1 cup	2 to 3 cups
Mixed Filling for Sandwiches (meat, eggs, fish)	1½ quarts	2½-3 quarts
Rolls	4 dozen	8 dozen
Meat, Poultry or Fish:		
Chicken Salad	2½ quarts cooked, diced chicken	5 quarts cooked, diced chicken
Fish, Fillets or Steaks	7½ lb	15 lb
Fish, large whole (round)	13 lb	25 lb
Ham (bone in)	14 lb	28 lb
Hamburger	9 lb	18 lb
Turkey or Chicken	13 lb	25 to 30 lb
Wieners	6½ lb	13 lb

Food	25 Servings	50 Servings
Salads, Casseroles, Vegetables:		
Baked Beans	¾ gallon	1¼ gallons
Cabbage	4 lb	8 lb
Canned Vegetables	1 #10 can	2½ #10 cans
Macaroni Salad	5 cups cooked	10 cups cooked
Mashed Potatoes	9 lb	18-20 lb
Potato Salad	4¼ quarts	2¼ gallons
Scalloped Potatoes	4½ quarts or 1 12x20" pan	8½ quarts
Rice	2 lb raw	4 lb raw
Fresh Vegetables:		
Carrots (3 oz or ½ C)	6¼ lb	12½ lb
Lettuce (for salads)	4 heads	8 heads
Tomatoes	3-5 lb	7-10 lb
Desserts:		
Cake	1 10x12" sheet cake or 1½ 10" layer cakes	1 12x20" sheet cake or 3 10" layer cakes
Ice Cream	3¼ quarts	6½ quarts
Brick	2¼ quarts	4½ quarts or 1¼ gallons
Beverages:		
Coffee	½ lb and 1½ gallons water	1 lb and 3 gallons water
Lemonade	10 to 15 lemons, 1½ gallons water	20 to 30 lemons, 3 gallons water
Punch	1½ gallons	3 gallons
Tea	⅓ lb loose tea	¾ lb loose tea
Ice	1 lb per person in hot weather	Same
Liquor	1 bottle hard liquor	2 bottles hard liquor

Miscellaneous Information:

20 slices in a long loaf of bread
4 cuts per slice of bread
1 design per slice of bread
1 pint mayonnaise for 2 loaves of bread
1 quart salad dressing for 75 people
½ keg of beer serves 200

INDEX

E

283

Junior Woman's Club of Manassas, Inc.
PO Box 166
Manassas, VA 20108

Please send _____ copies of *The Virginia Hostess*   @ $17.95 each _____

Postage and handling   @ $ 3.00 each _____

Virginia residents add sales tax   @ $ .81 each _____

Total _____

Name _____

Address _____

City _____ State _____ Zip _____

Make checks payable to *Junior Woman's Club of Manassas, Inc.*

- -

Junior Woman's Club of Manassas, Inc.
PO Box 166
Manassas, VA 20108

Please send _____ copies of *The Virginia Hostess*   @ $17.95 each _____

Postage and handling   @ $ 3.00 each _____

Virginia residents add sales tax   @ $ .81 each _____

Total _____

Name _____

Address _____

City _____ State _____ Zip _____

Make checks payable to *Junior Woman's Club of Manassas, Inc.*

- -

Junior Woman's Club of Manassas, Inc.
PO Box 166
Manassas, VA 20108

Please send _____ copies of *The Virginia Hostess*   @ $17.95 each _____

Postage and handling   @ $ 3.00 each _____

Virginia residents add sales tax   @ $ .81 each _____

Total _____

Name _____

Address _____

City _____ State _____ Zip _____

Make checks payable to *Junior Woman's Club of Manassas, Inc.*